Colm 'Gooch' Cooper is the most outstanding Gaelic footballer of his generation and an iconic figure in Kerry football since his inter-county debut in 2002. He has played club football with Dr Crokes, winning a prized All-Ireland Club Championship with the Killarney side in 2017. Cooper won eight All-Star Awards and five All-Irelands with Kerry. He announced his retirement from the inter-county game in April 2017.

Vincent Hogan is one of Ireland's top sports journalists; he writes for the *Irish Independent*. His previous books as co-writer include Paul McGrath's *Back from the Brink*, which was William Hill Irish Sports Book of the Year in 2006, as well as autobiographies by Eddie O'Sullivan, Nicky English and Henry Shefflin.

T0096388

www.transworldireland.ie

www.penguin.co.uk

GOOCH

The Autobiography

COLM COOPER

with

Vincent Hogan

TRANSWORLD IRELAND

TRANSWORLD IRELAND PUBLISHERS
Penguin Random House Ireland,
Morrison Chambers,
32 Nassau Street, Dublin 2, Ireland
www.transworldireland.ie

Transworld Ireland is part of the Penguin Random House group of companies
whose addresses can be found at global.penguinrandomhouse.com

First published in the UK and Ireland in 2017 by Transworld Ireland
an imprint of Transworld Publishers
Transworld Ireland paperback edition published 2018

A CIP catalogue record for this book
is available from the British Library.

ISBN 9781848272194

Typeset in 10.75/13.35 pt Ehrhardt MT by Jouve (UK), Milton Keynes.
Printed and bound in Great Britain by Clays Ltd, Elcograf S.p.A.

Penguin Random House is committed to a sustainable future
for our business, our readers and our planet. This book is made
from Forest Stewardship Council® certified paper.

5 7 9 10 8 6

To my parents, Mike and Maureen

Contents

Prologue

'I wanted people to ask why was I retiring, not why wasn't
I retiring'

– A. P. McCoy, in *Being A.P.*

In the end, people probably wanted me to be somebody that I
could never be.

They wanted sentiment. They wanted emotion. Maybe they
wanted tears even. But after all these years it seemed they still
didn't quite get me. That's what I said to Eamonn Fitzmaurice,
sitting in the kitchen of his house in Tralee six days after the All-
Ireland Club final. I'd been at a work event in Cork and had driven
across to bring some kind of closure.

I knew it was time. Eamonn had texted me after that Dr Crokes
win, just a single congratulatory sentence: 'Well done, we'll catch
up soon . . .' He needed clarity, and, in some respects, maybe I
needed it even more than him.

So after a little gentle dancing-around-the-houses banter with
Tina, we left her with the baby and settled down over two cups of
tea. And Eamonn began selling the attractions of another year
with Kerry. Telling me how they could tailor my training. How
there wouldn't have to be any flogging of an ageing body. He reassured me that I was playing well and could still add value to the

group. And he suggested that I think about how it might feel, drawing the curtain down on my Kerry career with a September finish in Croker.

Then, finally, the bonus offering. 'And remember,' he said, 'a Dr Crokes man will be captain!'

It seemed the whole world assumed that I'd go another year, but I'd been explaining to Eamonn why my instinct was to walk away. I'd endured another year of almost relentless physical niggles – a shoulder issue after the Corofin game, a stiffening back during the build-up to the final. Right up to that game with Slaughtneil it seemed I was nursing something, trying endlessly to coax my body to an effort it simply wasn't happy to make. I felt tired and, if I'm honest, maybe even slightly soft now.

Eamonn, to be fair, was respectful of what he was hearing. He'd seen the shit days, the head-wrecking days when I was down in the dumps but trying to put on a brave face so as not to drag others down with me. He knew me too long and too well to recognize when I was putting on a front. More than anything, he recognized that I knew my body's limits. That reconciling those limits with what I needed to put myself through to get to the point of being ready for inter-county represented a massive challenge. Even after club matches now I end up sore for days. My recovery time keeps growing.

But as he started selling me the fairytale, I felt a need to tell him something he didn't seem to know.

That he was selling the fairytale to a cold fish.

Retirements were never an emotional issue for me and this one was going to be no different.

'Listen,' I said. 'I didn't pick up the phone when Aidan [O'Mahony] or Marc [Ó Sé] retired. Great friends, great teammates, but that's not me. The show goes on, no matter who it is that walks away. I might drop them a text a few days later, but that's all. I was still a Kerry player, they weren't. Fuck it, we move on. They can't help me get my hands on Sam any more.'

And I told him it was the same when Darragh Ó Sé went, when any of the other big dogs left. There was no RIP stuff from me. No sentimental bullshit. I'm just not the type of person who buys into that stuff. I said, 'Listen, Eamonn, I didn't give a fuck about you when you retired!'

He burst out laughing at that.

'I don't mean it that way . . .' I protested.

And Eamonn goes, 'I know, I know. But you're dead right. Listen, if somebody can't help me win the All-Ireland, I have to move on too.'

I could tell he didn't want me to leave his house that night with the door completely closed. And after fifteen years, that was fair enough. But, deep down, I recognized that the very things he was selling me – the personally tailored training programme, the indulgences that would probably never be considered for others: the special treatment in other words – would, if anything, just amplify all the doubts now splashing around inside my head.

To be hard enough for Championship, I needed to be hard enough in how I prepared. That meant ten more weeks of torture. Another weights programme. Another slow, hard grind for the big explosion. Worse, I needed to do it with all the squinting eyes that would be upon me. And the fact I was even questioning my capacity to go through that seemed, to me, to be more or less answering the question now. Did I have the hunger? The appetite? The anger?

No. No. No.

So when I heard Tony McCoy utter that sentence in the TV documentary on his final year's racing, it was as if he could see inside my head. I was fine with people asking me why I was retiring, but the idea that they'd ever get to the point of wondering why I *wasn't* would have cut me to the core. I'm a lot of things you see but, above anything, I'm a proud bastard. I like to think I've a good manner with people, but I don't play this phoney humble-Joe stuff either. I know I was good. On my best days, I sometimes felt almost anything was within my powers.

So the idea of being a five- or ten-minute man? Of, maybe, being a non-playing captain? Nope. Not a hope in hell.

None of this was ever explored with Eamonn, mind. How could it be? He was honest enough to promise nothing in terms of game-time because to do anything else would have been to sell a lie. And we've too much respect for each other to go down that road.

I stayed for maybe an hour that Thursday evening and agreed to mull over things for the weekend. But, if I'm honest, my head was already clear.

The only soul-searching I'd done had been with myself, and that was for a reason. Because if I'd allowed any bit of sentiment into the decision, I'd have been back training with Kerry. I knew that. I needed to be cold and calculated in terms of not letting public or media or friends or work colleagues influence me. I needed to remove myself from all those influences and distil it all down to something brutally simple.

The decision had to be about what I knew I could do. Not what other people believed.

Two nights earlier, Johnny Buckley and Fionn Fitzgerald had called to my house, looking to 'sort out' the Kerry captaincy. One of the three of us would have the honour and the club's way was, usually, to leave us to decide that kind of thing between ourselves. What the two boys didn't know was that earlier that day I'd sat on the same couch they were now sitting on, jotting down the pros and cons of staying for another year in the green and gold.

And it seemed to me that the cons carried a lot more weight than the pros.

'Look boys, before ye even start,' I said, 'I don't know if I need to be involved in this conversation. To be honest with ye, I don't think I'll be back.'

Fionn, especially, seemed taken aback.

'You what?'

'Are you sure?'

'Jesus, I've never seen you train better.'

What he hadn't seen, what people generally hadn't seen, was Ger Keane calling to my house at ten p.m. at least three nights a week to give me physio sessions that just about kept my body going. They didn't understand the recovery work required, the struggle to conceal so many years' wear and tear.

So I made sure that that conversation was short and to the point, asking them to keep the content to themselves. But, essentially, the Kerry captaincy was a matter for the two of them now.

I was yesterday's man.

The following Monday, I made that final call. Came in the door from work, suit still on, and dialled Eamonn's number. It's not the calmest I've ever felt in my life, the heart thumping, perspiration running down my back. My head was a blizzard of questions. How would I replace the adrenalin? The buzz? The thrill of playing in front of 80,000 people? Truth is, I don't suppose I ever will.

All anyone can do is get on with the rest of their life.

Eamonn's response was calm. 'OK,' he said, 'I got that sense last week you weren't for turning.'

Then he started thanking me for my service, and, in the way of a typical Irish male, I wasn't entirely comfortable with that. I didn't want *plámás*, no matter how sincerely intentioned. And I kind of needed my own space now, if for nothing else just to get the heartbeat down again. This, after all, was the final act of my Kerry career. The moment of absolute closure.

We agreed that we'd delay any announcement until after that weekend's League game against Tyrone.

And you know something? Hanging up, all I felt was huge relief.

I'd taken sentiment out of the decision, weighed up everything completely logically, and made the jump.

After a quick call to my girlfriend, Céitílís Ní Bheaglaoich, I took maybe twenty minutes to gather myself. Then I pulled the Andy Merrigan Cup out of the boot of the car and went walking up through the estate on a personal mission. Two elderly neighbours of mine, Tom McCarthy and Evelyn Regan, had been in the wars a bit with their health.

I called in to Tom first, an old Crokes stalwart, now confined to bed. And while we chatted about old times, about games he'd gone to with my father, about trips that sometimes ended up with them having 'a shot of pints' on the way home, it struck me that his hand stayed firmly clamped to the silverware. He'd actually become emotional when he saw it. And that emotion, I'll admit, made my own eyes fill.

Then around the corner to Evelyn – two house calls that took me no more than ninety minutes to make. And I felt completely uplifted walking back home after with the cup.

Just realizing the effect that seeing it had on them brought home to me just how selfish I'd become throughout my career. How defensive even. In some ways, I'd turned the avoidance of people into an art form. The art of staying in my own private bubble for fear somebody might say something I didn't want to hear. For years, from the moment I climbed out of bed in the morning, my head would have been full of training and diet and recovery.

I'd become hopelessly tunnelled because that's what I felt I needed to be.

If there was no milk in the house, I'd go without rather than call up to the local SuperValu for fear of who I might bump into. I lived in dread of being asked about training. About injuries. About a likely team for the weekend.

Maybe, from the outside, I might have looked really cool with things. And that certainly would have been the case in my early days. Like the Friday before the 2004 All-Ireland final against Mayo, I was on the counter in AIB, Killarney. Back then, even people who had no business in the bank would come up to the window just to chat. 'How will ye do this weekend?' The joke was I'd have a special queue to myself. It wouldn't knock a thing out of me. People wishing me well in the final and I'm meeting them with an easy smile.

'Thanks!'

That changed completely over the years. As I got older, I was never front of house in the build-up to a big game. I just wouldn't have been able to handle that. I began to carry the weight of the world on my shoulders.

Now, within minutes of ending my Kerry career, I already felt more at ease with myself. More open.

Of course, both Tom and Evelyn mentioned how sweet it would now be if I could bring home the Sam Maguire in September too to complete the set. And all I could do was lie to them. Tell them that it was the last thing on my mind now.

And, in a sense, my silence now was lying to everyone.

Kerry beat Tyrone that weekend to unexpectedly make the National League final, but Eamonn was happy that I go ahead with the announcement. 'Might even take a little heat off us,' he told me. So I texted brothers and sisters the night before. 'Look, keep this to yourselves, but this is breaking tomorrow . . .'

If that sounds impersonal, that's just the animal I am. Thinking about it, I couldn't help wonder afterwards if that text might even have come as a bit of a relief to them. Finally they could go to Kerry matches and not be fretting about how I did. Maybe there'd be some pride too. I'd hope so. But I didn't need them telling me that there and then.

The phone went into meltdown at work the following morning and my boss, Sean Healy – a passionate GAA man – let me away home. A brother of mine, Mike, called over and we headed to Killarney Golf Club for a quiet nine holes. I hadn't wanted to go when he suggested it, but it proved the perfect escape.

Believe it or not, the only conversation we had the whole way round was about yardages!

On our way out the door, Shane Lowry texted from Augusta. 'Is it true?'

'It is man, my time is up!'

'Ah bollix. Well good luck with it, we'll catch up soon!'

'How's your game?'

That was my reflex, I suppose. Diverting the conversation away. Not so much running from it as taking a giant sidestep. Shane had more than enough on his own plate, yet here he was thinking about my retirement. Two days later I'd be sitting on a high stool in McSweeney's, watching him go two under in the US Masters.

If I'm honest, that week comes back to me now as a bit of a blur. The breadth of tributes astonished me. To have people from other sports like Lowry and Brian O'Driscoll and Ronan O'Gara and Henry Shefflin and, yes, Judy Murray saying such kind things gave me a lot of pride. But some of those closer to home meant every bit as much. Some of the stuff from team-mates especially meant a lot. Likewise things said by opponents, particularly lads I might have had my share of battles and scrapes with over the years.

When you're a player, the first thing you want is the respect of your own people. But then when you sense it coming from a quarter you assumed just hated your guts, well, that means a hell of a lot too.

The evening before the League final I played a county league game against An Ghaeltacht. Marked by my old friend, Marc Ó Sé. The two of us were laughing as we had the pre-game handshake. 'Fuck it, is this what we're reduced to now? County league?'

That night we celebrated the fiftieth birthday of a mutual friend, Mick Culhane, in Ventry. And sitting in Páidí's place, at the same table as Darragh and Tomás, the stories flying over and back had us nearly crying with laughter.

Tomás: 'Do you remember me and the bottle of red wine?'

Me: 'Never mind that, do you remember me in Vilamoura?'

More about those later, but the night was really special. It just felt like so many worries were gone. Nobody paying much attention to me or my retirement, all the focus on the birthday boy. Céitílis and I hurried back to Killarney the following day because I wanted to be in my own place to watch Kerry taking on the Dubs.

A quick, anonymous lunch in Treyvaud's, then time to settle down in front of the TV. For some reason, paranoia probably, I didn't want to watch the preliminaries and made a point of switching channels to the soccer rather than hear the half-time conversation. Did the same at full-time. Even *as Gaeilge* on TG4, I had a suspicion I might feature.

So I had no idea that the GAA decided to mark my retirement with a tribute on the giant stadium screens. Just a few texts came through that night, describing it as a beautiful collage of moments that was warmly applauded by both sets of supporters.

Hearing that meant a lot to me.

But my time was over. You could say 'The Gooch' had been decommissioned, but then I doubt that will ever really be the case.

Funny how that name caught such traction from the moment our old Dr Crokes goalkeeper Peter O'Brien came up with it on the basis that I, apparently, bore a passing resemblance to those red-haired 'Goochie' dolls that were all the rage back in the late eighties, early nineties. I'd have been no more than eight years old at the time, but people I've known my entire adult life have never addressed me as anything other than 'Gooch'.

In many ways, only my family ever communicates with me as plain Colm.

Of course, Céití was treated to a running commentary (whether she liked it or not) as the boys, finally, turned the tables on Dublin. She said afterwards that she didn't recognize the creature ranting at the TV, that she'd never seen me so animated. And it did feel strange watching a game from afar in which I had a fairly intimate sense of the tactics being applied.

So I was all 'They've got to press up here!'

Or, 'Go Dave go, pop into that pocket!'

It's fair to say I was wired by the finish, and seeing Fionn go up to get the cup filled me with pride. You could see what it meant to him, what it meant to Kerry. We needed that win.

But not once, not for a single second, did I sit there thinking 'Shit, I left a League medal behind me!' And that fact was telling me now that I'd made the right decision.

The final over, we slipped out of the house, down towards the cathedral and took ourselves for a walk in the National Park. Just ordinary people doing the most ordinary thing on an ordinary Sunday evening.

The whoops and hollers of Croke Park could have been on another planet.

1

'The Dirtiest Child in Killarney'

There's a photograph I treasure above the million other snap-shots taken during my football career.

It brings me back to an October day in Tralee seven years ago, specifically to the end of the county final. The *Kingdom* newspaper ran it across their front page that week with the gold-lettered caption 'That's my boy'. It's just me and my mother, Maureen, running towards each other to embrace.

I suppose every Irish son believes they're the apple of their mother's eye but, in my case, I pretty much knew it. My mother fussed over me in a way she never did my four brothers and two sisters. She was endlessly protective towards me, maybe especially so that day in 2010.

It was Dr Crokes' first win in ten years (we'd lost three of the previous five finals) and, accordingly, our first title since my father, Mike, passed away suddenly in 2006. Unlike in 2000, I was the only Cooper boy in action this time in Austin Stack Park and I suppose there were a lot of different emotions fizzing between my mother and me as we ran towards each other that day.

I'd just shaken my marker's hand when, before I knew it, she was there in front of me. No words were exchanged between us. It was just pure emotion, the kind that words probably could never adequately convey. Even thinking about it now makes my eyes sting.

My father's death affected me a lot more than I understood at the time. You tell yourself you're fine, but you're not. He died on an April Monday and I actually came on in a League game against Dublin six days later. Why? Just something that Maureen said encouraged me to do it.

Something along the lines of 'Do whatever feels right to you, but I think your father would want you to play.'

So less than seventy-two hours after watching my father's coffin go into the ground up in Aghadoe, I was running around a football field trying to convince myself and everybody else that I was doing fine.

I wasn't in a good place for a while. Actually, I think it was a year on before I really started to deal with it. When someone dies suddenly, it's hard to avoid a feeling of bitterness. You question things. Why did it happen?

A year earlier I'd lost a really good friend of mine, Kieran Cahillane, in a drowning accident. The tragedy occurred in the early hours of the Sunday that Kerry played Mayo in the '05 All-Ireland quarter-final. There's a diving rock on Moll's Gap, not far from Ladies View, a spot that lads were inclined to go up to for a bit of craic. I'd never gone there myself and I'm not sure if in Kieran's case it had just been a one-off. But he went up there this evening with a gang of lads from town and never came home.

Look, we've all done unwise things in our lives and lived to tell the tale. Tragically, on this occasion, Kieran didn't.

He was a very bubbly fella, seldom in poor form, and we were great buddies. We'd have collected glasses together in Tatler's when we were younger, but then he was hugely popular with everyone in Crokes.

There was a seven-a-side soccer tournament played in Killarney every summer, one that Crokes would always put a team in. We'd call it the 'Tatler Toffees' and Kieran would usually be on it. Sometimes I'd operate as manager, though I use that expression loosely. Basically, the job of manager would entail bringing a bottle of water and picking seven out of ten players to start.

I remember Kieran as just a good, close friend. Someone in whose company I was always comfortable.

Management took a decision not to break the news to us until after the Mayo game.

I'd been talking to Kieran that Saturday night and we were going to meet up for a pint when I got back down from Dublin. Dr Crokes had a Munster League game the day before in Tipperary. He went up with two or three others and they were in a car accident on the day. They'd all escaped injury and he was almost laughing about it afterwards. 'We were lucky,' he told me on the phone.

So we won the quarter-final and once back in the dressing-room the three Dr Crokes lads – myself, Eoin Brosnan and Kieran Cremin – were called into an ante-room, where the drug-testing is done. The door was locked and Patrick 'The Bag' O'Sullivan began, 'There's something I need to tell ye . . .' I could see his eyes were welling up.

And do you know, I'd seen Patrick come out of the hotel lift that morning in the Crowne Plaza and remembered thinking he just didn't look himself. That his eyes seemed a little watery. Now my first thought was 'There's something wrong at home'. But then, why had he brought the three of us in?

You're just after playing in front of maybe 60,000 people and suddenly it means nothing.

I got the train home, went to Kieran's house in Pinewood and saw him lying in a coffin. He was nineteen. All I could think was 'This can't be true. I'm going to wake up out of this horrible dream any minute . . .'

Do families ever really recover from tragedies like that? I'm not sure it's actually possible. A part of you must be broken for ever. To this day I meet his parents, James and Eileen, and on some level – when I'm talking to them – it's Kieran's face I see. Same when I see his older brother, James.

Emotionally I was all over the place when it happened, taking the week off work and missing training.

And, in a way, Kieran's death maybe began getting tangled up in my mind when my father passed away a year later. You expect to be doing different things with your friend or with your father and that's gone out of your life without warning. There's a big hole. Things move on but, on some level, you're reluctant to move with them. You feel bitter.

We all as a family went through a little bit of that in 2006 I think.

I grew up in working-class Ardshanavooly, a children's paradise just off Park Road in Killarney.

Small terraced houses, three up, three down. Mam, Dad and seven of us squeezed into a tiny space. I remember it as idyllic when for my parents it must have been anything but. Actually, my childhood comes back to me now as a bit of a minor miracle. You see, we had everything and nothing. Mike and Maureen Cooper worked incredibly long hours that only now, in hindsight, register fully with me and, I suspect, my siblings.

My father was a general labourer on building sites six days a week. My mother worked in the Laune Bar and also routinely did double shifts in a restaurant, The Flesk, downtown. They basically grafted around the clock just to keep us fed, clothed and warm. I had no appreciation of that at the time. How could I? I hardly had time to catch my breath.

My sister Karen still jokes that I was 'the dirtiest child in Killarney'. My nails, my face, my hair always seemed clogged with muck. There's a green space both front and back of Ardshanavooly and it was on those two stretches of grass that I lived out my fantasies. It's also, I suspect, where I came to understand the importance of self-sufficiency.

Maybe being the youngest of five boys (Danny, Mark, Mike and Vince in that order), I was always going to have that quality given the brothers didn't exactly spare me physically in games. But there was a democracy to life in Ardshan too that went deeper than immediate family. On a summer's evening, nearly every house in the estate could be represented in our soccer games and the age profile of those playing could range between ten and thirty.

It would be hell for leather stuff that would frequently end in tears for the smallest and lightest.

Those two words – small and light – attached themselves almost permanently to me through my teens as a Gaelic footballer and, given I had barely turned seventeen when I first played Senior Championship with Dr Crokes, I am often asked if I ever felt physically intimidated in that time. The honest answer is no. Games on the Ardshan greens genuinely steeled me to survive against older, stronger players. I learned there how to deal with pain and, maybe more importantly, how to avoid it.

Those games hardened me to everything: falls, fights, scrapes, being told you were 'useless', 'too weak', 'too small', getting the instruction 'Go away home to your Mam now' whenever the tears might start to flow. I remember my own brother, Mike, absolutely lamping me with a tackle once after I'd nutmegged him on the green and, in his mind I suppose, humiliated him. So off home I went, tears streaming down my face. Those were the rules of engagement, even with your own flesh and blood. No quarter asked or given. Every match we played meant something to us and we became hungry, fiery bastards. That's certainly where my competitive streak comes from. If it's a game of marbles, I'll want to win.

It's funny, I was up in the Newstalk studio in 2016 doing an interview for the Club Championship when Joe Molloy put it to me that he got the sense from me that I was a pretty happy-go-lucky character. That if I won, great. If not, it wasn't the beginning or the end of the world.

And I started to laugh. 'No, no, no, that's not me at all. You've got me completely wrong there!' The truth is, a defeat can hang with me for a whole winter. Defeat cuts me deep. It lingers with me. I enjoy the highs as much as anyone, but the setbacks probably send me down lower than most. I care so much, I end up peppering myself with questions.

Fuck it, why didn't I perform?

Did I cut corners?

I review everything, almost to an obsessive degree.

Fuck it, should I not have eaten that extra bowl of cornflakes?

It could get ridiculous at times and, in recent years, I've consciously tried to get more rational about things. But happy-go-lucky Joe? Lord Jesus, not a hope.

Soccer was the main game we played in Ardshan, if only because it was the simplest. But we moved with the seasons, mimicking everything we saw on TV.

If it was April and The Masters, we were up the back building our little golf course with twigs for flags and mounds of sand for bunkers. At a squeeze we could probably fit seven holes into a stretch of grass running up to the basketball court behind what is now Deerpark Shopping Centre. You might have thirty of us in fourballs, playing for a 'pot' of fifty cents, which could buy you a fair bit in the local newsagent's.

In May, we'd be playing FA Cup finals at Wembley. Come July, the tennis racquets would be out on the road to recreate Wimbledon. Endlessly, we just adapted and improvised. There used to be a hotel just across the road, The Torc, that had a tennis court and we'd sometimes slip across there too when it was quiet, the staff knowing full well we weren't guests' children but leaving us be to bang balls at one another as Andre Agassi or Pete Sampras.

I particularly remember the thrill of Italia '90 and being down on the front green, every one of us wanting to be Paul McGrath or Ray Houghton for the night.

To survive in Ardshan, you had to be able to play multiple sports. Not necessarily excel at them, but at least compete.

Everything seemed so easy back then. We hardly ever had money in our pockets, but fun didn't come with a price tag. Above all, life felt safe. Some summer mornings a few of us might just head away out to Muckross on our bikes, always with the message 'Bring the ball!' If you could squeeze a few bob off your Mam or Dad, well and good. If not, just grab something out of the bread bin. We barely had time to eat, let alone grow hungry.

You could be gone from ten a.m. to eight p.m., yet nobody worried. Ours was a world without mobile phones. With no endless monitoring. People just looked out for one another, kids included.

Another day it could be a trek up to Deerpark Pitch and Putt, just beside the main Crokes field (which then, incredibly, was a pond full of tadpoles) on Lewis Road. Up through a farmer's field and in a back fence to escape the inconvenience of paying. I'd say we were the bane of the owners' lives up there. And, because of the geography, Ardshan boys developed an intimate knowledge of the holes on the back of the course.

Only a mug ever bet against one of us on nine, ten or eleven!

I imagine a lot of kids today would read this and groan at the simplicity and innocence of our young lives. But it was Heaven. I wouldn't swap the memories for anything.

I mean, I see my nieces and nephews now and their days seem so wrapped up in technology and social media and communicating in just about every way imaginable bar sitting down and having a chat. Don't get me wrong, they have their lives too. I do get that. My older sister Geraldine's daughter, Ciara, plays with the Kerry Minors. She's already won three All-Irelands and likes to remind me that she's catching up on me.

But the first thing she does when she comes into my house is charge up her phone.

'Jesus, Ciara,' I say, 'would you just leave the phone down for a second?'

And she'll look at me as if I'm something prehistoric. 'Colm, relax . . .'

The day before my father died, Dr Crokes won a county league game against Rathmore and Mike Cooper was sitting in his usual spot that evening, sipping a pint in Jimmy O'Brien's. We met at home beforehand and I mentioned to him that I needed to get my car taxed. He said he'd sort it out for me in the morning. Those were the last words we spoke.

A massive heart attack took him away from us and the sadness and loneliness took a long time to go away. Sometimes Maureen would be babysitting some grandchildren and I'd arrive home to a completely empty house, the starkness of everything just exaggerated by the silence.

I suppose I was lucky that I had the football but, looking back at '06, I just wasn't myself that summer. Losing my father affected me a lot more deeply than I understood. I went on automatic pilot. We won the All-Ireland, but I played quite poorly throughout most of it. I just didn't seem to have that hunger. I was going in training only because everybody expected me to be there. But I was only there in body.

I remember I met Dr Con Murphy for a pint in McSweeney's that October and, somehow, I think he could see it in me. He told me it took him two years to get over his own father dying and I was standing there, telling him, 'I'm fine Con, honestly I'm fine!'

But I wasn't fine. There was an emptiness there, maybe an anger still inside me. And I think that anger takes something from you, just from how you carry yourself. It had a very big impact on me and took me maybe the best part of twelve months to properly deal with it.

The lads in Jimmy O'Brien's probably knew my father better than anyone. They'd tell me stories of fellas coming into the pub from different parts of the country, gabbing away about Kerry football when one of them might almost inevitably ask, 'Does Gooch live near here?' Jimmy would stand there behind the counter, peering out over his glasses with a smile, knowing that there wouldn't be a word out of my father.

Dad loved that. Just him and his pint, never letting on that I was his son, regulars grinning from ear to ear at his silence. That was his style, always keeping his cards close to his chest.

He was the same at home, never coming out with any big opinion about how one of us might have played in training or during a match. He'd always be inclined to hold fire. A few days later, one of the brothers might say something to me like, 'You were going well the other night. What did you get, 1–2?' And before I had a chance to answer, he'd look up from behind his paper and say flatly, 'Yeah, but what about the two points he missed?'

In his house, no son would ever be allowed to get ahead of themselves.

Mike Cooper didn't play much football himself but I think it's fair to say that he loved the game. He was a Dr Crokes selector for a good few B teams, mainly social outlets where the biggest challenge for management would be to find fifteen guys available at the same time. There'd always be a few pints after those matches because craic was the glue that held those teams together.

Tuesday nights, he'd routinely head off to see a game somewhere in the county that might have zero relevance to Crokes. Say Glenflesk against Spa, just to see it for the sake of it. Always he'd bring me with him, and it never ceased to amaze me that Dad seemed to know everybody at these games. He'd like nothing more than to be in Jimmy's the following Friday, telling the lads about this fella or that fella who they'd be hearing about down the line.

His way at home was to stay largely undemonstrative. When I won my first All-Ireland medal in '04, I remember him coming up to me in The Burlington with just a shake of the hand and a pat on the back. That was it. No big speech. No great show of emotion.

And I think we all pretty much inherited that from Dad. We've never been big as a family on expressing our emotions to one another. Maybe a lot went unsaid, with the boys especially, but that wasn't coldness. In fact, it was anything but. My father communicated his pride in every one of us in his own quiet, gentle way. None of us doubted for a second that he loved us.

But he was a creature of routine and an unashamed homebird. He and Mam had spent a little time working over in Cricklewood when their romance was still young, but Killarney was home and, other than Dublin in August or September, I don't think he ever had any great interest in leaving town. It was as if his time in England convinced him that travel was overrated.

In fact, the idea of going on a foreign holiday would have been laughable to Mike Cooper. I'd say he couldn't imagine anything he'd like to do less. All he wanted was the comfort of routine. Of work, home, family, Jimmy's on a Friday and Saturday night, a match on Sunday.

In later years, when we were all earning and keen to give something back to Mam and Dad, we'd sometimes propose a little holiday abroad. 'Will you go for a week to Portugal with Mam and the girls?' And he'd look at us as if we were aliens.

'Not a chance,' he'd say with a grin. 'But don't let me be stopping the rest of ye!'

His death made me question why we take ourselves so seriously in this life. Football is sport. Work is your job. Neither is the beginning or the end. I remember in the early days after he passed, I'd go home and be looking at that empty chair and just feeling there was such a gap in my life.

Maybe they were the things that got to me most. The quietness. The empty chair. No car in the drive.

They were great friends, him and my mother. Mam was from Cromane originally, just outside Killorglin. Dad came from Cummeenavrick, Clonkeen, on the Kerry/Cork border – not far from Séamus Moynihan country. The lads from Ballyvourney used to have some craic slagging him about that in Jimmy's.

'Jesus, Mike, if you were only another mile up the road, Gooch would have been a Corkman!'

And him laughing, 'Well thank God it was all downhill to Killarney because my chain was broken!'

We couldn't have asked for a better upbringing. Like we never had much, but we always seemed to have enough to get by. We joke about that among ourselves now. One of the brothers might be bringing the family to Portugal for two weeks and we'd be slagging him, 'Jesus it's far from holidays to Portugal you were reared!'

The truth is I look back on my childhood as the perfect grounding. Growing up in an estate of maybe 115 houses where there was a huge amount of young people, everyone out till all hours in the summer, playing games. Mam would be cracking up because I was endlessly sneaking out, diving around with a ball, even if it was pelting down with rain. I literally could not walk to the shop without a ball in my hand.

The neighbours, sometimes, would come out at eleven o'clock at night, asking, 'Colm, do you realize what time it is?'

Maybe they were just sick of the noise, worn down by the relentless thud of a ball hitting concrete. But there was a real community warmth there too. Still is. And the thing is, nobody worried. We were in a safe place, full of big families that mirrored our own.

When I think of growing up, the amount of sport we played is what dominates my memory. Not just the soccer and Gaelic, the pitch and putt and tennis, but basketball too, up on a court at the back before the nets were cut down. The sport had a massive following in Killarney back then with St Paul's playing in the National League and drawing the likes of Ballina (with the McHales and Deora Marsh) or Star of the Sea of Belfast down to the Presentation Gym.

When the nets up the back did go, left behind were the severed stanchions, two metal bars no more than 4 feet high and maybe 2 metres apart. From the age of eight or nine I practised my kicking relentlessly through those bars, left foot, right foot. Usually I'd be alone, but I'd love it when there was someone who'd come up with me to kick the ball back. Nobody told me to do it, but my right wasn't as strong as I wanted it to be. Looking back, I think my skill level has always been high largely because of the work I did up there, between those metal bars.

I can't remember having a best friend as such because you could actually play with seven different people in as many days. Sometimes when I meet old friends now, they say to me, 'How in God's name did our families raise us? Sure none of us had anything.' It's true, we didn't. But the beauty of those days was it never felt that way.

When Mike died, Maureen pretty much took on the role of joint mother and father to us. She made a point of getting out and about a little more, going to matches with the two girls when previously she'd been quite happy to leave that to the men.

And I think she really began to enjoy the craic that came with following Dr Crokes around. That win in 2010 became the first of four consecutive county final victories and I've great memories of bringing the cup down the town for a parade, meeting for a drink and seeing my mother, smiling broadly, coming through the door. She'd sit down with us and have a glass of Guinness, the kids dancing around the cup like moths around a light. She loved meeting the other players, asking after their parents.

When I think about that now, I know I'll never be able to thank my two sisters enough for encouraging her to do that, for getting her out of the house. You could see the realization slowly dawn in Mam: 'Do you know, I like getting out like this!'

And almost always after a game, her opening line to me would be 'You'll never guess who I met . . .'

She started coming to Kerry matches in Dublin too but they played havoc with her nerves. Sometimes she just stayed in the hotel across Jones's Road, hearing the roars of the crowd but choosing to wait for the girls to come back over and tell her the news. The building of that hotel was a godsend to her. It meant she could be right next to the action without actually having to sit through it.

And you've never met a prouder woman. Proud of her family. Proud of her house. She'd go to bingo on Sunday nights, just around the corner. If Kerry had won that day, people said they could see an extra bounce in her stride, coming through the door. A staunch Crokes woman, wearing her pride lightly.

And Maureen, above all, could read me like a book. She knew instinctively when I wanted to talk about something and when I just needed some space. There's a great comfort in having someone like that in your life because there's no effort required when in their company.

Maybe it's the ultimate friendship.

Our house, inevitably, was full of football. Five boys who lived to play, a father who was addicted and a club – Dr Crokes – who'd have Mike Buckley (Johnny's dad) doing circuits of the town in his bus every Saturday morning to bring kids up the Lewis Road to training.

'Twas the highlight of our week to be sitting on a wall at the entrance to the estate for that 10.10 a.m. pick-up. Ahead lay an hour of Heaven on the small pitch behind Fitzgerald Stadium where, on the really good days, a Crokes senior like Connie Murphy or Pat O'Shea might take charge of the session.

They were our heroes. You see, Kerry hadn't a great team at the time and my earliest memories of Munster finals would be of triumphant Cork supporters. You have to remember that after Kerry's last All-Ireland win under Mick O'Dwyer in '86, the county won just one of the next nine Munster Championships. We were, effectively, in the doldrums.

For a child of that era, then, the video machine became a godsend. The day we got one was a monumental one in the

Cooper household, not simply because we could now rent movies from Mike Stack's shop down the town, but because we could now tape matches off *The Sunday Game* too and, most importantly, watch incessant re-runs of *Kerry's Golden Years*.

I'd say, in time, every house in Ardshan had a copy of that video, the commentaries becoming so familiar to us we had all but learned them off by heart.

So we'd be out on the green, doing our 'Phoenix from the Flames' thing, with Micheal O'Hehir's, Mick Dunne's or Ger Canning's words pouring out instinctively.

'And Paddy Cullen, oh dear, oh dear . . . Paddy Cullen adjudged . . . oh a goal in the greatest freak of all time . . .'

'John Egan . . . Kevin Moran can't hold on to him, and I mean hold on . . .'

'John Egan heading through . . . oh Paddy, what are you going to do?'

Those men were gods to us, but faintly distant gods. They belonged to another lifetime. Kerry's biggest star of my childhood was Maurice Fitzgerald, but he was nine years playing for the county before he ever got to Croke Park in September. Maurice Fitz was a sublime talent at a time when Kerry had few enough of them. So the men I wanted to emulate were Crokes players. Neighbours. Brothers.

I was eight when Crokes brought me to Croke Park as their mascot for the '92 All-Ireland Club final against Thomas Davis of Dublin. Two of my brothers, Danny and Mark, were in a tiny (by today's standards) squad of just nineteen players and I had been a virtual ever-present up at training, endlessly kicking balls back on to the field, handing out water bottles.

From memory, it was Teddy Counihan and John Keogh, the club's chairman and secretary back then, who called to the house that week to make the announcement. 'Colm, we want you to be our mascot above in Dublin.' I looked at my parents blankly. Hadn't a clue what they were talking about. Didn't know what it was that mascots might be expected to do. Come to think of it, I didn't even really understand that this was going to be an All-Ireland final.

I knew it was a big thing for the club becoming kingpins of Kerry in '91 because they'd fallen at the final hurdle a few times. For some reason I specifically remember the devastation of them losing a final replay to Kenmare in '87 even though I wouldn't have been old enough to go to that game.

But I suppose I was a part of the Crokes furniture by '92, always allowed in the dressing-room and on first-name terms with men who, to me, were the biggest stars around.

And the club did things in a style appropriate to that status, the players all kitted out in blazers with crests on the breast pocket and their tiny mascot given a specially tailored tracksuit that, believe it or not, remains in the Cooper household to this day. I was beyond euphoric when I realized what it entailed. Being part of the official party meant that I travelled up with them on the train, staying overnight in The Grand Hotel Malahide. This, to me, was the nearest I'd ever come to foreign travel. Croke Park existed only on the telly to me, almost a place of make-believe. I remember thinking that, in their blazers, the players looked like a professional soccer team from England – and, being honest, I couldn't imagine anything more glamorous than that at the time.

Memories of the day?

The old dressing-rooms in Croke Park were down at the corner where the Hogan Stand met the Canal End, the pitch accessed through a concrete tunnel that saw its share of skelping across the years. As the Crokes players went jogging out for their warm-up, a steward made to block my way.

'No kids or mascots allowed on the field,' he said.

Peter O'Brien was our goalkeeper and a neighbour from Ardshanavooly. 'Open the fucking gate!' he roared. 'He goes where we go!'

The steward knew better than to argue and, pretty soon, there I was standing on this magical field, trying to look important and busy, yet all the time snatching glances into the stands to see if Mam and Dad or, better still, some school friends might see me in my tracksuit.

Part of the warm-up involved fellas cracking low, hard shots at Peter in the goal, and when someone threw me a ball I did the only thing that came naturally, rattling it into the Canal End net. Next thing, I could see Peter's expression darken. There he was, getting himself psyched up for the biggest football day of his life, and an eight-year-old had just rattled one past him. Just the thing for confidence.

'Will you ever fuck off over to the dugout!' he roared.

What I maybe only realized much later was that, for virtually all of the Crokes players, this was a first time in Croke Park. Psychologically, the challenge ahead was massive. Connie Murphy – who would win Man of the Match – would have been the only Kerry panellist on the team, and even for Connie trips to Dublin weren't exactly commonplace. So this was a once-in-a-lifetime opportunity, and they didn't want to let it slip.

I remember watching the game intently without fully understanding its importance. But I still shared in the general exultation when the final whistle blew with Crokes winners by the narrowest of margins, 1-11 to 0-13.

Heuston Station that evening was party-central for anyone heading to Killarney.

And the fuss afterwards was intoxicating to me, the cup being brought around to schools and a realization beginning to dawn that this team of neighbours and friends, under the management of Eddie 'Tatler' O'Sullivan, was officially the best in Ireland now. I remember thinking that to be a Dr Crokes man was to feel utterly bulletproof.

It's funny, the twenty-fifth anniversary of that winning campaign was acknowledged the weekend of the 2016 county final, the players paraded at half-time and were invited to deliver the customary ceremonial wave. I heard there was a good session the night before too and everything was done with a bit of style. Just before Christmas I was slagging Vince Casey, one of the club stalwarts, about it over lunch in The Royal.

'Ye're fucking milking this, Vince,' I said, laughing. 'The great one-in-a-row team!'

When I got the bad knee injury that ruled me out of 2014, my mother was the one who seemed to best understand the emotional minefield I was now picking my way through. By then I'd moved into my own house out in Ballydowney on the Killorglin Road and, by and large, liked keeping to myself out there. In the early stages of recovery especially I just wasn't much company for anyone.

To be fair to Mam, she'd say to my sisters, 'If he wants to stay at home, leave him be!' The bond I had with her used to crack them up. They'd say I was spoilt rotten. And I was. My mother would do things for me that she wouldn't dream of doing for the rest of them. She could have something arranged on the Saturday before a Munster final, but wouldn't hesitate to cancel so that she'd be there to make me dinner. I knew she'd have preferred to have me living at home, if only to make sure I was eating properly. Like most Irish mothers, I suppose, she was a worrier. I'd say she had the rosary beads worn to nothing over the years, praying that I'd come to no harm.

So 2014 really knocked her out of kilter. To suddenly hear a story of me being injured making the *Six One News* would have been unsettling for her. Hearing that I was likely to be out for a year would have been a real jolt, and it certainly didn't help that there were people on local radio even speculating that I might not play again.

My mother was old-style, you see, in the sense of believing that if somebody said something on radio, it must be true. She'd nearly see that as having more legitimacy than what I'd be telling her myself. And I could sense, instinctively, that she was worried about where I might be psychologically that spring. In a sense, she had every reason.

But her faith always sustained Maureen through good and bad, and it would need to be especially strong that summer. It was amazing to see the comfort she drew from it, the store she put on sending Mass cards and saying novenas or decades of the rosary. She'd go to Mass in The Friary regularly and knew everything that was going on in the parish. I remember thinking that she was so deep in credit with the Almighty it was only right that I could count almost a dozen priests at her funeral Mass.

To some degree, I envied her the certainty of that devotion.

Like I always go to Mass the morning of a big game in Dublin, but am I an avid Mass-goer? No, I couldn't say I am. As Declan O'Sullivan said to me once, 'We always go to Mass when we want something.'

The cancer diagnosis came our way that March.

I remember Kerry playing Tyrone in a League game in Killarney around that time and Mam just saying that she didn't feel herself. When subsequent tests confirmed our worst fears, we had a lot of difficulty getting her a hospital bed before – with Dr Con's assistance – we finally got her a spot in the Cancer Unit of Cork University Hospital.

My mother hated hospitals and found the next four or five

weeks especially hard. We were taking turns to go over and back but eventually we reached a compromise that she could come home, reporting back to the hospital once a week for radiation and chemotherapy treatment. I'm not sure if she was thinking the worst back then; we certainly weren't. But I do vividly remember her saying to me one day, 'Look, whatever way this is going to pan out, I'm not going to go back to hospital!' All she wanted was the comfort of her own home and she was, instantly, happier once inside the front door.

My sisters were in regular contact with the doctors but, deep down, we could all see her declining in front of our eyes. Geraldine rang me one day to confirm what I think we'd all been quietly suspecting.

'The treatment isn't working.'

Soon enough, the prognosis came that she had, at best, a few months to live. I think Geraldine's words were 'Look, she'll be doing well to see September'. The moment I heard that my heart skipped a beat, even if I can't say I was surprised. I look back now and I see that she was putting on a brave face for our benefit. She'd constantly be telling us that she was 'grand' when, in hind-sight, she must have been feeling desperately ill.

But my mother was the most unselfish person that you could ever meet. She just didn't want to be the centre of attention in any way.

As she began to fade, I think the morale of everyone around her hit rock bottom. The girls were fantastic, a thousand times more useful and practical than us boys. We kind of rotated the times to sit with her, but Geraldine and Karen took the brunt of it. A loved one dying puts an awful strain on families and I can't really imagine how we'd have coped if my sisters hadn't done as much as they did.

Kerry played Galway in an All-Ireland quarter-final on 3 August and, with Eamonn Fitzmaurice now involving me in squad matters again, I travelled to Dublin with them. Eamonn, I suspect, was trying to help take my mind off matters at home, and my sisters fully understood the psychological boost that would give me. And Maureen herself was still sufficiently alert to be telling them, 'Make sure he's on that train to Dublin.'

But then, over the next few days, the life just began to drain away from her.

On the Wednesday night we were all in the house, knowing the end was near. Essentially taking turns to sit with her on the basis that we couldn't bear the thought of her passing without someone being by her side.

It's almost funny looking back at how her pride would not allow her to lie in a bed even for those last harrowing hours. Home to her was the couch in the sitting-room, from where she'd always watched television, read the paper or just listened to the radio. That was her definition of a home place and she wasn't about to vacate it.

I'll forever take comfort from the fact that I just happened to be sitting with her as she breathed her last. She was kind of in my arms, me just rubbing her hair. Then this gentle gasp and, suddenly, my mother was gone.

She is buried above in Aghadoe with my father now, the breathtaking perch of the cemetery offering a view of The Lakes and Carrauntoohil and, if you crane your neck to the left, Ross Castle. It's one of the most beautiful resting places you could imagine. And, strangely, the grave next up from them, no more than 12 feet away, is that of my old friend Kieran.

I hope they're sleeping soundly.

2

'Colm, Bring Up Your Boots . . .'

Kieran Donaghy sometimes says to me, 'Gooch, you were always going to play for Kerry!'

My usual response isn't printable. It's bullshit you see, this idea that I was some kind of protégé always on the radar of those who mattered in the county. I wasn't. You probably had to be on winning teams to have that status and I'm not exaggerating when I say that, from the age of twelve to minor, my group in Dr Crokes hardly won two games in a calendar year.

I was dealing with a lot of failure and, to be honest, not dealing with it especially well. I'd get unbelievably frustrated.

The problem was that I cared far too much when some of those I was playing with palpably didn't care at all. In fact, they really didn't give a toss whether we won or lost, and that was constantly wrecking my head. I remember an under-14 game against Kilcummin one day – a neighbouring club – and they must have been hammering us by twenty points. With every new adjustment to the scoreboard I was becoming a bigger Antichrist on the field.

Even though I was tiny, I was having to play midfield, the idea being that I'd catch a few kick-outs, carry the ball upfield and maybe feed the lads inside. Problem was, no one seemed to be communicating to the lads inside that this might be happening. Every time I kicked a ball in, it came straight back out as if off a gable wall.

This came to a head when, having been fouled, I went to take a quick free. Glancing up, I could see that the lads inside weren't even looking in my direction. As I put it to Pat 'The Bag' O' Sullivan – who was on the line, monitoring my preciousness – they were 'too busy looking at fucking flowers or whatever'.

In a temper, I just kicked the ball out over the sideline. 'Just take me off!' I said in a huff. And Pat was fit to be tied.

There I was playing the martyr rather than swallowing my pride and just doing my best for an outclassed team. And Lord Jesus he gave it to me between the eyes on the way home that day. 'Colm, you need to cop yourself on boy!' Without realizing it at the time, I think that day taught me a lesson. It sowed a seed. If I was already developing a hard edge from the games in Ardshanavooly, that day flicked another switch. I was getting too angry and impatient.

All well and good, but I needed to channel it in the right direction.

The trouble was I'd have been going to school in The Sem with a lot of those Kilcummin players and the thought of just seeing them the following morning killed me. I knew I was a lot better than some of the fellas giving us these hidings, but we just couldn't win. We were always carrying too much dead wood.

I couldn't understand why fellas didn't care, why they'd walk off the field after a hiding like that still chatting and joking as if the scoreline hadn't actually registered. Me? I cared too much. I wouldn't be able to sleep that night with the frustration of what had happened. And that wasn't healthy or natural for a fourteen-year-old.

I would have been a First Year in The Sem at the time and still a million miles from making any waves as a player. 'Nice footballer, but too small' was all I ever heard. It was like an echo.

One that would follow me all the way into a Kerry jersey.

My schooldays were confined to three buildings all within a square quarter mile of one another off New Road in Killarney town.

Fourteen years spent strictly local then, starting in 'The Mercy' (Holy Cross Mercy National School), then 200 yards down the street to 'The Mon' (Presentation Monastery), and finally across the road to the ivy-clad walls of 'The Sem' (St Brendan's College).

When I think of it, in thirty-four years I haven't stirred very far from my roots. When Mam died, I even moved back into the family home in Ardshanavooly. Apart from a short stint working in Tralee, the geography of my life today has changed very little from what it was in my childhood.

The Sem is a bit of an institution in Kerry football with a record number of senior Munster college titles to its name, not to mention the 2016 Hogan Cup as All-Ireland champions. It has given some of the county's most legendary names their first real taste of serious competition, including the likes of Páidí Ó Sé, Johnny Culloty, John O'Keeffe, Pat Spillane and Seamus Moynihan.

And it's probably fair to say that, for a time, pulling on The Sem jersey felt like a bit of a release to me. It was considered a big thing to be in the college colours because it put a player in the shop window in terms of county advancement. Seán Kelly, the future GAA President, was a teacher there at the time and took charge of a couple of teams I was picked on. We won the Russell and Moran Cups (Kerry and Munster under-15 titles), but it would be wrong to suggest that I was living out any kind of dream here.

Yes, it was better than the routine hammerings I'd become accustomed to with Crokes, but I was playing soccer with Killarney Celtic (sweeper, striker, left side of midfield) too and, being honest, was a little torn between which of the sports I was enjoying most. I'd actually stay playing soccer until called up to the Kerry minors, but that was still a long, long way away.

I did get called up to Kerry under-16 development squads, but that experience had zero positive impact on me. If anything, it made me angry. I was always a sub you see, even though I firmly believed I was better than a lot of those playing. Again the stigma of being on so many losing Crokes teams seemed to be following me around. And I'd be sitting there absolutely boiling with temper.

Why the fuck am I even here?

The truth is I didn't really care what jersey was on my back. I just wanted to play.

Declan O'Sullivan would have been on those development squads and clearly already signposted to be a future star, himself and Micheal Meehan two of the big names at senior colleges level for Coláiste na Sceilge and St Jarlath's respectively. Me? I wasn't even mapped at that stage. Even when I broke on to The Sem's senior team, there weren't exactly trumpets blaring around the county in celebration of a new star.

That's the point I keep trying to get across to Donaghy. My early career was a very reluctant slow-burn, largely because people still seemed fixated on my slight physique. Only in Crokes was anyone inclined to look beyond my size and recognize that here was somebody who could really play.

By the age of sixteen I'd begun training with the senior team and was flirting around the edges of our Championship squad.

And that's when the rhythm of my football life began to quicken. I was really stepping up to the mark in training, often against men twice my age, and I have a suspicion that someone in the club eventually rang Charlie Nelligan, then the Kerry minors manager, and said, 'Listen, you really should have a look at this fella.'

Because I was called in to a trial in Tralee and we played a game against the Kerry juniors. That evening I motored well, scored something like 1-4, and it was as if eyebrows suddenly started to rise all around me. A case of 'How is this fella not even in on our extended squad?'

From that night on, I was in.

So the launch pad wasn't The Sem or Kerry development squads, it was the belief of people in Dr Crokes. Contrary to what so many people imagine, the timeline really was that stark. I began breaking on to the senior Crokes team around April 2000, roughly two months before my seventeenth birthday. Only then did the Kerry minors come calling.

And, even when they did, there was still an element of management hedging their bets.

You wouldn't have put a dog out that July day in 2000 that changed my life in football.

My Senior Championship debut for Dr Crokes was against our nemesis, South Kerry, in a county quarter-final that might as well have been played on an oil rig. Waterville was under siege from the skies that day and not many fancied an ageing Dr Crokes team to come out the right side against opponents who had Kerry's best player, Maurice Fitzgerald, in their ranks. Visiting teams generally didn't win down there. And, in such atrocious conditions, the assumption would have been that the odds were tilted even more heavily against us.

'You'll be on at the weekend, just go in and do your thing!' was the beginning and end of manager Harry O'Neill's instruction to me. This was a day simply to sink or swim. I was seventeen years and fifty-seven days old.

We won 1-4 to 0-6 and I scored the only goal. It came midway through the second half, a scuffed Noel O'Leary (Kieran's uncle) effort for a point dropping short and me just diving full-length to get a touch so perfect, if I tried another hundred times I'm not sure I'd be able to replicate it. Even now Noel will still joke, 'Gooch, I made you with that goal, don't forget me!'

Maybe this was the day I really started putting to bed the idea that, physically, I wasn't able for serious football. South Kerry didn't take prisoners and, in horrendous conditions, I doubt very much they were too worried about the wisp of a corner-forward getting his first Championship start.

The other lads, naturally, were fairly protective towards me. They had to be. They didn't want to see me pushed around. As my reputation grew over the next few years there would be no shortage of lads looking to take cheap shots. That came with the territory. I might drop a dummy solo, kick a point, and the roar of the crowd would confirm the view that I'd just made a fool of my marker. Always, I knew what was coming then.

You could almost read the words forming in his head: 'This little cheeky fucker needs to be brought down a peg or two here. He won't fucking do that to me again!'

Then you'd get the bang.

He'd have no choice. He'd have fellas in his ear: 'Give that little runt a dig and soften his fucking cough.' I wouldn't call it verbal intimidation as such. Certainly not on the level that's become fairly commonplace today. But you'd always know the clip was coming from lads just looking to see what you were made of.

As I got fitter and stronger across the years, I became better equipped to deal with all of that. Maybe I even came to learn a few of the dark arts myself, dropping the odd sneaky shoulder or elbow into a lad when he least expected it. The law of the jungle I suppose. Eat or be eaten.

All five of the Cooper boys played that day in Waterville and there was a famous picture taken of us after, standing on the field like drowned rats. Mike scored a big point towards the end of the game and it was, I don't doubt, one of my father's proudest days.

We beat West Kerry in the semi-final, another filthy day, and would have been considered outsiders against Ghaeltacht and the Ó Sés in Tralee on yet another waterlogged pitch for the final. If I'm honest, we were haunted to win. They missed chance after chance and probably wonder to this day how on earth they left the Bishop Moynihan Cup behind them.

I have lovely memories of a huge Crokes crowd moving next door to the John Mitchels club afterwards and us being applauded into the clubhouse in our blazers. Now, at last, I knew people were looking at me differently. I was someone who 'had the stuff', as we put it in Kerry. People had always seen the skill, but now the competitive streak was obvious too.

To be a student wearing that blazer in John Mitchels that evening will forever stay with me as one of my favourite football memories.

The following day, myself and Eanna Kavanagh brought the cup down to The Sem, still in our blazers, classmates looking up at us on stage with smiles of mild disbelief. The street cred it gave Eanna and me, two Leaving Cert students, was absolutely massive. Still, I could see the expressions of surprise too. After all, I'd gone from a history of winning virtually nothing to claiming a senior county title with my first shot.

Those three games for Crokes in the 2000 Kerry Championship were the ones that really announced me, delivering my first major achievement in football. A Kerry county title had status all around the country, I knew that. People in other counties tended to know the identity of the Kerry champions.

For all the time my brothers had played, their only previous win had been in '91.

Unfortunately, it being millennium year, it was decided to run a separate competition to decide who would represent Kerry in the Munster Club Championship. Glenflesk won it, but we had the cup that mattered most to us.

One of Charlie Nelligan's minor selectors was Mikey Sheehy, and just to be in such close proximity to my favourite player off the *Kerry's Golden Years* video was a treat. I've gotten to know Mike well over the years and all I can say is that the familiar line 'you should never meet your heroes' doesn't apply.

Put it like this. I've met mine, and they didn't just deliver, they went some distance beyond that.

Mikey's a thorough gentleman and we're really good friends today. Some people you just have a connection with, a spark with, I suppose. In my case, he's one of them. On team trips over the last couple of years, the first golf fourball declared would always be Mikey, Eamonn Fitz, Donaghy and myself.

It's funny, we were at Anthony Maher's wedding last December, Donaghy, Mikey and myself just hopping balls off one another at the bar. Anthony's bride, Megan, is a Limerick girl, and standing just across from us were these two elderly boys, their ties loosened, watching everything that moved in the place. And I overheard one of them saying as he looked across, 'Christ, that'd be a fair full-forward line over there!'

I love that about the GAA. The idea that heroes are kind of ageless and that people don't forget.

The Kerry team that won those eight All-Irelands in twelve

years have a place in the game that I doubt will ever dim. More than two decades after they'd finished, Paul Galvin and myself would sometimes recreate the things they'd do in training. We might be just doing the warm-up and I'd look across.

'Right Paul, who did this?'

'That's Egan's goal celebration!'

Giggles.

When I was injured in 2014 and, for a time, moping around with my chin on the floor, Patrick O'Sullivan rang me one day. 'Come away with us to America, Gooch, it'll be good for you!' The trip was a regular fundraising effort for our new Centre of Excellence out in Currans, near Farranfore.

I didn't want to know.

But Patrick was adamant. 'Look, it'll help if we have a current player as well as all the boys.'

The boys? That'd be Bomber and Mikey and Ambrose and Seánie Walsh. That'd be Pat and Tom Spillane. That'd be Mick Galwey. That'd be Darragh and Tomás. Reluctantly, I agreed to travel, little realizing it would lift my spirits hugely.

Sure I'd had pints with all these lads before, but I'd never spent a sustained period in their company, never really gotten to know them beyond the superficiality of a post All-Ireland Monday pint before you rush for the train. In New York, we had a lot of morning meetings followed by lunches that tended to take on lives of their own. You'd be sitting there with a beer in front of you when, suddenly, Bomber's on his feet, singing 'Hallelujah'. Next thing, there's a three-hour sing-song in full swing and locals who've just come in on their lunch break are taking the rest of the afternoon off because they can't drag themselves away from the craic.

I remember sitting there thinking 'I hope my life is like this when I retire and that I still have these types of friends, travelling around the world and pretending we're twenty-one!'

Honestly, the enjoyment these men still got from one another's company was intoxicating. I couldn't take my eyes off them. How could you not be inspired by them? And the last thing on my mind for those few days in America was my ruined knee. It was perfect.

I suppose I spent my whole career wanting the approval of these people because of what they represent. It was always important what they thought of me because they'd done it themselves. They knew what it was all about. I wouldn't obviously ever have broadcast it, but to get some compliment from any one of them in a newspaper column or on TV always meant a huge amount to me. It felt as if they had my back, that they appreciated what I was doing.

There was a big dinner, $10,000 a table, with some of the most influential Irish in America attending. I was asked to speak, and I felt a little out of my depth. Because the trip had really emphasized how the men of '75–'86 had a unique status in the game. They were the ones under pressure for pictures, not Darragh, Tomás or me.

I got a bit of a laugh by opening with 'These lads were gods to me growing up, but after seeing them the last few days . . .'

The trip taught me just how strong the Kerry brand really is, how it stands for something across the world. It showed me how people in America are just as passionate, if not more, about the GAA as we are at home. It means so much to them. You could tell in conversation that they were fully connected with what was happening back in Kerry. They'd listen to Weeshie Fogarty's *Terrace Talk* on the internet. They got all the papers. They saw everything on TV.

That specific trip to the US raised an astonishing €1.1 million for the Centre of Excellence. It pulled in massive business connections from all over North America. Without the help of the highly successful construction businessman Maurice O'Regan in

New York, none of it would have been possible. South Kerry man Eoin Moriarty also played a major role in the fund-raising drive. But Patrick was the one who instigated those trips to America and, for me, that one in 2014 was a real eye-opener.

More than anything, it reaffirmed the sense that that team of Kerry footballers, that generation, had something that every generation to follow will always aspire to.

I have often thought since of how greatness really is in front of our noses in Kerry.

When I was briefly based in Castle Street, Tralee with the bank, I was surrounded by legends. To my right-hand side, across the road? Seánie – seven medals. Darragh, down the road? Six. Mikey? Eight. Bomber was only over the way, Charlie Nelligan's bakery around the corner. I'd see Ger Power and others going down the street together, just heading for a coffee. And it always struck me that these men had set unbelievably high standards for the rest of us to follow.

They're quite simply football royalty.

I didn't get a run in the first round of the 2000 Munster Minor Championship, started the final in Limerick, but we were beaten by a James Masters-captained Cork team. I remember they had a player called Conrad Murphy and if ever you'd have picked out someone on the field that day guaranteed to make it at senior, he'd have been the one. I suppose it shows the fickleness of sport that, for one reason or another, it never happened for Conrad.

It would be 2001 then before I really felt a part of things in a Kerry jersey. That minor team had a cracking attack, particularly the inside line of myself, Declan and an absolute flier from the Gaeltacht, Conall O'Cruadhlaoich. All three of us were already playing Senior Championship football with our clubs and we duly won the Munster Championship, beating Cork by three points down in Páirc Uí Chaoimh. Sadly, a good Dublin team with the likes of Bryan Cullen, Paul Griffin and David 'Dotsy' O'Callaghan on board then edged us out in a high-scoring All-Ireland semi-final.

But, at least, I was on the county radar now.

There would have been a succession of trial games on Saturday mornings early in '02 for the Kerry seniors and they started bringing me in, essentially to make up the numbers. And, after a while, I think the penny might have dropped with manager Páidí Ó Sé and others. 'Fuck it, this fella is doing a little bit more than just making up the numbers!' To be honest, I was scoring freely nearly every time I went in. My size wasn't stopping me.

I was, by now, heavily involved with the Kerry under-21s too, with Jack O'Connor as manager. The structure of the under-21 competition was a bit daft with the provincial championship being played in March and April, then a delay till later in the year for the All-Ireland semi finals and final. Clare were our opponents in the Munster final and we played really well as a team in Ennis, winning 3-15 to 2-11.

After that, a good few of us – myself, Declan Quill, Séamus Scanlon and Ronan O'Connor – were formally added to the senior panel.

I knew I was flying, but it was still a surprise when Páidí rang the week of our Division Two National League final against Laois. 'Colm, bring up your boots for the weekend, we're going to give you a go. The boys will be in touch.'

It was only a fortnight to Championship and I was about to climb aboard a rocket ship.

3

A Rag Doll Among Juggernauts

Páidí's passion was a human firework show, but in dealings with me he was inclined to keep the matches unlit.

I took it that he was giving me space, letting me settle. He'd say little enough to me beyond offering encouragement to go 'do your thing'. It was something I'd become well accustomed to in a Kerry jersey. Nothing ever became too prescriptive. Every Kerry manager I'd play under seemed to see me in much the same light. The bird-not-to-be-caged thing I suppose.

Starting out, I thought senior inter-county would be a different world, a different philosophy. I imagined it would be far more tactical and mentally exacting. It seemed strange to be a teenager being sent into senior battle now without any real instruction.

But Páidí's way in the middle of a group was to light fires in people. To poke our pride with a stick. He was brilliant in full flow. What he did was give you a sense of the history you were representing. The tradition. The honour. Sometimes his words would have the hair up on the back of your neck like the teeth on a comb. He'd place big store on the people who had gone before us. He'd show clips of past Kerry teams, grainy images of lads running around The Blaskets. He'd push home the respect these men had for the jersey and how wearing it brought a big responsibility.

I loved watching and listening, soaking it all up. I was learning things here that I needed to learn. If they wanted to keep me in there 24/7, I'd happily have done it. Because Páidí's word was gospel. The man could have sent me off to climb Carrauntoohil in the dead of night and, fuck it, I'd have volunteered to do it twice. That was the buzz I was getting now.

Prior to stepping into his dressing-room, probably the big image I'd had of him was that left hook smashed into the side of Dinny Allen's face in the '75 Munster final. Hard-man Páidí. Dinny had just caught him with an elbow and, well, it wasn't in Páidí's constitution to allow a forward to take any liberties. But people maybe forget that himself and Dinny walked away from that incident in a big embrace.

In some ways that captured the Kerry–Cork thing. Hatred is too strong a word, but at times in games it doesn't feel a million miles away. Familiarity breeds contempt, and we meet each other too often to ever find the space for an adult relationship. Páidí's view was that Kerry needed to be 'right' twice in a Championship season. First, to beat Cork in Munster. Second, to win an All-Ireland final in September.

That, obviously, was an attitude spawned prior to the invention of the Championship 'back door' and the inception of All-Ireland qualifiers. But there's still a grain of truth in Páidí's vision today. Every summer, Kerry's first real sense of how we're travelling will almost always come courtesy of a game against Cork.

And my first Championship season was no exception.

I'd scored a goal with my first touch in that Division Two League final against Laois. Tomás Ó Sé kicked a ball down the line to me and, as I started cutting in, I was waiting for people to come across and block my way. Just assumed I'd end up having to offload. But they came a little bit slower than I'd anticipated. So I stepped inside the corner-back and was surprised the way everything opened up. Next thing, I'm one-on-one with the goalkeeper and, BANG, I roll it past him, wheeling away and thinking to myself 'Jesus, this is perfect!'

If I'm honest, I went into that game hoping that if I played well I might have an outside chance of making Kerry's Championship squad. That was the height of my ambitions. You have to bear in mind I hadn't been involved for a single League game up to that moment. I hadn't been training with Kerry. I'd been just going in for the odd trial game and now, suddenly, I'm wheeling away with a big grin on my face after scoring a goal in a League final. I'm sure people were looking in, thinking 'Where are they going with this child? One proper belt and he'll be gone!'

If so, I couldn't blame them. I felt a little out of place myself.

Like I'd never played with Mike Frank Russell and I remember once making a run across him, getting the ball, turning and kicking it over the bar. But soon as I kicked it, I felt like apologizing. 'Fuck, sorry, that was your space.' That's where I was – nearly apologizing to lads if I got in the way. And yet, at the same time, trying to show everyone that I had 'the stuff'.

Páidí didn't say much when it was over, other than to warn me that I should steer away from any boys looking for interviews now. I didn't really know that evening if he thought I'd been good, bad or indifferent.

That was his way. He'd leave you to figure things out for yourself.

As it happened, I subsequently made my Championship debut the same day as Marc Ó Sé, a ropey enough four-point defeat of Limerick in the Gaelic Grounds on 12 May 2002. Cork were next up in Killarney, the same day Ireland played a last-sixteen game against Spain in Suwon at the World Cup. We togged out across the road in Crokes and it's fair to say our focus wasn't exactly where it needed to be. Heads should have been full of the red jersey but, instead, a few were leaning low to radios now. Mine included.

So picture it . . .

Outside, the rain is pelting down on a half-lit Killarney and Páidí's trying to get us ready for what he knows is going to be a war. There are puddles forming on the pitch. Are we ready for it? Our whispers probably tell a tale.

Páidí: 'Now lads, every last one of ye be ready to drive your man right back on his fucking arse today. This is our fucking patch and—'

Whispers: 'Yeeeeeessssss, Robbie Keane, one-all!'

We go across the road and all but get our arses handed back to us. Páidí takes me off just before half time, says nothing. Owen Sexton's definitely been getting the better of me, but it feels as if we've all been just hunted down in packs. The whole team is floundering, and whenever that happens, a light, inexperienced corner-forward becomes instantly disposable. I've no complaints. Kerry aren't exactly short of high-grade forwards when you think of Johnny Crowley and Mike Frank Russell and Liam Hassett and Dara Ó'Cinnéide and Aodán Mac Gearailt and Seán O'Sullivan and Eoin Brosnan. Colm Cooper? The past month or so has been such a blur, I reckon this is a reality check that's always been coming. And I presume that's me done for the year. They might keep me on the squad, but I won't see any more action.

But there's also a voice in my head, leaving the Killarney dressing-room that day, saying something along the lines of 'Whatever it fucking takes, that won't happen to me again.' I feel I've been caught a little off-guard.

The game ended in a draw, 0–8 each. Afterwards, someone told Páidí about the radios and about fellas being tuned into the happenings in South Korea. He couldn't believe his ears. The man was fuming. 'Do ye not think we've enough on our fucking plates, lads?'

Two days later, Micheal Ó Sé died suddenly. Páidí's brother. Darragh's, Tomás's and Marc's father. Darragh was our captain for the year but, now, football was the last thing on people's minds. Instead we were all heading to a funeral in Ventry out of solidarity for a manager and three team-mates whose lives had just been hit with a bomb. Micheal was buried on the Thursday, and three days later Cork gave us a nice trimming in Páirc Uí Chaoimh.

And here's where the selfishness kicked in.

You see, I didn't quite understand the Cork thing yet. I didn't get the personal nature of the relationship and what losing to them represented to someone like Páidí. In a sense I'd maybe been listening to his team-talks without really hearing what I needed to hear. Because I came away from Cork that evening thinking one thing and one thing only: 'Well I held my end up!'

I'd been surprised that Páidí started me at wing-forward and heartened that, if I wasn't exactly pulling up trees against Sean Levis, at least I did OK. So if there was a lot of doom and gloom about the place leaving Cork that evening, I felt kind of immune to it.

A general decision was taken that the best thing for fellas now was maybe a night on the beer. We were heading into uncharted waters with the second season of All-Ireland qualifiers pitching us into a game against Wicklow seven days later. Sports scientists would have had a canary at the medicine we took.

Personally, I didn't want to be too public about it, but the idea of a few pints appealed. It's not the done thing now, but back then a blow-out sometimes achieved far more than any number of team-meetings. The alcohol loosened us up, and with that came openness and honesty. Maybe enough candour even to get fellas squaring up to one another. Sound, so long as it didn't get out of hand. We needed soul-searching. We needed things thrown out on the table.

'Christ Almighty, you're playing like a man who needs his hand held crossing the street!'

'Are you training as hard as you fucking need to be?'

'What the fuck are you planning on doing about what happened to you today?'

The thing is, Kerry can't get hammered by Cork and there not be consequences. No matter the circumstances, something has to give. We knew there was a cull coming because Cork had made fools of us. That was how it felt. I could see the bitterness in the older lads. It wasn't said out loud, but the broad view was that we'd let the Ó Sés down especially. Was that how we honoured the boys' father? Páidí's brother? By letting Cork walk all over us?

That Monday morning I had to get a scan on my hand in Tralee. Just a knock I'd taken on a bone they don't like taking chances with. There was speculation that I mightn't be fit enough for Wicklow in Portlaoise. I was in the car that Friday, coming home from physio I think. There was a Championship preview on the radio and they hit upon Kerry's first ever All-Ireland qualifier.

'Now there's speculation that Colm Cooper might not be available,' said Brian Carthy.

'Sure even if he is, what difference will he make?' interjected Pat Spillane, one of the Kerry golden circle. And Pat threw out the familiar line about my size and the question marks over whether or not I really had 'the stuff'. He didn't know me, but was still happy to pass judgement.

I got the distinct impression he didn't rate me. It stung.

I turned the radio off. 'Fuck him, he knows nothing about me.'

There was no real dynamic through all of this between Páidí and me. Few enough chats, little enough instruction. Just the occasional hand on the shoulder and a reminder: 'We need you to be fucking tough the next day . . .' That was the beginning and the end of it really. Be tough. Take no shit. I don't think he imagined I was ready to process too much beyond that. He might have been right too. My only thinking was 'Thanks be to God, I'm in again!'

You see, hearing Spillane's little barb reminded me how much I yearned for the approval of that generation. Páidí was showing huge faith in me, but what did the others think?

In successive weeks, we hammered Wicklow and Fermanagh. Then we trimmed Kildare by eight points in Thurles. And that was the day I really sensed we were on to something.

Because Kildare had a serious team. They'd got heavyweight operators like Glen Ryan, Anthony Rainbow, Dermot Earley, Brian Lacey and Martin Lynch and had just given Dublin a right rattle in the Leinster final before a packed Croke Park. But I got a goal after maybe two minutes and immediately felt bomb proof. Too fucking small and light did you say?

At the beginning of August we played Galway in the All-Ireland quarter-final and I went well again, this time against Kieran Fitzgerald, the reigning 'Young Footballer of the Year'. Páidí was wrapped up in the swell of things now and pulled a stroke the night before by getting us into Croke Park for a little walk about. Don't know how he managed it, but I suppose if any man had connections it was our manager. The win gave us a semi-final against Cork.

And that's when I started to realize what Kerry–Cork really meant.

The intensity rose in everyone. In Páidí, in the senior players, in those of us learning on the hoof. Training had a different feel to it. Fellas were finding something more within themselves. It might be only 5 per cent, but they were finding it. There was plenty of skelping now in practice matches without complaint. It was time to find the hard edge in us. I was nineteen and no different to the others.

It was being made clear to me that whatever ball went in to a Kerry corner-forward had to stick. If it was coming straight back out, there were lads on the bench who'd take Páidí's hand off for the chance to replace me. On one level, I was loving the stony seriousness of it all now. On another, I couldn't help wonder if it was all a big mistake.

Like, twelve months earlier I'd been playing minor county league games, being beaten by twenty points maybe but knowing I was better than most of my opponents. Just stepping past fellas as if they were training cones. Some of them were still children, fifteen-year-olds still growing into their bodies. Now I was going to war with men. The clipping was vicious, the message unrelenting: YOU DO NOT TAKE A BACKWARD STEP HERE!

I should have been intimidated, but I wasn't. I had such trust in my skill levels, I just believed I could figure out a way to beat my marker even if he was bigger and stronger and more experienced (which just about all of them were).

And by fuck were we ready now for Cork. We won 3-19 to 2-7. One-way traffic. I got Man of the Match. They were talking about me on *The Sunday Game* now. If I could go that well against a marker as good as Anthony Lynch (Sexton was taken off me early on), the suggestion was that maybe Kerry have found a gem here. But more than that, people were talking about the team. After a horrible June, Kerry had begun lighting up the summer. We'd scored fourteen goals in our last five games.

Just one more bit of business left to tend to now. Kerry stood seventy minutes away from a thirty-third senior All-Ireland. Our opponents, Armagh, had yet to win one.

It was hard to look at that statistic and not imagine that history would carry us home.

Sometimes I look at old photographs of '02 now and what I see is a rag doll among juggernauts.

I weighed 10 stone that summer. Bananas. I often laugh that if there was a strong breeze it could have blown me over the cross-bar. What happened to me that year wouldn't happen to a young footballer now. I can say that with some certainty. Today's minors already have two or three years of strength and conditioning in the bank before they pull on the county colours. They're already steeled for high levels of physicality, whereas I wasn't. Beyond what I took from the front and back greens of Ardshanavooly, I had no real physical foundation for what was coming.

Joe Kernan understood that and, naturally, had every intention of exploring just what this Killarney wraith was made of. Why wouldn't he? His Armagh team was hard-nosed and ruthless and, yeah, unscrupulous in the way you had to be if you had designs on surviving the attrition of an Ulster Championship. They had serious players too, particularly men like Kieran McGeeney, Ronan Clarke, Stevie McDonnell, Paul McGrane and the McEntee brothers.

Kernan's Armagh will probably go down as the county's greatest. But in my head, we handed it to them.

The memory still sickens me because we should have been out the gap at half-time. We were four up and Brossie had a goal chance that flew inches wide. Seven up and it would have been over. The rest comes back to me as a blur of poor shooting, rash decisions and, eventually, panic.

People ask me if I was nervous beforehand. I wasn't. Páidí had told myself, Marc, John Sheahan and Seán O'Sullivan, the new kids on the block, not to get too involved in the media stuff. 'There's enough pressure on ye, lads.' Honestly, that suited me fine, but I didn't really care. Back then, a pre-All-Ireland press night was an absolute bun fight, journalists free to sidle up to anyone they cared. Balls would be flying over heads and, sometimes, deliberately lamped down on top of them as the media did their thing during what was supposedly a normal training session.

Páidí did his damnedest to give everything a sense of normality, but that never really works with an All-Ireland final. You are getting measured for suits, fielding requests from long-lost friends for tickets – everybody around you wants to talk about the very thing you're being advised to try and keep at arm's length. Suddenly there's a kind of artificial dimension to your dialogue with people. Your sentences are overrun with 'yerrahs', your shoulders shrug on reflex.

By now we were doing a lot more video work after training. We'd eat in The Gleneagle, then out with this old-fashioned video recorder, Páidí in charge of the remote. It all seems comically primitive now compared to the digital world we live in today. And Páidí and the remote rarely saw eye to eye. He'd be trying to rewind one minute, fast-forward the next. The clip he'd want just couldn't be found. And his patience would wear thin.

'Ah fuck it. Marc, come up here.'

We stayed in the Tara Towers the night before, a typical Páidí piseog. 'Tara Towers . . . it never did us wrong.' I was rooming with Ronan O'Connor, who was very close to making the starting fifteen. We'd come through from the under-21s together and Ronan was perfect company for the weekend. Only twenty-one, but a mature twenty-one. No giddiness, no bull.

Even though we were in the final, Páidí was hugely conscious of some belly-aching in Kerry about there being too many representatives of An Ghaeltacht in his squad. There might have been half a dozen of them at the time, including of course his three nephews.

They were all good players, fully worthy of their places, but Páidí knew people were trying to pick holes.

Anyway, the morning of the final he's down in the hotel lobby when the lift door opens and out stride the An Ghaeltacht six, shoulder to shoulder. Páidí takes one look and barks, 'Ah for fuck sake lads, I'm under enough pressure, will ye ever spread out like?'

Enda McNulty marked me in the game and it's fair to say he was more intense than anything I'd come across. I'd learn over the years that Ulster corner-backs were just cut from different stone. But, to begin with, things were going fine for me. I kicked two points in the first half. I was moving nicely, getting on a lot of ball. Yes, Armagh were physical but, to be fair, I could never describe them as dirty.

I did take a few belts, but they were largely good, fair ones. I remember Liam Hassett giving me a pass down the Cusack Stand side once, just along the sideline, and I was like a man balancing on a tightrope trying not to cross the whitewash. McGeeney had a 10-yard run at me and, naturally, could not resist the invitation. Ten stone of roadkill awaiting collection. He gave me a good belt in the rib cage but, having seen it coming, I managed to get the return ball away to Hassett. Tried not to show it but I was fucked for a few minutes after. Maybe it was a kind of rite of passage because one thing I would take from that day was that I couldn't logically be going to battle with boys like McGeeney again if I only weighed 10 stone.

Anyway, the game changed with Oisín McConville's second-half goal at the Hill End. It shouldn't have, but it did. We were still four points up after fifty-four minutes, but the goal was a sucker-punch. It put wind in their sails I'm not sure they truly expected to get. Worse, we pretty much retreated into our shells. For the last quarter of an hour Armagh were better than us. Tougher, hungrier, more streetwise.

And the scenes at the end have, of course, gone down in history. Maybe I should have been happy for them but to this day all I feel about that game is anger. Nobody hands you an All-Ireland, they tell you. Well, that day we disproved the theory.

Because that day we gave Sam to Armagh on a silver fucking platter.

There was a lot of noise in Kerry afterwards, especially as the team had been hammered the year before (fifteen points) by a Meath side that subsequently lost the All-Ireland final to Galway by nine. The day of the Meath meltdown, I'd been on a Kerry minor team beaten by Dublin.

Heading home that evening, all you could hear on the train was 'Kerry won't be back in Croke Park for a long time . . .'

I suppose that's the rhythm of life in Kerry football. We expect things, and when that expectation isn't met the reaction tends to be severe, often irrational. According to everybody around us, Kerry were in the doldrums now. For other counties, a narrow All-Ireland final defeat might be considered decent return for a season. In Kerry, as the light bled out of 2002, it was seen as a portent for some kind of famine.

Now there was a good deal of warmth around the place initially. I was staggered by the amount of people that came out for our homecoming and it really struck me looking down off a trailer in Killarney that ordinarily I'd have been down in the middle of that throng. There was a kind of unusual outpouring of emotion. I just think everybody wanted us to win that year, particularly for the Ó Sés.

But it wasn't to be, and Páidí was under pressure now. That much was obvious. Even though he'd delivered two All-Irelands as manager, I got the impression a lot of people in the county looked on him as some kind of West Kerry lunatic, just pounding up and down the sideline, shouting and roaring. He was actually far more astute than those people realized.

It's true, compared to today's managers he wasn't into the same level of detail. But I don't think anyone of his era was. His strengths lay in passion and motivating people. He wouldn't be sending you video clips, but he'd know if a fella wasn't cutting the mustard. No one could hoodwink Páidí. He could make a judgement on a player fairly quickly, and that judgement was usually made on the basis of whether that player could win an individual battle. Was he tight enough? Was he winning the ball inside? Did he have 'the stuff'?

I'm not sure he could operate in today's environment with its emphasis on sports science, on dieticians and nutritionists and performance coaches, and everything being broken down and monitored by GPS systems. That wasn't how he'd make a call. He was much more 'Can he stand up to the heat?'

He'd make a straight-line judgement and then would live or die on that call. Managers today delegate constantly. They rely hugely on the calibre of people around them. Don't get me wrong, Páidí surrounded himself with good people too. But in many ways he was an island. He took things on his own shoulders, and that wasn't always appreciated by those around him.

Famously, one such case blew up in his face when we were on our subsequent team holiday in South Africa.

That would be a magnificent trip, though it probably tells you something about Páidí's sense of where Kerry football stood in the greater scheme of things that he seemed endlessly convinced Nelson Mandela might come striding through the door, looking to meet the Kingdom's finest. I actually heard him asking a member of staff one day 'Is there any chance Mandela would be around?'

As it happened, the great man never did come over on a visit. But pretty soon we found ourselves in a blizzard of media attention that couldn't have been any more intense if he had.

The day we touched down in Cape Town, an interview with Páidí appeared in the *Sunday Independent* in which he gave the following quote: 'Kerry people I'd say are the roughest type of fucking animals you could ever deal with.' In the context of the overall interview the quote was unremarkable, simply stressing how demanding Kerry supporters could be. For those of us on holiday now, it barely even registered.

But it kicked off a controversy at home that started to blow out of control. I was rooming with Marc and I remember walking up from the pool with him one day and him saying, 'Fuck it, there's war at home over Páidí calling the Kerry supporters animals.'

I didn't understand the severity of what was happening at all. None of us did. The trip was like Disneyland to me: I was travelling with many of my heroes, staying in nice hotels, being given spending money each day. Fuck it, that was dreamland to me. It was only when we began to hear of the fallout surrounding another quote from the interview that it really became a topic of conversation. You see Páidí had said something about 'taking a more hands-on approach' in the preparation of the team for 2003, a line that many interpreted as veiled criticism of our physical trainer, John O'Keeffe.

Johnno hadn't travelled to South Africa with us and the word from home now was that he was massively offended by the words of the Kerry manager. Like, the two of them were great friends and, of course, former team-mates, so the idea of a rift between them now suddenly had our attention.

If I'm honest, the idea of losing Johnno was of far more concern to us now than any PR fire-fighting Páidí found himself compelled to do.

I do remember Kerry County Board issuing a statement, dis-associating itself from Páidí's comments and apologizing to anybody who was offended. And Páidí had to deliver one too, maybe the most important part of which was a clarification that he'd sought in no way to disparage Johnno. It would take a little while for things to be resolved between the two of them, but at no point did it really feel as big a deal to those of us on holiday as we were hearing it was being portrayed back home.

For our last couple of days in South Africa, wives and girl-friends went home, leaving Páidí centre stage to outline his immediate plans. And I have a memory of our final night on this beach by the shores of Table Bay, a jazz band playing and a bar-becue in full swing when Páidí strips down to his togs and disappears out into the ocean.

The craic is mighty until, after a while, someone mentions that Páidí hasn't come back out of the water. Where the fuck is he? Suddenly everyone's looking for our manager who seems to have disappeared into the Atlantic.

People are just beginning to get edgy when that familiar bullet head materializes out of the surf and he comes marching towards us, beaming from ear to ear.

And Páidí breaks into a familiar cackle. 'Had ye fucking going men, didn't I?'

4

A Different Script

Páidí didn't see the sucker-punch coming, but the truth of it is that none of us did.

The big black dog of Tyrone just showed up on Kerry's porch one Sunday in August 2003 and we had no answer to its bark. I won't say that we ran scared but we certainly didn't front up to it and go nose to nose. The truth is we didn't know how to. Tyrone just devoured us with their ferocity, putting a stamp on the game that survives to this day.

Personally, I was never really going well that year because of a torn adductor in my right groin. This meant I couldn't ever train properly, and the injury would require surgery that November. Now I'm not suggesting that made a blind bit of difference to our fate. It didn't. In '03 we came up against a football force that had our measure in every single way.

As a team we'd never really got moving the way we had for a time the year before. Limerick beat Cork in Munster and we were anything but impressive during a subsequent five-point defeat of them in the provincial final. Then Roscommon scored three goals against us in the All-Ireland quarter-final. Maybe the writing was on the wall there and we just didn't see it.

Football's conventional rules of engagement were about to be tossed in the bin.

History isn't kind to Kerry in assessing our Championship relationship with Mickey Harte's team. And '03 was the start of it. What they did to us in that year's All-Ireland semi-final would ripple through the next decade and beyond. I suppose the famous picture of Eoin Brosnan trapped in a scrum of eight Tyrone players went to the core of it.

Harte came up with a system in which his players hunted us down in packs. Theoretically, the idea of eight Tyrone players corralled in one corner of the pitch should have meant huge prairies of space for the other fourteen Kerry players. But theory stood for nothing against Tyrone's intensity.

I'll put it this way. I'd won an All-Star for my breakthrough season in '02 when the essence of what I did had an absolute simplicity. I was used to coming on to a ball, turning, kicking points. Now, suddenly, there was no room to do that. The space had disappeared. Against Tyrone I could beat my immediate marker but always there was someone else waiting to intercept me. The openings I'd previously presumed would be there were no longer accessible.

It shocked me. And on some level it fed a certain resentment. An almost arrogant this-isn't-fucking-football kind of rage.

There was a lot of that in Kerry's general reaction to how Tyrone played that year. In an RTÉ studio, Pat Spillane famously labelled it 'puke football'. We were up on our high horses – and that was the worst place imaginable we could be.

Because Kerry needed the humility now to understand the game was changing. What is often lost in our county when people talk about that Tyrone team is just how talented a group they were. Ordinary footballers couldn't have done what Tyrone did in 2003. Yes, their system was the key. But that system wouldn't have won an All-Ireland without outstanding players to implement it. Men like Peter Canavan, Sean Cavanagh, Philip Jordan and Brian McGuigan were as good as anything seen in football at the time. And Harte, obviously, had a tactical astuteness that made Tyrone incredibly hard to break down.

They killed us in that semi-final. I think I got Kerry's first score in the twenty-fifth minute, by which time we were already trailing 0-0 to 0-6. They were hungry, fresh, energetic. Mouthy? Yes, a little of that too, though not on the level they would take it to in later years. The truth is they didn't need to sledge us that day in Croke Park. Kerry's grand total for seventy minutes of football was a paltry six points. Appalling.

I'd never come across anything like it, this compression of space around the ball-carrier and the creation of wing-forwards who essentially worked the full length of the field. When you think of what our modern understanding of wing-forwards has become, the kind of rampaging play we see now from defence to attack in men like Ciarán Kilkenny and Diarmuid O'Connor, Tyrone were the ones who created the template.

In time they found a role for someone like Brian Dooher that, suddenly, every other county felt a need to replicate.

Before '03, football was largely man-on-man. Given fitness levels were usually uniform, the more skilful team invariably won, and that suited us fine in Kerry. Now Tyrone were writing a different script. The ferocity of their play was a shock that year, not simply to Kerry but to everyone. And losing so badly was an absolute disaster for Páidí.

Towards the end of the game an elderly Kerry supporter came down on the field and took a swing at him. It was kind of a defining moment I suppose. Maybe the 'animals' line was coming home to roost. Either way, Kerry's last three Championships had ended in defeats to teams they'd been expected to beat. We were getting a label for softness, for not having the stomach to put it up to Northern teams especially.

And for someone cut from the stone that Páidí was cut from, I'd say that kind of charge offended every fibre of his being. A Páidí Ó Sé team being labelled soft seemed almost perverse.

I'd say he knew the writing was on the wall now. To begin with, I think he wanted to stay on, but a meeting with county chairman Seán Walsh made clear to him the board's view that it was time for a fresh voice in the Kerry dressing-room. Unfortunately, that information reached Páidí through a third party before the chairman got to have his say.

He was angry, and for Walsh, a personal friend, that can't have been easy. But a few days after their eventual meeting Páidí called a press conference in Killarney. He would not be seeking another term as Kerry manager.

The firework show was over.

5

'The Outsider' Comes Good

We needed to get pig-headed in Kerry, but we needed to back up that pig-headedness with science. That much was crystal clear.

Con Houlihan once said something along the lines of us always needing someone to blame in the county when our summers go sour. He reckoned we handled victory with relative calmness, but defeats meant 'the search is always on for scapegoats, not to mention scapesheep and scapeasses!'

Con had a point. Losing cuts us to the core. It offends us. I mean, I was sorry to hear Páidí was gone because he'd put such massive trust in me when others undeniably had doubts. But the way Tyrone had just pushed us aside was never going to sit easily with people. The blade was always going to fall on someone, and Páidí was a static target. I was out for a night in Cork with some friends when I got a text confirming Jack O'Connor as the new Kerry manager.

The news came as a small relief. Jack knew me from the under-21s and the impression I got was that he had a high enough opinion of me.

That was probably no harm given the feeling that everybody was open to the axe now. Not just Páidí, even the lads who won the All-Ireland in 2000 had used up all their credit as Jack set out to put his stamp on things.

But that wasn't going to be quite as easy as it sounded because, in a way, Jack himself was on immediate trial here. Ten days after that Tyrone defeat for the seniors we'd played an under-21 Munster final against Waterford in Walsh Park and lost to a last-minute sucker-punch of a goal scored by Shane Walsh, subsequently better known as an inter-county hurler. The defeat was an unmerciful shock to the system. It was Waterford's first ever Munster title in the grade and their supporters in a 5,000 attendance went absolutely ballistic at the finish.

When you think that the likes of myself, Declan O'Sullivan, Séamus Scanlon and Declan Quill started that game and that Kieran Donaghy came on as a sub, you get an idea of how big an upset it felt at the time. After all, three of us had played in the senior semi-final. If I'm honest, I was left scratching my head after, wondering was this inter-county lark for me at all?

So, for Jack, there was now a need to be seen to hit the ground running. To make clear he'd put that Tyrone defeat behind him.

He started by appointing Pat Flanagan as physical trainer, and the impact was immediate. Pat was a former sprinter who believed in pushing weights like nobody we'd worked with before. With Páidí and Johnno we had free access to The Gleneagle gym, but use of it always felt optional. There was no structured schedule to follow, no formal monitoring. Pat believed in checks and balances though. He wanted everything written down now and boxes to be ticked. There were individualized gym schedules he wanted people to follow.

It didn't apply to me yet because I was still in rehab after that groin operation. For now, the focus was on strengthening my core. The weights could wait. But I knew they were coming.

I sidestepped a training week in Lanzarote where Pat had his first real opportunity to get into the players' heads. The feedback was hugely positive. Pat was very technical about things like posture and the way people ran. He believed injuries could be avoided by simple adjustment. The week in the Canaries got a big thumbs up from the squad then, albeit the one night out they were permitted turned a little sour when one of the younger lads, Dan Doona, had his jaw badly broken when trying to act as peacekeeper in a fight. I often wonder would Dan's career have turned out very differently had that incident never happened. Because his predicament was the last thing Jack now needed as he tried to put his mark on things.

Then a week before the commencement of the 2004 National League, Galway gave Kerry an almighty hammering in a challenge game near Sixmilebridge. The new management team wasn't a wet weekend in the job but already there were grumbles.

It would get worse before it got better. Kerry's first League game took them to Longford on the first weekend in February and they came a cropper. My rehab had spared me the indignity so I was at a club match when the news came through. Next thing, I could hear heated conversations sparking up all around the field.

'You're fucking kidding . . .'

'Longford?'

'Beaten by a point?'

'Jesus Christ, where are Kerry fucking headed?'

Jack's a stubborn type who knew he was in a war zone here. You see he's not one of what he calls 'the golden circle' and reckoned, because of that, he wasn't really rated. His immediate predecessors as Kerry managers were all on first-name terms with the Kerry public. We'd gone from Micko to Ogie to Páidí.

Now we'd Jack O'Connor from Toorsaleen in the south of the county, who kept being reminded that he was manager of a Kerry under-21 team that lost a Munster final to Waterford.

Pretty quickly Jack communicated a view to us that he didn't believe too many of the four-in-a-row team had his back. He didn't come out and actually say as much, but it was soon pretty clear that he reckoned he was rowing against a wicked current here. Some of the old heroes weren't slow in having a little cut at him in newspaper columns after the defeat in Longford.

Jack's view was they wouldn't have done that to one of their own.

Anyway, Kerry bounced back, by winning their next two games against Cork and Dublin. Turns out the win over the Dubs was our first in Parnell Park for eighteen years. Next thing, Jack was on a roll that carried Kerry all the way to a League title. They won it with little enough contribution from either me or the Ghaeltacht boys who'd reached the All-Ireland Club final. We got back in from the semi-final on, by which time Jack had learned a hell of a lot about the strength of his panel.

It felt a proper League win too because Kerry had to work for it. We would win other League titles on cruise control, but not this one. In that April semi-final we beat Limerick by two points, a really sticky team that would give us plenty to think about before the year was out. Then we'd a solitary point to spare against Galway in the final in early May.

It was clear that Jack still didn't feel accepted but at least he'd won over the dressing-room. His way was to be very hands-on with the players, having a lot more one-to-one chats than we'd previously been accustomed to. I found he asked me my opinion a lot because he was interested in the chemistry between players, forwards especially. Who was most comfortable with who?

But I got the impression he was reading every line written about him too. It was clear he was oversensitive to it.

In time, I think he discovered that the first thing any Kerry manager needs to acquire is a fairly thick skin. They need to pull their collars up against the climate of endless overreaction. And Jack wasn't at that stage yet, still bristling at some of the gods in the county.

We went to Ennis in the first round of the Munster Championship and beat Clare with a fairly mediocre performance. The broad view as we trooped back to the dressing-room was something along the lines of 'a win is a win'. But Jack was having none of that. He lost the plot. Tore strips off us. He let us know in no uncertain terms that standards were being set on his watch and those standards hadn't been met.

I'd never seen him like this before, so his outburst was a surprise. In hindsight, probably a good one too.

We devoured Cork next day out in Killarney and then it was up to the Gaelic Grounds for a Munster final against our old friends from Limerick. Except, of course, we weren't especially friendly with each other. They were a serious team with the likes of John Galvin, Eoin Keating and Stephen Lucey at the top of their game and they'd have liked nothing better than to take the Kingdom's scalp.

One of the differences in working with Pat Flanagan now was he still had us doing weights in the middle of the Championship season. It became clear that himself and Jack had a longer-term plan here than simply winning a Munster title. They'd Croke Park in the autumn on their minds and, no question, that felt like a bit of a gamble. Because we looked heavy-legged in Limerick.

There was plenty of clipping in the game too and Jack's view, rightly or wrongly, was that referee, Gerry Kinneavy, was being harsh on us. He gave it to him down the banks eventually and there was something in his anger, justified or not, that felt welcome. He'd begun asserting himself here. Taking no prisoners.

Kinneavy was given a garda escort off the field as the game finished in a draw, everyone feeling wound up.

In some ways, maybe we came away thinking our work was done with the replay set for Killarney. That innocence was knocked out of us fairly swiftly one week later when we found ourselves seven points adrift after twenty minutes. There was a lot of mouthing on the field and plenty more coming from the line. Water boys, everybody having their say about how the big show ponies of Kerry were fucked. Jesus wept, losing a Munster final in my home town was something I knew I could never stomach. Losing it to Limerick? Nightmare.

But we hung tough and, under a blazing July sun, the game went right down to the wire. Darragh, especially, was immense as we saw it home. Kerry 3-10, Limerick 2-9. Of course, we shook hands at the end, but there was no love lost here. Limerick hadn't won a Munster title in over a hundred years and maybe on some level I should have felt sympathy for them.

I didn't. The bastards nearly had us.

Next up felt like the biggest game I'd ever played in. The Dubs in a packed Croke Park, the Hill giving it socks. It's what I'd always dreamt of ever since that *Golden Years* video first came into our house. Kicking frees towards that human cliff of blue challenged me now in a way I probably hadn't been challenged before. They called me everything under the sun and, as I'd be lining up a kick, the sound was like a kettle coming to the boil. On some level that seemed to get my juices flowing. I felt comfortable with the pressure.

We ran out winners by seven points but, deep down, we knew it hadn't been a seven-point game. I still have a vivid memory of a first-half Alan Brogan shot snapping back off Diarmuid

Murphy's crossbar. But we saw the game out really well and two weeks later had six points to spare over Derry in the semi-final. Jack, the self-styled outsider, was just one game away from a clean sweep.

To this day it's my favourite goal, the one that helped us beat Mayo in the 2004 All-Ireland final.

Why? Because I needed all the skills to score it. Eamonn Fitz lamped a high ball in (he claims it was a pinpoint pass, but it was actually fairly agricultural) that I caught above my head. Pat Kelly was marking me but, the moment I landed, I sensed a goal was on. My speed on the turn was going to lose him. After that it was just solo – little basketball hop bounce inside and a nice calm finish, rolling it into the corner.

Just everything about it captured the qualities I respect most in the game. Above all, I love seeing a composed finish from a forward when the pressure is at its highest.

We went into that final with a brutally simple game-plan: attack them in the air. Jack was very smart here, pointing out that the Mayo inside forward line wasn't exactly the tallest, so chances were their backs weren't dealing with too much high ball in training. They wouldn't have been stress-tested. To this end, he brought back Johnny Crowley for a job on the edge of the square at the expense of Mike Frank Russell.

It was a big call given Mike Frank's skill levels, but Crowley and Dara Ó'Cinnéide were so strong in the air, Jack felt this was the way to hurt Mayo.

He was proved right too, the two boys cleaning up and Kerry creating mismatches all around the field. Mayo had got off to a flier with Alan Dillon's fifth-minute goal, but that would be the high point of their day. We just gave a complete team performance, and for me particularly, it felt as if everything I touched turned to gold. With eighteen minutes to go we led 1-17 to 1-6, Mayo players clearly shell-shocked at what had just happened to them.

I remember a surreal moment around the sixty-fifth minute, just catching my breath and looking up at the giant Hill End screen with the luxury of knowing that we were champions.

Even then we weren't giving an inch. I suppose there were too many of us – myself, Marc, Brossie, Mahony – chasing our first All-Ireland even to countenance easing back on the throttle. My 1-5 would get me Man of the Match, a Texaco award and untold levels of personal fulfilment. It seemed as if nobody had mentioned my size all summer.

And Jack, naturally, was hugely pumped after. He felt, justifiably, that he'd proved the doubters wrong. From that opening League defeat against Longford, Kerry had kicked on and won the lot – League, Munster, All-Ireland. Little more than six months on from people telling us that we were fucked, we were market leaders again.

Golden circle or not, Kerry had a new maestro.

6

'Whatever You Do, Don't Retaliate!'

'Then you start, lads . . . you insult his mother, insult his grandmother, his sister, his family, every generation of them. Insult the shite out of them, annihilate them, lambast them. Make sure that man hits you. When he hits you, you hit the ground. He gets the line, we'll get the free. Fifteen men down to fourteen . . . lads, ye don't even know how to play the fucking game.'

– D'Unbelievables

The legendary Timmy Ryan was ahead of his time with that team-talk to the under-13 hurlers of Glengooley.

I reckon Jon Kenny was doing his famous sketch a good decade before real life began imitating comedy in inter-county football. Tyrone didn't invent sledging in the GAA, let's be very clear about that. As long as I've been playing there's always been a mouth or two determined to make themselves heard. Fellas trying to get into a player's head to make him lose concentration or, better still, his temper. Probably been there since before Noah and the Ark.

But Tyrone were different.

They were the first team I came up against who seemed to regard trash-talk as being just as fundamental to the game as tackling. And they were relentless in 2005. Right from the throw-in, a constant commentary.

Fuck you're playing awful shit Gooch, I'd say you're not long for the hook.

Bet ya I'll beat you to the next ball that comes in . . .

Harmless enough in comparison to some of the stuff I've heard reported since, but heading in one direction. Ryan McMenamin would be my marker in that year's All-Ireland final and Ricey, as he likes to be called, almost prided himself on being able to wind a forward up. Personally I never minded playing on him because he was never the stickiest corner-back in the world. Maybe his mouthing was to compensate for that.

He'd hit you the odd dig into the back too and try to annoy you with these little pinches, hoping you might throw an elbow back and get the line. Tyrone were pushing the boundaries that year, maybe overstepping them at times – and who could really blame them? Pushing those boundaries would bring them their second All-Ireland in three years. We'd felt we were better than them that year, but history tells us we were fooling ourselves.

They had it both ways you see. Players like Peter Canavan, Seán Cavanagh, Owen Mulligan and Stephen O'Neill who'd have made any team with their talent. And fellas to do the other stuff. If they were getting away with that other stuff, what did we honestly expect them to do? Hand us a written apology and vow to change their ways?

Bottom line, if winning demanded Tyrone be nasty, they were more than willing to be that. It didn't make them unique in the annals of Gaelic football, did it? Some of the most successful teams in history would have cut a family member in two just to get past them to a ball. I get that. Kerry haven't exactly been angels when it's come to use of the dark arts. But sledging? No, that's not really us.

Anyway, Tyrone didn't give a shit then about what anybody thought. They didn't care if people hated them. If anything, I suspect they took energy from that idea. Got a kick out of it. And they particularly got a kick out of pulling the rug from under a fancied Kerry team.

Part of that, I suspect, was in reaction to the way Pat Spillane and Joe Brolly had become a kind of Punch and Judy show on *The Sunday Game* once Pat had patented that term 'puke football'. All of that just added fuel to the Tyrone fire. 'Everybody hates us. Fuck them!'

I'm often asked was I one of those who came to hate them. My honest answer is I hated the fact that we couldn't beat them. And, yes, they were hateful to play against, no question. They were testing you in every single way. But the big issue for me was that they were allowed to do it. That's the bit I really hated, the stuff that would go unpunished.

But then, maybe that's the 5 per cent they feel got them across the line.

Was the sledging actively promoted within the Tyrone dressing-room? Only they can answer that. But almost every last one of them seemed willing to do it. And when you think about it, there was no penalty for it. A referee could never hear it so, in every way they could, Tyrone just played the system.

There are different kinds of hatred. I mean, I can hate Bernard Brogan or Ciarán Kilkenny for the damage they've inflicted on Kerry in recent years. Same thing with Canavan, Cavanagh, Mulligan and O'Neill back then. But it's not real hatred, is it? If anything, it's grudging respect. But the hatred you feel towards those who just make it their job to niggle? That's different. That's closer to the real thing.

This anti-football stuff. Winning by hook or by crook. Horrible.

There was an incident in the '05 final that had an adverse effect on me for much of the first half. I was making a run in around the penalty spot, just trying to lose my man. And Tyrone's goalie, Pascal McConnell, kept charging out towards me, as if trying to block my run. On this one occasion his glove made contact with my face.

I got this horrible sensation of grit in my eye and immediately went down. And all around me became a symphony directed towards the referee, Mick Monahan. 'Diving, ref, diving, diving, diving . . .' They were like squawking birds on a wall.

I'm telling them to fuck off with themselves when Monahan comes across to me and says, 'Whatever you do, don't retaliate!'

So I'm sitting on my arse in Croke Park, barely able to see out of one eye, and the ref's telling me not to retaliate to something that hasn't, it seems, even merited a free. There are two umpires standing, hands behind their backs, no more than a few feet away. Don't retaliate?

'Well are you going to fucking take action or what?' I ask Monahan.

His silence is the answer I expected and I'm rattled now. Maybe we're all rattled. Rattled and frustrated. Rightly or wrongly, I reckon I've just been taken out of the game. Was it premeditated? It's possible, I don't know. But what kills me is, the ref's only response is to tell me not to hit back.

We'd talked beforehand about how Tyrone were likely to have something up their sleeves.

My form that summer had really come good. I'd always believed it would.

Funny, the Monday after our '04 All-Ireland final win, myself,

Johnny Crowley, Jack and a couple of others found a quiet spot in The Killarney Avenue when all the homecoming formalities had been completed. Just to 'sip on a couple of sodas' as we like to put it. The rest of the town was absolute bedlam, but here we could at least hear the sound of our own voices.

And I remember Jack looking me in the eye and saying flatly, 'You'll have to be better next year.'

And, sure, I was pure brazen and bould. This big grin on my face, telling the Kerry manager not to be worrying. That being better in '05 would be 'no hassle' to me, 'no problem'.

Years later, he'd recount that exchange to me, grinning. 'I told you in '04 you'd have to be better in '05 and you, you fucker, you were!'

I mean, Limerick used four different markers on me in the Gaelic Grounds and we'd beaten Cork at Páirc Uí Chaoimh in the Munster final, always something sweet. By the time we met them again that year, in the All-Ireland semi-final, I was absolutely at the top of my game. Niall Geary marked me both days and was taken off after twenty minutes in Croke Park where we beat them by thirteen points.

So Tyrone were never going to go holding doors open for me, were they? We knew something was coming, but what do you do when it lands? Maybe the lack of anger in us as a group that day said more about us than we were willing to absorb at the time. Because all we gave Tyrone in return was just noise.

I'd started well, had kicked a point and was beginning to motor. Next thing everyone's barking and roaring and squaring up for an argument and, without knowing it, the game is being played on Tyrone's terms. Was the McConnell thing premeditated? I can't honestly say. And let's be straight, it wasn't what lost us the match.

Tyrone were hungrier than us, meaner than us, better. Take away the mouthing and they still had something over Kerry.

Their small men hit our big men harder than they'd been hit before. Stopping fellas in their tracks, big Kerry bulls getting bounced back on their arses. Balls getting turned over.

Canavan scored a class goal on the stroke of half-time from a Mulligan knock-down, then Harte took him off for a breather before sending him on again to close the deal. More evidence of how they were rethinking the game. Improvising. Setting different standards. We ended up chasing the game, and in the dying seconds Canavan pulled me down with a virtual rugby tackle as I sprinted to take a return pass. Their best player doing whatever it took. Not giving a shit what anyone might say on that evening's *Sunday Game*.

He'd been blackguarded himself enough across the years, so could you really blame him?

So Tyrone were in our heads, dominating our thoughts by the end of the year. Exactly where they wanted to be.

The All-Stars trip had been to Hong Kong that January and, in hindsight, maybe offered us an early glimpse of what was coming down the line.

Myself, Paul Galvin, Tom Sullivan, Diarmuid Murphy and William Kirby were the Kerry tourists and it's fair to say we didn't spare ourselves. I remember an English pub in the basement of the hotel we were staying in and every evening seemed to finish on a high stool down there. Telling stories, skulling beer, happy tourists without a care in the world.

The Tyrone lads had a different tour. Mickey Harte was one of the managers in Hong Kong and I have a memory of his players always having bottles of water in their hands when you'd meet them in the hotel lobby. They were using the hotel gym too. And when it came to the exhibition game, they played it as if it was Ulster Championship in Omagh.

At the time, I suppose we were almost tickled by their seriousness, telling ourselves that they'd probably be on the tear like the rest of us only for Mickey watching their every move. We misread them.

We didn't understand the depth of Tyrone's hunger.

> 'I know what they're thinking, they're thinking Timmy Ryan is too hard on us. Well I'll tell ye something lads, I'm not. Ye'll know all about it next year when ye're playing under-fourteen!'
>
> – D'Unbelievables

7

'Comin' to Get You Goochie!'

I am sitting on a hotel bed in Melbourne, eyes hurting from the flickering of the TV screen, ears ringing like a fire alarm and someone drilling away with a jackhammer inside my skull.

The instruction from Dr Con is not to go to sleep. 'Go home,' he said, 'but don't go to bed!' A worry with the early stages of any suspected concussion is that bad things can be camouflaged by sleep. At least if you're awake, the symptoms become self-evident. You can communicate what you feel.

So this is how the trip of a lifetime ends.

Sore.

Nauseous.

Agitated.

Watching shit TV.

The Aussies have just given us a hiding. An aggregate series win of fifty-seven points for two Tests and a technical knockout in the physical stakes. Put simply, they've beaten us up, humiliated us. And now – with everyone else out on the tear, drowning their sorrows – I'm sitting alone on the far side of the world thinking one thing and one thing only.

Never again. Never fucking again.

It's October 2005 and I've finally scratched an itch that has been bugging me for some time.

I'd wanted to represent Ireland in an International Rules Series and maybe had been a bit presumptuous a year earlier when called up to Dublin for a trial. Physically I felt in the shape of my life, had just won Man of the Match in an All-Ireland final, and was heading for an All-Star and a nomination for Footballer of the Year. Maybe playing for my country felt like the next logical step in my progression. But Pete McGrath evidently saw things differently.

I'd been seriously pissed off when overlooked for his squad, maybe even more so when Ireland then gave the Aussies a good thumping in the series, playing a brand of football that I reckoned would have suited me down to the ground. So I was on a mission in '05. After the disappointment of losing the All-Ireland to Tyrone, I suppose I just reckoned three weeks in Australia might be just what I needed to recover psychologically.

Now, given Tyrone players would dominate the squad selection, it mightn't have seemed the wisest way to go about it, but the idea of living and training like full-time professionals – even for that brief spell – had always appealed to me. There was also the attraction of running out into storied Australian venues like the Subiaco Oval in Perth and Melbourne's Telstra Dome, places I'd only seen on TV. So this time I made sure Pete saw just how piped into the concept I had become and was thrilled when confirmation came that I'd made the cut.

That, sadly, would prove just about the high point of my International Rules experience.

Maybe we should have seen the cheap shots coming, but we didn't. I doubt there's any need to go into detail about what hit us, given the Second Test especially is remembered as one of the worst exhibitions of thuggery ever witnessed in the series. And that's saying something.

After their hammering the year before, the Aussies had appointed the grizzled old Essendon coach Kevin Sheedy as their manager. It might have been just coincidence of course, but his appointment seemed to change their attitude towards us. Suddenly there was a vibe that only over their dead bodies would a bunch of Irish amateurs come to Australia and embarrass them on home soil.

So while we had a decent squad with a good captain (Galway's Pádraig Joyce), we were just sitting ducks for the physical viciousness coming our way.

They had done their homework on individuals too, which astonished me. Like, it was clear they'd heard of a footballer called 'The Gooch' because, from the off, they were full of verbals towards me. 'Comin' to get you Goochie, don't you worry mate.' I was just about getting over the idea of being so well known in Australia when the digging began to start.

The worst of their offenders would be a little tub of a chap called Chris Johnson who also just happened to be one of Sheedy's co-captains. I thought that said everything. In the Second Test especially, Johnson seemed hell-bent on just hurting people. Everyone remembers the clothes-line tackle on Philip Jordan I suppose, but he was ridiculous from start to finish in that game. It was as if there could never be enough fights in the game as far as he was concerned. He spent the day just trying to nail people.

Anything went in that game. Punches, kicks, straight-arm tackles. I'd never come across anything like it in my life.

It wasn't so much that the Aussies were over-physical as the sense that they literally wanted to do damage. Tackles became assaults, and all the time you got this kind of smirky condescension from them, a sense that they just didn't rate us at all as footballers or people. Guys could have been seriously injured with some of the Australian antics that day. Worse, it was clear they felt they could do what they did without any fear of retribution.

I remember talking to Tadhg Kennelly about this after. Tadhg had been due to be part of the Irish squad, but – lucky man – had to withdraw because of injury. He said the Australians were taking liberties because they knew there was no question of any suspension carrying over into the Aussie Rules season. So they basically felt they had a free pass to do whatever they wanted to do against us.

Deep down, I think I'd already decided it wasn't for me even before I took the late hit. It was a cheap shot, zero intention of getting the ball. To this day I don't even know if my attempt to score went over the bar or drifted wide. Haven't a clue either about the name of the lad who hit me. But the impact arrived maybe two seconds after I made contact with the ball.

BANG.

Comin' to get you Goochie . . .

I would go home with a very sour taste in my mouth after that. Why bother putting your health on the line for a glorified exhibition game against opponents intent on inflicting physical damage? The atmosphere was just appalling out there. One Irish player was even head-butted.

Before we'd left the stadium I think I said it to my room-mate, Eoin Brosnan. 'I won't be playing this again Brossie, not this shit.' Just felt I was better off at home, looking after myself for Dr Crokes and Kerry rather than risking having my career ended by some Australian clown doing a decent impression of a thug.

And that's what the voice in my head is saying at three a.m. as I finally turn the TV off in Melbourne. Still no sign of Brossie coming home, but my head has settled and the ringing in my ears is quiet.

Never again. Not this shit.

8

A Father's Son

They say at home that I'm very closed as a person, and I suppose my father's death proved it.

I give little enough away at the best of times, but when I lost him, I pretty much went into a shell. I became selfish with my sorrow, if that makes any sense. I shut people out. I moped. I sulked. I bristled. I internalized everything, communicating to everyone around me an impression of preciousness that I now regret.

It was as if I was taking exclusive ownership of the family's grief.

No question, I inherited my passion for football from Mike Cooper. When I was a child, if there was a game he wanted to see, he assumed that I wanted to see it too. It wouldn't require an actual conversation. Just a throwaway 'We might head over to Glenflesk tonight' would be enough. Soon as he'd have the dinner down, away with us in the car. The conversation wouldn't ever really feel like father and son. He'd toss things out to me as if I was one of his buddies hunched over a pint down in Jimmy O'Brien's.

I'm not saying we were exactly full of chat every time we sat in the car, but I could almost pretend I was an adult when it came to dissecting what we'd see. Now he mightn't have been paying a blind bit of notice to anything I had to say, but I suppose the beauty was it never felt that way.

The suddenness of his death had a brutal impact on us all. I can see that clearly now. But at the time, I behaved as if I was the only one dealing with a terrible loss. As if I was his only child.

I was working the counter that morning in the bank when an ashen-looking Patrick O'Sullivan came through the door.

The early-morning rush had just finished and I was tidying things as he came to the window. I could see immediately that something was seriously wrong. 'Gooch, come away with me, something's after happening to your father up the road.' The 'up the road' Patrick was referring to was a building site just at the back of Ardshanavooly where Deerpark Shopping Centre was under construction. Patrick didn't let on, but he already knew my father was gone.

The word had already begun sweeping down the town, as bad news tends to do. *Mike Cooper's just dropped dead above on the shopping centre site.*

My father took his last breath no more than 200 yards from our front door. Just walking across the yard when cut down by a massive heart attack. Driving up in Patrick's car now, I could tell he was very frazzled. A journey of no more than five minutes, but it was all questions and no answers.

'I don't have any detail, Gooch . . .'

'Just got a phone call saying something happened . . .'

'Wait till we get up there . . .'

My poor mother was coming out the front door as we pulled up, but the reality hadn't really dawned on me. I remember thinking that Dad might have had a fall or maybe been hit by some kind of machinery. In my head he was still with us, injured but alive.

But they were just putting him into the back of the ambulance as we arrived, their efforts to resuscitate over. And that's when my heart sank. 'Very sorry,' the medics mumbled, their heads shaking. They let us climb into the back of the ambulance, closing the door behind us so that we could say a private goodbye. Just two or three last minutes with my father, poor Mam near hysterical.

Then they took him away to Tralee, leaving us to stumble back to a house that would never feel the same.

The days that followed are a blur. My sisters took charge of organizing the funeral, the rest of us really just sitting around in a daze as the house became flooded with friends and neighbours. Everybody well-meaning, everybody trying to help, but nobody really knowing what to say. The body was brought home and we laid him out in the front room. I remember shaking a lot of hands but, largely, just sitting there in silence. I couldn't really talk to people, couldn't even acknowledge them.

It was as if a bomb had gone off inside my head.

Dad had no history of heart trouble, but he'd been quite sick at home with pneumonia through Christmas of 2005 and I'm not really sure he ever managed to shake that. Like Mam, and most of their generation, he was a smoker, and we could tell he wasn't really himself for a long time after that. He just looked and sounded washed out, but yearned for the comforts of routine.

In the end, I'd say he was nearly lying to himself just to get back working. Telling people he was 'the finest' when having little or no energy. I don't honestly know if the pneumonia had anything to do with what happened to him that April morning. All I do know is his death felt cruel and unfair to every one of us.

His funeral Mass was held just a few hundred yards down Park Road in the Church of the Resurrection, which he'd helped build.

The days that followed were incredibly tough on my mother. The two of them did everything together and their plans for his retirement would have been simple and inexpensive. They had no desire to travel the world but I suspect that, having raised seven children, they'd looked forward to having more time to themselves. To being able to enjoy their grandchildren, but then have the luxury of handing them back!

The only wealth the pair of them ever aspired to was their house and a healthy family. That was as good as a Lottery win to them.

Women are far more open than men in how they deal with grief and Geraldine and Karen would have cried a lot with Mam. The boys? We did what most Irish men do in these circumstances and stayed buttoned up, hurt, maybe resentful even. Me more than anyone. It felt disrespectful to laugh at anything. To smile even.

When someone is taken from you so suddenly, I think you lose the motivation to do anything for a while. There's a feeling that life should almost stop right there and then, that it's inappropriate to be happy.

I didn't verbalize any of this because, as I said, that's just not what an Irish male does.

But I became full of self-pity in the months after my father died. As if the whole world was against me. People were constantly reaching out and I kept pushing them away. Not in an aggressive way. Just by being that 'closed book' my sisters often refer to. By being constantly cranky.

'What are you trying to help me for?'

'I don't need your help!'

Everyone was kept at arm's length. Not just family and friends, team-mates too. I had the barriers up, shutting everybody out. Acting tough, I suppose. As if I could fight the world on my own. I was too immature to understand what I was doing, too young to see the bigger picture. I was twenty-two, still growing up essentially, internalizing everything to try to communicate an inner hardness that probably didn't exist.

And I kind of resented the publicity my father's funeral drew, with photographs in the papers. That didn't sit well with me at all. Because of my profile, the event was considered a news story. A national news story even.

And all I'm hearing is *How is Colm?*

This would go on right through the summer of '06 and, fuck, it wrecked my head. I felt as if I was living in a goldfish bowl. I could be walking down the street to get a sandwich at lunchtime and get stopped by some family for a conversation. They might be down in Killarney on holidays. Complete strangers.

'How are you since your Dad?'

There were days I thought my head might explode, but what can you say? They don't mean any harm. The last thing you want is to have that conversation, but the only alternative is to be rude. To blank them and walk past. I couldn't do that. I can't.

So I'd just swallow hard. 'Everything's grand, thanks for asking. Have a great holiday.'

Being famous in a small town, people presume so many things about you. It's like they consider you some kind of local ambassador nearly. They expect there to be an open line to you at all times. Everybody means well, but it can start to feel suffocating. Total strangers addressing you as 'Gooch'. Not Colm. Gooch.

It's friendliness and warmth and 100 per cent well meaning, but I don't have a big house with electric gates to go home to when I want to hide.

One thing I do understand is that I have a huge connection

with Killarney and Kerry people in general. Killarney people have had access to me all the time. I'm one of their own. I'd say some maybe can't believe how successful I became, that I got to be a national star.

But I've always been *their* star.

I could be sitting in a coffee shop and someone might even invite themselves over to join me at the table. I'd never be rude. There would have been plenty of times across the years when I just wanted to be on my own, yet I'd still just sit there and listen. They might be talking about the weather or telling me about something that's going on out in Muckross or asking did I see such-and-such match? And I just got on with it. I was reared to be polite with people.

Probably in my younger years that was harder, though. There'd be days I'd be sitting there thinking 'Fuck this'. But I'd do it anyway. Over time, I came to understand that it kind of meant something to people. Just to be able to go home and announce, 'I met Gooch inside in town, he says things are good in training!' They'd feel they had some kind of inside track and that meant a lot to them. Maybe some of the affection I've got from people is related to that. To the fact that I was easy to access.

But I wanted to hide in the summer of '06. I wanted to be invisible. But how could I do that, sitting at a counter in AIB on Main Street? Walking down the street with an instantly recognizable face? Training above in the park?

I was visible everywhere and it felt, at times, as if I was trying to handle my grief in full public view.

Then there was the pressure of expectation. The football talk. The worry about my form and how it might impact on Kerry's hopes of winning the All-Ireland. Even grieving, that remained. All I wanted to do was get the fuck out of Dodge, but people still wanted things from me. They wanted me to be Gooch.

Above: Where it all began: Dr Crokes Team, officials and 'mascot' leaving Killarney railway station en route to the 1992 All-Ireland Club final.

Left: First trip to New York, 1995.

Below: The five Cooper brothers after winning the 2000 County Championship – my first one. From left to right: Colm, Vince, Mike, Mark and Danny.

Left: Croker introduction: my first game in the Coliseum, 2 September 2001, All-Ireland minor semi-final against Dublin.

Below: In with the big dogs: 2002 All-Ireland senior final, escaping the clutches of Armagh's Enda McNulty.

Bottom: My favourite Kerry goal: All-Ireland Senior Football Final Mayo v. Kerry, 26 September 2004.

Above: A clean sweep: Dr Crokes Social '04 with Sam, Munster Championship and National League trophies. *Front:* Mam, me, Dad; *back, left to right:* Mike Murphy (brother-in-law), Vince Cooper, Geraldine (sister), Danny Cooper, Helen (sister-in-law), Noreen (sister-in-law), Mark Cooper, Annette (sister-in-law).

Below: Dad, me and Mam after Kerry won the '04 All-Ireland.

Left: A familiar foe: one of many battles with Tyrone's Ryan McMenamin, 3 April 2005; National Football League, Division 1A, Fitzgerald Stadium, Killarney.

Above: High fliers: All-Star trip to Hong Kong after winning the '04 All-Ireland. *Left to right*: me, Tom Sullivan, Diarmuid Murphy, Paul Galvin, William Kirby.

Right: Myself and my good buddy Kieran Cahillane (RIP), just a week before he died.

Above: Calm before the storm: Australia, International Aussie Rules '05.

Below: Up close and personal: tackled by Dale Morris, International Rules Series, game two, Australia v. Ireland, Telstra Dome, Melbourne, 28 October 2005.

Above: Stairway to heaven: rolling the ball past David Clarke as we take early control of the 2006 All-Ireland final against Mayo.

Left: Same goal, different angle.

Below: Help from above? Collecting Sam with Declan O'Sullivan after an emotional roller coaster of a year, 17 September 2006.

Above: My nephew Aaron meeting his heroes and Sam Maguire. *Left to right*: Darragh Ó Sé, Marc Ó Sé, Kieran Donaghy, myself, Aaron and Tomás Ó Sé.

Left: Home is where the heart is. *Back, left to right*: me, Mark, Vince, Mike and Danny; *front, left to right*: Karen, Mam, Geraldine with 'Sam'.

Below: Trip of a lifetime: Mam, Karen and me in Central Park, New York.

Above: Days you dream about: Munster Championship Football final, 1 July 2007, Kerry v. Cork – pre-match parade in Killarney.

Right: History in the making: tackled by Graham Canty in the first-ever Kerry v. Cork All-Ireland final, 16 September 2007.

Below: We've come a long road: celebrating with life-long friend and Kerry manager, Pat O'Shea, at the end of the '07 All-Ireland final.

I had zero interest in playing against the Dubs that Sunday. Zero. I knew there was going to be a minute's silence for my father beforehand. I knew people would want to pay their respects. But even the thought of that was draining to me now. I wanted to be a million miles away from it all. To be left alone. Jack O'Connor called to the house that Friday and said he wouldn't push me either way. That they'd love to have me tog out, but the decision would be mine.

When he left, I turned to my mother and said, 'I'm not playing. I've no energy for that. The week has worn me out.'

And that's when she said that my father would probably like me to tog out.

And I was 'Fuck sake . . .'

What could I do? To be fair to Mam, she didn't give a shit about Kerry in this situation. She was concerned only about her family. But she was always thinking about what would be 'the right thing' to do and, just as importantly, to be seen to do. Initially I was even angry about that. I didn't want to be put out there in front of everyone. I didn't want to be the centre of attention. I had barely slept all week and felt emotionally and physically drained.

But I did what she said, came on as a sub, scored a point with my first touch, and the place went absolutely mental. And, if I'm honest, that moment gave me a little surge of energy. But it was artificial energy. In an ideal world, I'd have taken time out. But this wasn't an ideal world. I was Kerry's key man and people needed to know where they stood with me. We were coming into pre-Championship training and I had no energy, no zest, no enthusiasm for the game at all. I was a walking shell.

Jack, to be fair, was trying to give me space. We won the League almost without trying, but I was way off where I needed to be. He knew I was too stubborn to talk things through with anyone. My family knew too. I got a few bollockings off the brothers in that time, just having a little go at me over 'the way you're acting'.

Of course my view was that they just didn't understand. They weren't public property. They weren't getting stopped in the street.

I look back on that summer now and I see they spent the entire time walking on eggshells when they were around me. I was completely selfish, carrying the weight of the world around on my shoulders. Communicating this 'Give me fucking space' message when they were trying to get over their own grief while raising kids.

My only defence is that I was really just a kid myself. I thought I had all the answers. But the truth is, none of us had.

Until you're personally affected by a sudden death, it's almost something abstract in your mind. It's a voice on the RTÉ *Six One News*, giving the detail of a murder or some horrible accident. You hear it but don't really absorb it. Until it lands on your own door, you've no appreciation of what its impact will be on those who are left behind. None.

The shock that runs through you almost pulverizes your whole system. You can't just take a tablet and be cured. I suppose my father dying forced me, eventually, to grow up in a way that took some time for me to understand.

And my family weren't the only ones who needed to be patient.

9

'You Didn't Believe Me, Did You?'

Jack O'Connor's trying to see inside my head, but not getting very far beyond the front door.

He's been here before, but I don't suppose that makes it any less tricky. When Kieran drowned last August, Jack spent a few days just leaving me room to breathe. I appreciated that. I needed it. No point asking me how I was doing when I didn't even know the answer to that myself. I'd missed a couple of training sessions, but there was a team to manage and a game to win and, at some point, he needed to know.

So two weeks before that year's All-Ireland semi-final against Cork, he rang. 'Gooch, I'll meet you in town at five and we'll just head away and have a chat.'

In my naivety, I thought he might have some new tactic in mind, but next thing I knew we were down in Kenmare, sitting with two pints of Guinness before us and ordering dinner off a menu in Sheen Falls. I remember sitting there at first thinking 'Has this man lost his marbles?' Imagine the noise someone could make locally with that image of the Kerry manager supping pints with a key player two weeks before an All-Ireland semi-final.

But that was why he wanted me out of Killarney. For a bit of privacy, a bit of space. He reckoned a couple of pints might, at least, get me to open up because Jack wouldn't have been the only one who saw me as a cold fish. But he knew too that there was still a cloud hanging over the whole town of Killarney because of Kieran.

It's fair to say he didn't get a great deal out of me that evening, but he did get just about enough to conclude that I was determined I'd be ready for Cork. My form was solid that year and, once I was right mentally, it was unlikely to desert me. And it didn't.

But this is different. If football felt a rescue of sorts after Kieran passed, it's more of a suffocating pressure now. On some level, I don't even want to know. Or at least I don't want the endless commotion, the squinting and questioning that follows me around as a Kerry footballer. The trouble for Jack is I can play decent football even when my heart is only half in it. I mean, I have a good League final against Galway, scoring freely, but my body language tells him I'm still in a solitary place.

Then the Championship starts and, I suppose, that body language doesn't soften. My form is poor. I look back on that time now and it brings home to me the complexities of man-management, of just trying to read and maybe manipulate the minds of thirty individuals.

In this instance, to begin with, when Jack comes looking for answers, he's not getting them.

We draw with Cork in Killarney, then get well beaten one week later in the replay at Páirc Uí Chaoimh. So much for the team that's on a mission to dethrone Tyrone. Within an hour of the final whistle in Cork we are in a crisis meeting at Hayfield Manor. Feels like we're in big trouble here. After four games in this Championship our goals return is zero. Even Waterford and Tipperary have managed to frustrate us.

Jack's got problems in every section of the team, but he's mostly got them with an attack in which two of his star men, Declan O'Sullivan and Colm Cooper, just aren't motoring. When he looks across the dressing-room at me, I can more or less hear the voice in his head.

What the fuck do we do with this fella?

At the meeting, people say their pieces but nothing's really resolved. Nothing ever is at these meetings until lads get back on the field again and start walking the walk. 'The knockers will be out in force now,' Jack tells us. Seamus Moynihan gets the juices flowing with a rousing call for the men in the room to start being counted. But, mostly, lads are just looking at the floor. We've no experience of winning an All-Ireland through the qualifier route and there's a sense here that we've just run out of things like hunger, desire, heart. Maybe bottle.

Everybody wants the same thing, but nobody's really sure how to bring it about. I can tell Jack wants me to be a leader here, to play the role of a senior figure in the dressing-room. But that Colm Cooper's nowhere to be seen.

I'm going through the motions, moping about, feeling sorry for myself. I'm not performing on or off the pitch and something has to give. Jack decides that that something will have to be Declan. It's a horrible call for him to have to make given the two of them are Dromid clubmates, and I know he might just as easily have made the call on me. But Declan was booed by a section of the Kerry crowd when taken off in that Cork replay, something that sickened every last one of us to the core. Maybe Jack reckons he just needs a break here. But Declan's demotion means that I become Kerry captain. Maybe that's part of management's psychological wish list now, the hope that this added responsibility might kick-start something in me. Bring me out of my shell.

But we need more than words now. We need chemistry. We need a forward line that carries some kind of goal threat.

And that's when Jack pulls a fairly big rabbit from the hat.

I know Kieran Donaghy of course. I've played county minor with him. He's been in and about the senior squad now for some time, but we all think of him as a midfielder. That's where he spends most of his time in training, trying to get himself noticed in direct opposition to a monster like Darragh. Donaghy's 6ft 5in and a bit of a monster himself, but against Darragh he's an apprentice.

Then one night Jack sticks him in on the edge of the square, he catches a few balls, sets up a few scores, and I suppose – maybe desperation being the mother of invention – that's Kerry's eureka moment.

Until now, Jack's been trying Bryan Sheehan and Declan at number 14. It hasn't been working, but then nothing really has. Now none of us has any idea yet if the giant we know as 'Star' is really up to senior county standard. We certainly don't know if he's even related to an inter-county full-forward. But Jack sidles over to me in training one night.

'We have to take a punt on this man.'

The idea was that someone of Donaghy's size would take the focus off lads like myself and Mike Frank Russell and we might avail ourselves of the extra space inside. But Jack in his wildest dreams couldn't have imagined what's about to happen. We draw Longford in the qualifiers, score 4-11 against them in Killarney, and Star is directly involved in 4-4. Brossie gets a hat-trick of goals and I manage 1-3. It's not exactly classic Kerry football, but there's a pulse in us again.

That pulse comes as much from Star's personality as his size. His enthusiasm is infectious. Coming off the field that day, he gets swamped for media interviews. He's about to be named *The Sunday Game*'s Man of the Match. Darragh and I are looking at him, grins across our faces. Because Donaghy's in his element here. Jack spots the commotion around his new hero and says with a chuckle, 'Just fucking leave him at it!'

He's right too. Whatever it is that Donaghy's after bringing to this team, the last thing we want to do now is curtail it.

His switch to 14 means I'm no longer Kerry's primary ball winner inside. That's a big relief. I'm sick and tired of having two fellas fucking horsing off me under every ball when I don't have the energy to fight even one. We have become too predictable with me at 13, Mike Frank at 15. Teams have been watching us do pretty much the same thing for three years. They know exactly how we are going to play.

What's that they say about it being the definition of insanity to do the same thing over and over, yet expect different results?

Suddenly, Star's giving our midfield the option of just lamping ball in on top of the square. Now I can make a run off the ball. Now I can double back on that run as the ball is descending, knowing he can slip me a pass inside. It sounds simple but it isn't. In time, Cork will try to replicate what we do by reinventing Michael Cussen as a number 14.

But Cussen is no Donaghy.

Kieran's switch gives everyone a boost and lifts energy levels in the team. No question, we're still a work in progress, still making silly mistakes. But at least we're talking. *You peel off the back post next time, Kieran, and I'll see if I can get you.*

And, fuck it, it's hard not to love the man. There's divilment in him. He comes to training in this purple '04 Opel Astra that he nearly needs a shoehorn to get into and which looks like it's held together by twine. But within weeks of that end-of-July demolition job on Longford he's got a sponsored Volvo. We see him driving through the gates and all anybody can do is laugh. Good luck to the fucker. He's after making our lives fun again.

By then, he's also put Armagh to the sword in Croke Park. And for this Kerry team, beating a hard-nosed Ulster team constitutes something a good deal bigger than rolling over Longford. I made a captain's speech before the match and laid my feelings on the line. Something about Armagh '02 and Tyrone '03 and '05, about those defeats convincing people that Kerry couldn't cope with Northern hardness.

'We're not losing to another fucking Ulster team on my watch.'

People reckoned Francie Bellew would eat our beanpole novice without salt. If we're honest, a few of us might even have considered it a possibility. This was a shot to nothing really, with the possibility that it might blow up in Jack's face. But Donaghy gave us an option nobody else could give us: the option of Darragh just catching kick-outs and lamping ball in on top of the square.

The year had been a fucking trudge for all of us until that light bulb went on in Jack's head. If it went out again, the truth is we were almost certainly goosed.

And for a long time it looked like that would be our fate. For half an hour Francie had Star in his pocket and I could see the humour drain out of Donaghy like corn from a sack. If anything he was trying too hard, running too early. He needed just to hang tough there. They were giving him loads of verbals, especially their goalkeeper, Paul Hearty. 'You have him bate up a stick Francie!' was Hearty's mantra. In that grown-up way of adults playing for a big prize, they were calling Star 'a cry-baby'.

I was worried about where his head was so I wandered over and said something loud enough for the Armagh boys to hear. I told him to relax, that all he needed was 'just one ball to stick'. I wanted to remind them that Star was like nothing they'd ever marked before. Wanted to remind *him* of that too.

Armagh were leading by four points edging towards the end of the first half, when Donaghy set me up for a point. Then Mike

Frank got another after Hearty made two good saves and the vibe going in at half-time was transformed by those two scores. Jack started bigging up Donaghy in the dressing-room.

'Fair play to you Donaghy, you could have turned your hole to it.'

Within minutes of the resumption we were level and ready for Star to reintroduce himself to the Armagh boys. A Sean O'Sullivan effort for a point started dropping short and Donaghy anticipated, rising to catch it over Bellew's head. As he turned to go inside, he went down on his knees like a young foal not yet able to stay upright on spindly legs.

Francie thought he had him, but Star threw one of those basketball shapes of his and was in the clear. He shot before Hearty managed to get close enough, and even as the net billowed Donaghy couldn't help but swing round and give back some of what he'd been getting.

'Who's crying now?'

There's a man who's been carrying me through a lot of bad days now and I don't even realize he's doing it.

We all know this is Seamus Moynihan's last year and there's no one we'd like to recognize more with a proper send-off. His way is to set his own standards, then see to it that others follow. In my time as a Kerry footballer he's never been captain but he's always been a leader.

Without me even realizing it, he's pushing my buttons now. 'Come on to fuck Gooch, we'll do a bit extra . . .'

He knows Kerry need me firing and I start doing this extra core work with him, not really realizing what his game is. He's got issues with his back and it's like he just wants company as he fights them. So I start doing extra physio work with him, without really stopping to think if I need it.

That's the way it is with Moynihan. He leads, you follow.

He starts collecting me on Wednesdays at six a.m. to head up to Ger Hartmann's clinic in Limerick, swinging into Henry Street before eight for some core work with Ger Keane before getting some physio. The way it runs, we're back in Killarney by eleven. Moynihan's had a word on my behalf in the bank. 'Look, we're trying to get this fella right . . .'

And, in Kerry, that man's word is like a bishop's decree.

So nobody's asking any questions. Maybe they're still giving me space because of my father, so I can swing into work three hours later than I should. And in my innocence, all I can think at the time is 'Fuck it, Seamus is killing me here'.

We beat Cork in the All-Ireland semi-final without ever seriously entertaining the idea of defeat. There's a rhythm to this rivalry now and it's one, I suspect, that's beginning to send them crackers. Beat us in Munster and, rest assured, we'll be waiting down the line with payback in Croke Park. This is '02 all over again. Their heads are surely melted.

Declan's pushing hard now too, we can all see that. When I think of the hardest bastards I've played football with, he'd have to be right up there. The way he's held himself together since being jeered off the field in Cork is a monument to that toughness. In some ways, he's gone to ground. Just put the head down and held his counsel.

But every night in the park, the hurt is in his body language. He's driving himself into everything with a message that says one thing only: I'll get myself back on that fucking team if it kills me. It's not sour the way he does it, not remotely. I mean, I can see him geeing up Donaghy some nights, telling him he's 'flying'.

The weekend before the final we head to Cork to get away from the crowds. Enemy territory for the space to breathe. Our last practice game in Páirc Uí Chaoimh is full of edge and contrariness, and at one point Paul Galvin and Listowel's Brendan Guiney end up wrestling on the ground. Jack is smiling.

He has us how he wants us.

When the team is named, Declan's in for Brossie. I'm gutted personally for my clubmate, but Jack isn't pulling any South Kerry favours here. I've been playing with Declan from under-14 up and I know that when he's on it, there's nobody will live with him. They have this expression in Kerry when passing judgement on a young player: 'Has he the stuff?'

Declan O'Sullivan has it in spades.

The news of Brossie's demotion doesn't go down too well in Killarney. Our first night training after the team announcement, I'm a little late on the field and start my warm-up alone. Jack sidles over. I think he's waiting for me to give some kind of reaction, but I just say, 'It's fine!'

I don't know, maybe he's waiting for me to say 'Fuck you, I was captain!' But how can I? It isn't about me lifting Sam Maguire. I don't care if Jack lifts it himself or if Brossie comes on and lifts it. I just get the impression Jack is waiting for me to say something smart to him. But I'm never going to do that.

Anyway, word coming out of Mayo is that they're confident this team is different. The way they came from seven points down to beat Dublin in the semi-final; the way they went and warmed up at the Hill End beforehand; the way Mickey Moran has put a bit of Ulster hardness into their attitude – all of it makes them feel as if they're on to something now.

Our view?

If I'm honest, we don't even see them. We are on such a mission to win this All-Ireland you can put the German army in front of us and we'll be ready to go for their throats.

Declan's on James Nallen, and the first ball that drops between them he's out of the blocks, dips the shoulder, and Nallen's left for dead.

I remember looking at that thinking 'No one's going to hold that man today'.

The game is over after twelve minutes. We're 2-4 to 0-0 up before I score a third. Mayo's 'difference' hasn't got them through the first quarter. It's annihilation.

Long before the end I start thinking about my father. About how, without really knowing (or at least admitting) it, I desperately wanted to win this All-Ireland for him. Maybe call it a personal debt of gratitude.

Declan is captain by rights again, but he insists on me coming up into the Hogan Stand with him to collect the cup. In his speech, he mentions Dad. I keep the tears at bay, but can't help looking up to the sky and thinking 'Fuck yes, this means something!'

It's been a horrible year for the family and I've had to dig really deep to lift myself out of that personal space. Just to be of value to Kerry again. Seeing my Mam at the function that night with the girls really brings that home to me. My brothers are downstairs in the bar. We're all smiling and it doesn't feel as if those smiles should carry any guilt now.

I've been on tenterhooks all summer and they have felt it. So, somehow, this seems like closure. As if I can finally move on. I'd gone up to the grave on Saturday and told him we'd be bringing the cup back. And it was as if I could hear his voice coming back at me crystal clear: 'Don't be too sure about that now, don't be too sure . . .'

It's maybe Wednesday before I get back up to Aghadoe again and I can't help but smile as I reach out and touch the headstone.

'You didn't believe me, did you?'

10

Some Class of a Rogue

The Tuesday after the All-Ireland final, Tomás Ó Sé and I were keeping the party going with a few recuperative lunch-time pints in Jimmy O'Brien's.

We'd both left the mobiles off, to keep the outside world at bay I suppose, and Jimmy was in his element having two of the Kerry team on site, telling jokes, spinning yarns and just generally letting the guard down. Next thing, the payphone in the bar rings, a voice on the end of the line enquiring whether Tomás might be on the premises.

'I'll check!' said Jimmy, cupping the receiver in his hand.

Tomás took the phone, and who was it but Páidí on a mission. He'd got two corporate tickets for that weekend's Ryder Cup in the K Club and wanted Tomás to travel up with him that Friday. But with Tomás due back teaching, he had no choice but to decline.

Now I've never actually been told this, but you wouldn't need to be Sherlock Holmes to figure out that I hadn't been in Páidí's initial plans. Basically, he asked Tomás if any of 'the lads' were in the pub with him. 'Ya Gooch is here,' I overheard Tomás say. 'Sure he'll be mad for road!'

So I was put on the line, and now it's 'Colm, Páidí here, well done, mighty stuff altogether. C'mere, the Ryder Cup is on Friday and I want you to come up with me . . .'

The way he spun it, Tomás was never any more than a go-between here.

I didn't care, I was thrilled. I'd taken the week off work and couldn't believe my luck to be getting to attend an event I've always loved watching on the TV. Páidí started talking about how we'd be wined and dined in a big marquee beside the 18th green and how I'd need to bring a suit and passport. He was on the board of Bord Fáilte at the time and, clearly, that job didn't put him in the way of too many mediocre tickets.

Páidí told me he'd collect me at the Crokes pitch at 10.45 a.m. that Friday – something I thought a little strange given he could surely just as easily have swung round by the house. But it was Páidí. Who was I to argue?

Friday arrived and I was up at the pitch, suit in a clothes holder, waiting for his car to swing in under the railway arch. No sign of him at 10.45. Still no sign at eleven. Around ten past I started thinking I might have been sold a pup here. Tried his phone, but got sent straight to the answering machine.

And all that was in my head was *Is this fucker after catching me here?*

But, next thing, I could hear it. Louder and louder in the Killarney sky, until a helicopter materialized overhead and began descending gently on to Crokes' main pitch. Out jumped Páidí, already in his suit, hunkered down low under the spinning blades like Sonny Crockett in *Miami Vice*, shouting across to me, 'C'mon, we're running late!'

And before I knew it we were zooming across the East Kerry

landscape at maybe 6,000 feet, heading north, Páidí holding court as if this was an everyday kind of thing in his life.

Jesus I was in Heaven. We had a day of days above, meeting everyone who was anyone and me, this young buck who'd just won an All-Ireland, walking around with the ultimate Kerry legend. Now I can't say we watched the golf too intently, but the day was just dream stuff, brilliant craic, belly-laughs from one end of it to the other. Let's just say I felt no pain.

The pilot was keen to get home in daylight, so we were just clambering on board again when Páidí swung away. 'Fuck it,' he said, 'I have to get a polo shirt for Pádraig.'

And off he runs, skipping every queue, apologizing every step of the way – 'Sorry now, sorry now, I'm in an awful rush' – and getting away with it only because he was, well, Páidí.

We were hardly in the air again when he announced that it would suit him better to get dropped off first. Ventry before Killarney? I'm doing the maths and laughing. The whole thing was such a novelty I couldn't have given a fiddler's if he'd wanted to do a loop up over the Falklands. And sure, deep down I think I had an inkling of what was coming too.

We were beginning our descent towards Ard an Bothair when he turned to me.

'Colm, you probably need to go to the toilet, come in for a minute.'

And there, in the pub, a kind of welcoming party for the two high-fliers.

Páidí just loved the idea of everyone seeing him arrive down from the K Club in a chopper and, better still, delivering one of the Kerry players who'd won the previous Sunday. Two pints later, the pilot was telling me if we weren't in the sky soon I wouldn't be sleeping in Killarney that evening.

So up we went, taking a little detour to Farranfore for refuelling, then across to Killarney for my safe return. The Lakes looked stunning as we swung in across the town, but then we hit a small problem. There was a hurling match on right in our landing area and another one on in the top field. So we hovered overhead for a little while, the pilot trying to get the message across that, well, the hurlers were a little bit in our way here.

So they stopped the game, he landed the chopper, and out I climbed with this big, self-conscious head on me, apologizing for the inconvenience. 'Bollix, sorry about that lads . . .' And away I skulked, the chopper already skyward again, my ears burning at the thought of what was being said behind me.

Who the fuck does this clown think he is? Wins a few medals and loses the fucking plot!

And all I could do was walk away home laughing. Thinking 'Isn't Páidí some class of a rogue all the same?'

11

'They All Think You're Mother Teresa'

Every end is a beginning in Kerry football. Time and memory just never stand still.

Jack's three years had pretty much emptied him, and we could see it. There was no huge surprise then when the text went round that he was stepping down. He said he needed to go find new energy, that he'd been feeling himself go stale. That's what the job does to people, I suppose. It sucks everything there is out of them. Tests them to the core.

Pat O'Shea was always the obvious replacement, although there was some talk that John Evans, then manager of Laune Rangers, might be in with a shout too. The complication with Pat was that as full-time Munster Council coach there was a stipulation in his contract that he could manage his own club team, but nobody else's.

Outside immediate family, I think it's fair to say that nobody has had a more constant influence on my career than Pat O'Shea. My earliest memory of him would be those Saturday mornings waiting for Mike Buckley's bus to take us up to Dr Crokes training sessions where, invariably, Pat would be the man coordinating numbers.

He's virtually part of the stonework on Lewis Road by now, a corner-forward on the All-Ireland winning team of '92, the man who guided us to the 2016/17 All-Ireland Club title, and one who, ten years earlier, led us to the final.

Crokes were beaten in the '06 county final by South Kerry, but divisional sides being ineligible to play in provincial championships, we carried Kerry's hopes all the way through the province and into Croke Park the following St Patrick's Day. It meant Pat having not simply to look for that Munster Council dispensation to allow him to become Kerry manager, but also to seek permission for what turned out to be three months of working two dressing-rooms.

When I think about it, I'm not sure in my lifetime a single year has passed when Pat's not been involved with one Dr Crokes team or another, be it As, Bs, senior, minor or junior. His wife, Deborah-Ann, is Eddie 'Tatler' O'Sullivan's daughter and equally passionate about the club. She runs the shop and is a member of the Ladies' Committee. It's probably fair to say the two of them have a path worn in from their house out the Tralee road.

When he was eventually confirmed as the new Kerry manager, Pat's style was to keep things strictly separate and formal. In Crokes, we got the news just like everybody else, through the official statement from county board chairman Seán Walsh. It was coming up to Christmas, we'd just won the Munster Club, and I suppose Pat didn't want us to lose focus on the possibilities immediately ahead. All I remember him saying to those of us involved with the county was 'We'll be having a meeting about that in January, lads!'

End of conversation.

Basically, he wanted no more Kerry talk inside the Crokes dressing-room.

That was a predominantly young Crokes team and we'd eventually lose the All-Ireland final in a replay to a great Crossmaglen side en route to winning three titles in the next six years to follow the three in four they'd won at the tail end of the nineties. Their exalted status offered little consolation though. We should have beaten them the first day and might have done but for a contentious late decision by Wexford referee, Syl Doyle.

We were a point up in Croke Park with the game almost over when from my vantage point, Oisín McConville seemed to take about a dozen steps, pivoting around his marker to level things. Doyle allowed the score to stand which, to me, was a bad call.

Crossmaglen beat us fair and square in the replay, but if ever a day proved to me that referees' decisions matter, 17 March 2007 was that day.

There's a Rottweiler inside the skinny frame of Pat O'Shea, and people who know him soon understand that it's best to avoid his bite.

I'll tell you a story to explain. We're warm-weather training in Portugal, spring of '07 – a few weeks after that All-Ireland Club final – and Pat's way is to immerse himself in the drills, quite literally to take part in training as much as organize it. I suspect it's the basketball man in him (he was a ball-carrier for St Paul's and played for Tralee Tigers), his way being to be right down in the engine room of everything, calling time-outs, explaining drills, setting standards.

He's a hands-on coach then, very much in the image of someone like Phil Jackson when he was in charge of the Chicago Bulls team that won six NBA Championships. Pat just needs to be in the middle of everything, running different scenarios.

He has an intensity to how he works that people maybe need some time to acclimatize to. I always sensed that someone like Kieran Donaghy loved Pat's attention to technical detail because it represented a world he was clearly familar with from the Tigers. Others, though, probably found it a bit of an information overload. Especially those maybe accustomed to a style with their clubs of just lamping high ball in on a big full-forward and hoping for the best.

Under Pat, Kerry would now vary their game a lot more, think a lot more about keeping possession.

Anyway, we're running this sideline play in Portugal, going through one of those scenarios that Pat believed could prove the winning or losing of a match. The idea is we protect the ball. Avoid gambles. Use our game intelligence, by running loops to take a return pass rather than committing to a poor percentage play.

The ball gets drilled down the line to Kieran O'Leary, a fellow Crokes man. He's being marked by Daniel Bohane, but cuts inside and kicks the most amazing point from out near the sideline. An unbelievable score, and Kieran's cock-a-hoop. We're all standing there, grinning. 'Fuck that's some point Leary!'

But not Pat.

'Stop, stop, stop, what the fuck are you at?' he roars at Kieran.

'Sure I put it over—'

'I don't give a fuck what you did, run the sideline like I said. In here, give the pass, loop fucking around.'

He's absolutely spitting fire. Kieran's just taken a shot to nothing, the very thing we are being programmed to avoid. He's taken a shot that might go over maybe one time out of ten. And for Pat, who's looking for as close as we can get to certainty in our ball management, that's committing a cardinal sin.

On some level I suspect he's probably seeking to communicate a deeper message too. A few weeks earlier, himself and Kieran were fighting shoulder-to-shoulder for an All-Ireland Club title, but here he is tearing strips off his own clubmate. The message is loud and clear: he is ready to give it to anyone between the eyes, Dr Crokes or not.

And that's always been Pat's style. He's never felt a need to apologize for giving someone a bollocking because, bottom line, he's 100 per cent straight with people. He thinks things through, talks things through. Some lads struggle with his intensity, and if they end up walking away, that's too bad.

With Kerry, he was always playing these seven-a-sides in training for building fitness levels. High-intensity matches in which you had to run and run. And he's especially big on understanding time management of a game. On making the right decisions at the right time.

His standards never slip. With Crokes last winter, 2016/17, we had a programme running through Christmas and into the New Year that involved sixteen training sessions in twenty-one days. He was doing double sessions some days up at the club just to facilitate different groups. One of Pat's favourite sayings is 'Fortune favours the brave'.

The day of a match, business is business with him and you're expected to take care of it. But you can have the craic too when it's over. If the day's gone well, he's got no problem even blowing off a bit of steam himself.

Sometimes, over a few pints, O'Leary might even remind him of that point in Portugal. 'Yerrah fortune favours, Pat,' he'll say, laughing.

'Fortune favours . . .'

✻

The 2007 Championship was all about our relationship with Cork and the psychological hold we felt we had on them.

We beat them in both the Munster and All-Ireland finals and, by a distance, the July game in Killarney was trickier than the September one in Dublin. That tended to be the rhythm of things between us. If they felt they had a chance against us in Munster, they seemed – somehow – to get it into their heads that that chance would just evaporate when we met in Croke Park.

In Kerry, losing to Cork leaves a different taste to losing to any other county. A sourer one.

They had a hell of a team in '07, one carrying legitimate designs on winning an All-Ireland. And we should have been vulnerable. Not alone had we the change of management, we'd lost defensive stalwarts like Seamus Moynihan and Mike McCarthy to retirement, while Eamonn Fitz was beginning to drift in the same direction too (eventually stepping away in April after a League defeat to Dublin in Parnell Park). We also had a new physical trainer, John Sugrue taking over from Pat Flanagan – so, I suppose, no shortage of excuses for expecting a season of transition then.

Kerry didn't make the National League semi-finals and there would have been a fair degree of local foreboding when Cork came to Killarney for the Munster final. But the truth is we actually dealt with them easier than the eventual two-point winning margin might suggest. Essentially we blew a six-point lead through carelessness and had to dig the win out of a dangerous place in the end.

I'm not sure we'd have ever forgiven ourselves if we hadn't.

By now I had come to understand the bitterness between us as counties. Each of us hated the other having something over them. We'd probably have had this opinion that the few enough times they beat us in Championship, Cork were inclined to believe they had reached their destination. In July!

Maybe hatred isn't the right word but any time I've been beaten by a Cork team in Championship, I've come away with this horrible low, sinking feeling of someone taking something that belongs to me. There have certainly been a couple of days I've walked out of Páirc Uí Chaoimh especially thinking 'Where the fuck do we go from here?'

Losing to Cork in the League never really registered as anything too meaningful. Losing to them in Championship was always seismic.

I work with a lot of Cork people and, honestly, you couldn't meet better. But, if I'm honest, I find it hard to rinse the sourness out of me when they beat us. I accept that doesn't say a lot for my generosity of spirit, but losing to Cork in a game that really matters? No, just not acceptable.

That attitude undeniably carries over into the Kerry media too. Local journalists will kick the legs from under you if you lose to Cork. It's because Cork are our yardstick. Every new Kerry player that comes through, the first question people will be inclined to ask about him is 'Could he do it against Cork in a Munster final?'

With the provincial title reclaimed, we almost got caught on a horrible day in an All-Ireland quarter-final against Monaghan that I remember most for the Mone brothers, Dessie and John Paul, giving Star and myself a running commentary on how bad we were, not to mention dispensing the obligatory few clips. A last-second Tomás Ó Sé point eventually got us over the line, but it was a late goal by Declan O'Sullivan that really saved the day.

Declan got the key goal again in our semi-final against Dublin, a huge game that we led for most of the way only for a late surge by the Dubs to almost snare us. I have a memory of Darragh making an incredible catch from a kick-out under the Hogan

Stand and the team stringing maybe thirty passes together before we got the final score of the day.

The calm way we finished the Dubs off, dealing so patiently with everything thrown at us, gave the team massive confidence now. And, of course, that meant Cork in Croker again.

A game it was simply unthinkable we could lose.

I remember Paul Galvin branding it arguably the most important game in Kerry's history during the build-up to that final. It probably sounded like hyperbole, but what Paul said was exactly how it felt to us. You can see things in people when the pressure comes on, sometimes good, sometimes bad. And what I saw at our team-meeting in Dunboyne the night before that final convinced me that we were going to win. Just the expression on certain people's faces. Key men like Darragh maybe, Declan and Galvin. Like Mahony, Tom Sullivan, Marc and Tomás. Every one of them had these cold, stony expressions. There was a hardness in them. I genuinely remember looking around that room and saying to myself, 'Yeah, we're going to win this.'

And this may sound arrogant, but I was absolutely confident that I would play well. My form was good. I was, physically, in good nick. Where I'd been in 2006 was a distant memory now and I suppose in some ways I wanted to communicate that. I wouldn't normally say much at those meetings, but that night I told the room, 'Listen, if ye get enough ball in, trust me we'll take care of business.'

Not really my form in normal circumstances. But this felt different.

I sensed there was a feeling in the room that our attack had struggled in the Munster final. I certainly felt that I had a point to prove. But the truth was I'd missed chances all around me. That was the problem, not the Cork defence. If I'd taken those chances, I'd have been down as having played a blinder.

Don't get me wrong, tight marking was obviously part of the reason I'd missed those chances. But sitting in that room in Dunboyne, I just knew I was dialled in for a big game. So that's basically what I told the group. That if they got ball in to me like they had in the Munster final there'd be a very different outcome. That's how confident I felt.

There was a lot of talk that week about how well Graham Canty and Kieran O'Connor were playing, how well Cork were motoring in general. It all just sounded like Leeside propaganda to me, stuff I felt ready to put in the shredder.

Galvin reiterated his view that all past Kerry victories over Cork would amount to nothing if they beat us in the first All-Ireland final meeting between the counties.

To be fair, sometimes words aren't really needed at team-meetings. You just need the right vibe coming from the right people. Big players setting an atmosphere.

I was rooming with Galvin that year and we always hit it off well. People who don't know Paul probably see him as this dark, intense figure. Some might say he's the polar opposite to me, but we'd actually have a good deal in common. Maybe he just carries himself a different way to me, but we'd both have the same kind of drive within. And, because of it, I suppose we'd both welcome the release valve of sometimes juvenile behaviour. The truth is, nearly everybody did.

I remember before one final we were staying in the Crowne Plaza, and on the morning of the game Tomás put my bed out on the balcony. He'd slipped down to reception when he saw me going into breakfast.

'Sorry, I've left my key in the room, it's 417.'

What's a receptionist going to say to a man in his county track-suit on All-Ireland final morning?

He denies it to this day, of course. But up I go for my precious pre-match kip, in the door, and all I see is an empty space where my bed should be. And all I hear is the sound of snorting laughter in the corridor. Fucking hilarious, Tomás.

There was always plenty of that kind of mischief about, just to release the tension. I remember one hotel where the room numbers could be unscrewed off the doors and a few of the boys created absolute chaos. My abiding image of that is Dave Geaney, one of Pat's selectors, coming up from breakfast, the *Racing Post* under his arm, and being completely bamboozled as to why his door wouldn't open. Looking at the key, then the lock, then the key again. Trying it maybe a dozen times before having to swing back down to reception with a mystery to be solved.

Childish stuff, absolutely. But people needed that switch-off. Mental stress drains physical energy and you just couldn't sustain the type of intensity we'd be bringing to Croke Park without having that bit of high jinks.

Rooming with Galvin was never boring. He'd be into his music and it'd drive him crackers if I started singing a song without knowing the proper lyrics. 'Listen man, don't sing the song if you don't know the fucking words,' he'd bark.

Outwardly, Paul was a hungry, tough bastard, willing to do anything to win. What people probably didn't realize is that I was that person too. We might have looked completely different animals but, when it came to those big games, I wouldn't have had too many scruples about what it took for us to get victory. The difference was public perception. I was Julie Andrews to his Glenn Close, boiling the rabbit.

If you asked Galvin, I'd honestly say he'd describe me as one of the dirtiest bastards he's ever played football with or against. I'd certainly get away with stuff that he wouldn't. He'd often say it to me. 'Fuck it Gooch, you get away with murder. You absolutely nailed yer man the other day and not a peep from the ref. They all think you're Mother fuckin' Teresa!'

At times I'd wind him up nearly out of badness.

We roomed together on a lot of Kerry trips and I have a particular memory of the one to Vegas and Cancún after winning the '04 All-Ireland. Now Darragh has painted a picture of me scarpering out of a Cancún nightclub to leave him fending for himself just as chairs and tables began to fly. But, well, that's not exactly how I remember it. Let's just say that, of the Kerry contingent on that holiday, there were more than two of us in Coco Bongo that night when it felt as if all hell broke loose.

I'm not entirely sure what started it, but some of the Kerry lads were definitely involved centrally. And Darragh's right to a point: I did make myself scarce soon as I saw the furniture start to fly. I remember thinking 'I'm not getting stuck in any Mexican brawl here'. Lads were fairly sheepish afterwards about what exactly had kicked things off and I suppose the beer consumption made it all a bit of a blur.

Anyway, Galvin's into his music, and on that trip I drove him spare by routinely mangling the lyrics of his favourite songs.

In Cancún he'd been trying to teach me the words to Green Day's brilliant 'Boulevard of Broken Dreams'. And what could I do but act the stooge?

So Galvin's deadly serious, talking me through the lines.

'Right Gooch, listen! "I walk a lonely road, the only one that I have ever known, don't know where it goes, but it's only me and I walk alone . . ."'

And I'm there, big, earnest eyes staring back at him. 'Yeah, I think I have it now.'

The truth is I was too bollixed most of the time to take on board what he was telling me, even if I'd wanted to. So I'd play along. 'Sound, Paul. Think I have it now.'

Then I'd get in the shower and, top of my voice, mangle the lines all over again. Rising him. 'I walk a lonely walk, just me and the lonely street . . .'

Then out I'd step from the bathroom and he's sitting on the end of his bed, a face of fucking thunder.

'Are you doing this just to piss me off?' he'd say.

And I'm 'Ah bollix, am I wrong again?'

After morning Mass the day of that '07 All-Ireland final I went back to the room for my usual little half-hour nap. Maybe about midday, just to recharge the batteries. I was good to go, the bag packed, the mind settled. But instead of a nap I slipped into a near-coma.

Next thing everybody's gathering in the meeting room. Everybody bar one. Galvin is dispatched upstairs and finds me above, away with the fairies. He actually has to give me a dig to get a stir.

'You might shake yourself there boss, we've a bit of a match at half three . . . Now c'mon to fuck before Pat starts losing the plot!'

It wouldn't be stretching things to say we pulverized Cork eventually. I scored 1-5 and was named Man of the Match, but – as Galvin put it – I was 'dead to the world at ten to two!' That pretty much summed us up as a group that day. We knew what we wanted to do and believed absolutely in our ability to deliver.

I got to a high Séamus Scanlon delivery ahead of Kieran O'Connor and Alan Quirke for a first-half goal, and Donaghy would get two more in the second. We basically played as a two-man full-forward line, Pat choosing to crowd the middle third. Our strong men stood up to be counted everywhere, none more so than Darragh in his collision with big Nicholas Murphy. Darragh was just so battle-hardened you never doubted for a second that he'd have anything but a monster game.

We won by ten points in the end, the first team in seventeen years to retain Sam Maguire. And we'd hardly reached the showers when, outside, the world of punditry seemed to be assessing our three-in-a-row credentials.

Every end just another beginning.

12

Written in the Stars?

Sometimes a green and gold *geansaí* feels heavier than it should. It labels you, defines you.

People don't see much beyond it because I suppose they don't ever really need to. But the way the seasons keep on squeezing so tight, you can end up feeling like a cartoon character the world has decided is publicly owned. That squeeze was getting on top of me towards the end of 2007 and I came to the conclusion that I might be in trouble if I didn't address it.

I came to realize I needed to get out of Dodge.

It was a build-up of things. Partly the fallout to my Dad dying; partly the fact I'd been working since the age of twenty-one and almost always scrambling to meet someone else's timetable. But also partly that I'd been playing inter-county for six years on the bounce now and for all but one of those Kerry's season had stretched into September. On one level this was fantastic of course. Beyond my wildest dreams.

On another, it almost certainly bred a mild resentment.

I'd see friends heading off on open-ended summer breaks and envy them the freedom. As a key player for my county, it probably never occurred to anybody that I might be feeling restless. That maybe I had a little more going on inside my head than just a compulsion to win football games. People felt no reason to do anything other than make that instant compute: Gooch would be bursting a gut to win that three-in-a-row.

I would too. But, first, I needed to get off the merry-go-round.

That October I sat down with Patrick 'The Bag' O'Sullivan to explore my options. I knew he had a share in a bar in Chicago and wanted to see if there was somewhere out there I could maybe drop anchor. He got in touch with his business partners the O'Donoghue brothers, Trevor and Mick, two Kerrymen whose father, Micheal, is a successful hotelier in Killarney.

I didn't know them well but, pretty quickly, contact was made and a message came back that they'd welcome me over with open arms. I'd arranged four months' leave of absence from the bank and, ideally, wanted to be away for three of those from early in the new year.

Pat O'Shea, meanwhile, had got clearance from the Munster Council to manage Kerry for another year, so I told him of my intentions. I said that I was feeling burned out and maybe a little stale. Pat wasn't entirely happy. He's not a man to do things in half measure and maybe a part of him was worried that one of his key players might go missing for the year.

'No problem with you having a break,' he told me. 'But I want you back by the first of April.'

Being honest, that worked for both of us. He wanted to use the National League to have a look at some of the players coming through and, unless I was dragging the arse out of things while away, I'd be able to catch up pretty quickly with a few weeks of hard training. There were no hard and fast instructions about me having to keep in shape. I suppose, bottom line, I was an adult and expected to behave like one.

I took out a ninety-day visa and would come home just twenty-four hours before it lapsed.

To begin with I went to Phoenix for the Super Bowl. Pretty much just added my name to a trip Tatler senior had arranged with a gang from Killarney. We didn't manage to get tickets in the end, but we all just wanted to be in a Super Bowl town on a Super Bowl day.

It was New England Patriots against New York Giants, the Patriots going for a perfect season. And the Giants did them.

Darran O'Sullivan was out there at the same time with his dad and another Kerry crew and we all headed up to Scottsdale for a day at the Phoenix Open too. Planted ourselves amid the mayhem of the par-three 16th where the atmosphere, famously, is more like Coppers in the early hours of a post-All-Ireland Monday. It was fascinating to see how some pros openly embraced the general sense of mayhem and disrespect, while others just quietly bristled.

The day before the Super Bowl we'd been in R. T. O'Sullivan's Smalltown Irish bar watching Kerry against Donegal in the opening round of the National League from a sodden Ballyshannon. A Saturday lunchtime throw-in. Kerry were winning most of the day only to get caught on the line by a late goal. Lost by a point. There were a few lads wearing Donegal jerseys right in front of the screen, giving it loads. They'd just beaten the All-Ireland champions and you could see what that meant to them.

Darran and myself were keeping ourselves to ourselves down the back. Wearing baseball caps. The Donegal crew hadn't a clue we were there.

'Where's the fucking Gooch now?' one of them roared.

The temptation to toss out a pantomime 'HE'S BEHIND YOU!' shout was nearly too good to be true. But we resisted it, kept the heads down, held our peace. Nothing to be gained. I remember thinking 'Good luck to them if a win in February could mean so much!'

When I finally hit Chicago, the cold hit me like a punch in the face. Oh Lord Jesus it was an education. You couldn't walk anywhere, not even a couple of blocks. But the boys looked after me like royalty, putting me up – free of charge – in a nice apartment in the middle of the city. Feeding me in the bar, The Kerryman, just off Michigan Avenue. Between the two brothers and another friend of Tatler's, Mickey Joe Murphy, I literally wanted for nothing.

The sense of freedom was incredible.

When I heard another group from Killarney was heading down to Florida for a week of golf, I invited myself along. Flew at short notice and slept on a couch in the house they were renting in Kissimmee. Man, what a trip. Golf every day, few beers at night. Eating stuff that would bring a nutritionist out in hives.

I flew to Boston another weekend. A Kerry dinner dance, the cost of my flights looked after. I knew Dara Ó'Cinnéide was going too, so felt comfortable accepting the invite. Stayed with Donal Mangan, a Killarney man, and his wife, Anne. Again, hardly put my hand in my pocket.

Through all this I had a plan in my head. I wanted to bring Mam to New York, and knew that wouldn't be simple. The biggest obstacle was the fact she'd be obliged to go seven hours without a cigarette. To a non-smoker, I'm sure it's hard to see how that would ever be an issue. But to my Mam it sounded like a prison sentence.

Karen kept selling the idea from home and, eventually, I think my mother agreed almost out of exasperation. She hadn't seen me for three months and could probably tell from our telephone conversations that I wasn't remotely homesick. Maybe a few alarm bells were even ringing that I might cut loose altogether and stay.

In the end, I suspect a voice in her head was saying, 'If I want to see Colm, I'll have to bite the bullet here!'

So she came with Karen for a week in March, and that week is one I will always treasure. My mother was a great people-watcher, you see. She could happily sit with a coffee for hours, just observing the world go by; trying to second-guess people's stories; smiling at the relentless rush of the place – the thronged streets, the unbroken hum of business. We stayed in The One Hotel near United Nations Plaza and then The Affinia, next to Madison Square Garden. I have a picture of the two of us outside the Garden and you can read the delight in her eyes to be in this place with its skyscrapers and yellow cabs and giant flipping billboards.

That's exactly the expression I'd hoped the trip would generate. To Mam, it was like standing on a giant movie set. She took a trip on the Metro. She went shopping on Seventh Avenue. To her, it was a once-in-a-lifetime experience. Something she'd never imagined would ever be possible.

When she got home, she couldn't wait to tell people where she'd been. She was so proud of remarking that she'd been to New York. 'Oh just popped over with Karen to see Colm!' As if it was like hopping across to Killorglin. We'd be sitting at home long after and some film would come on the TV with that familiar Manhattan skyline. And we'd be glued to it, waiting for our cue.

'There's The Plaza, Mam – remember, where we had lunch?'

'Oh yes, I do. Wasn't that across from the big toy shop . . .'

I stayed on for one final week after they headed home, using up all but the last twenty-four hours of that precious visa. Then it was time. I went online and booked a flight home, feeling ready for football again. I wasn't exactly coming home in mint condition, but my weight had gone up by less than a stone.

Bottom line, I knew my mind and I knew my body. Two weeks of hard training and I felt sure I'd be ready for road.

Pat wasn't standing on ceremony on my first night back and seemed to decide the best way to greet the returning tourist was with a big stick.

We were above in the top Crokes pitch, and soon as I turned for the gap as the session ended, he was on my case. 'Aha, not for you my friend.' There was a small group, just recuperating from injuries, who needed reconditioning. 'The Fat Club' we called them, four or five required to stay behind for extra running, a plume of fairly black smoke trailing along behind them.

Now I was a first-time member.

Straight away I could sense a new edge to business. During training matches Pat was inclined to leave the whistle in his pocket. A bad predicament for a forward. You could be hanged, drawn and quartered trying to get a score and he'd be looking the other way, whistling Dixie. I'm not sure if this was with half an eye on Tyrone, the one itch this Kerry team had yet to scratch. But Pat clearly wanted to up the ante in terms of physicality.

We were the team with targets on our foreheads now, he made that clear. The ones everyone would be keen to have a clip off. You see, if we'd beaten Mayo and Cork in successive All-Irelands, the Northern issue hadn't been resolved. People were still wondering if we'd have the mettle for a big Ulster team in a dogfight.

The message coming down the line was Kerry needed to be right for war.

So a few rows began breaking out, and one that got a bit of air-time beyond the training-ground gates was between Darragh Ó Sé and David Moran. We were doing a tackling drill, high-intensity stuff where accidental slaps in the face and bloodied noses could be fairly commonplace. David was only in the door at the time, a young buck keen to make an impression.

Anyway, whatever way he caught Darragh, the big fella wasn't having it. So he hit David a right clip and, I don't know, it just seemed bang out of order. I suppose the feeling would have been 'Fuck it Darragh, if you're going to clip someone, don't do it to a young fella!'

Now some lads might be racked with remorse in that kind of scenario, they might carry it like a cloud with them. 'Fuck, was I well out of line there?' Not Darragh. Not a hope. That man's just cut from different metal. I often thought it was maybe one of his greatest strengths as a player. He could brush stuff off and forget about it. Just take the view 'Shit happens, drive on.'

I mean, I'm sure he apologized. He'd have had big time for David, but maybe this was partly his way of putting down a marker too to the new midfielder. Only one big buck in this town. I can say for certain he wouldn't have felt any need to turn that apology into a ceremony. He'd have maybe mumbled a one-liner and kept on running.

Because Darragh didn't toss out too many apologies.

To be honest, we all had different moments as the intensity was ratcheted higher. I got into a scuffle one night with Rónán Ó'Flatharta. Handbags stuff really, but symptomatic of an atmosphere in which nobody was taking a backward step. Pat had the luxury of a big panel and I think a lot of people were getting edgy about their place in it. The three-in-a-row wasn't mentioned, it didn't have to be. We all knew full well what that would signify. The status it would bring.

For now, it was just about lads putting down personal markers. Marking their territory.

I got back in as a late substitute for a League game against Galway in Salthill and Kerry would go all the way to the final in what almost felt like third gear. We had bigger fish to fry now and Kerry hearts weren't exactly broken by a four-point loss to Derry in Parnell Park. The GAA reckoned the game would have been completely dwarfed in the open spaces of Croke Park, and they were right. Maybe 10,000 filed through the turnstiles in Donnycarney that day for a double-header.

I doubt three hundred of them were from Kerry.

Our next competitive fixture was a Munster Championship opener against Clare in Killarney in mid-June. We won by twelve points, but that's not what people remember. They remember a notebook sent tumbling to the grass.

It happened on the terrace side, and I remember standing a long way away from it, seeing the book fall and momentarily panicking that things might get even worse. Paul Galvin was our captain in 2008 and, from first whistle in that game, it was fairly obvious he was being blackguarded. A man known for a temper is an easy target and Paul already had what I considered a harsh booking to his name when, after another off-the-ball scuffle, Paddy Russell called him over.

Now Paul's a fairly deep sort who, if you know him, wears his heart on his sleeve. The thing is, not many do. Know him, that is. He's very guarded, doesn't let too many people in. The Kerry captaincy would have been a big thing to him that year, though he wouldn't have been the type to broadcast that. Trouble is, opponents knew him as someone with that short fuse too. They always believed that they could get to him.

Looking back, I think there might have been a voice somewhere in Paul's head saying, 'My big year and people are trying to fuck me up here!'

After the first booking he would have known he was walking a tightrope. But what do you do when people keep on digging you off the ball and nobody's offering protection? Just down tools and decide it's not going to be your day? Volunteer to be substituted? When he saw the second one coming, a fuse inside him blew. It was as if he felt the whole world was conspiring against him. Maybe he'd been playing with too much passion and aggression to prove himself a worthy captain too, but – hand on heart – I believe he was wronged that day in Killarney.

Anyway, that second yellow tipped him over the edge and he knocked the notebook from Russell's hand. Indefensible I know, but was it really the scandalous act it was subsequently portrayed as? I accept you must never raise a finger to a referee, but it was the notebook he made contact with, not Paddy.

The fallout was extraordinary. If he'd started flinging hand grenades around Fitzgerald Stadium that day I'm not sure the publicity could have been worse for Paul. And he paid a massive penalty: a twelve-week suspension and a level of media infamy more in keeping with someone clambering handcuffed into a garda van outside The Four Courts.

The incident left an impression on everybody – referees, public, opponents and, maybe most pertinently, the GAA authorities. It almost came to define Paul from that day on. People drew pretty definite conclusions about him. I sometimes look back on the famous battles he subsequently had, particularly against the likes of Noel O'Leary or Eoin Cadogan of Cork, and I think people's reaction to them was coloured by what Paul did that day to Paddy Russell's notebook.

I do know he was incredibly hurt by it all.

Now I'm not making him out to be a saint. Galvin himself would be the first to admit he could be anything but. Yet there's a lot going on behind those eyes that people don't understand. Often enough he gave people ammunition to come down hard on him. And look, you cannot raise your hands to the referee, end of story. Paul was wrong to do what he did. That's not up for argument. But there was a context to it, and context doesn't often get an airing in these cases.

Anyway, it meant that his captaincy was stillborn. For the next three months he wouldn't be allowed to train with Kerry, let alone play with us. He became a non-person in the eyes of the authorities. We all felt bad for him. Angry even. And maybe we needed to be channelling our emotions differently.

Because that anger came to feel like stones in our shoes.

Darragh and Marc both saw red in a five-point Munster final defeat to Cork. Although Marc's card would be subsequently rescinded, the sky above was black with trouble now.

Because we lay down that day in Páirc Uí Chaoimh. Our second-half collapse was spineless, setting off all kinds of alarms in our heads about where we were as a group. It pitched us down the qualifier route again, and if that had worked out well enough for us on Jack's watch in '06, a lot of that had been down to Donaghy's arrival down off a beanstalk.

Not for the first time we just had to maybe hope that we'd see Cork again that summer and find some energy in the bitter parochialism they had a way of igniting inside us.

Monaghan gave us a typically plain, hard-hitting contest at the beginning of August that we won by a goal; then Galway gave us the absolute opposite in a monsoon six days later. That was the day they had to close Jones's Road because of flooding and the lights were on in Croke Park from early afternoon. It all felt very surreal.

Micheal Meehan was outstanding for Galway that day, but in that quarter-final we gave probably our best attacking performance of the year so far to win a virtual shoot-out by 1-21 to 1-16. It was just pure football, last man standing declared the winner.

So Cork's biggest dread came to pass and, though they would

take us to a replay in the All-Ireland semi-final, we always believed there was no way they'd be beating us twice in the one Championship year. We cut it fine, no question. But we were actually nine points up in the replay, doing a familiar Croke Park number on them, when – inexplicably – we conceded 1-6 without reply.

Stupidity on our behalf. Carelessness. We had them in a head-lock, lost concentration and bent down to tie our laces.

I remember standing at the far end of the field, looking back down at this virtual meltdown, thinking 'Fuck sake, is this really happening?' For a while we just couldn't get the ball out past the halfway line.

But our reaction probably said a lot about where we felt we stood in relation to Cork. David Moran caught a massive kick-out and gave the ball to Darran who took off as only Darran can; he slipped the ball inside to me and I stuck it. End of story.

That was what I was there for, what I expected from myself. To be a go-to guy for Kerry. To dig it out when the chance arrived, close the deal. It's why Kerry people expected so much from me, why – for maybe twelve of the fifteen years I played for Kerry – they saw me as our top forward. Because they believed that all I needed was that half chance. And I loved that.

The sense that my own people could trust me.

In our heads at least, Tyrone were inclined to talk with their chests out, wearing their self-regard like a loud suit.

I remember reading a few interviews at the time and it seemed they were already christening themselves the 'Team of the Decade'. That stuck in the craw. We were now facing into our fifth All-Ireland final in a row. We'd won three to their two. They were full of it. We were biting our tongues.

No question, we would have considered them the perfect final stepping-stone to a three-in-a-row. But we blew it. We let them off the hook. That's how I look back on the '08 final. We weren't good enough to beat them in '03 or '05. But '08 was different.

Listen, good luck to them. Their third consecutive Championship win over Kerry would give them whatever bragging rights they chose. We got that. We still do. But they weren't really any better than us in '08. They didn't have it – as they liked to believe – over us psychologically.

The truth is we played poorly on the day, yet still should have won that final. When I think back on the game, maybe the stand-out moment is Pascal McConnell just about getting his big toe to a Declan O'Sullivan shot that was headed for the bottom corner. McConnell was a late inclusion because the father of their number one goalkeeper, John Devine, had died suddenly that Saturday night. He's a few inches taller than Devine and those inches proved absolutely crucial. The same starting position for Devine and the same shot from Declan hits the net. A Kerry goal at that point and I honestly believe we'd have won the Sam Maguire. I'll forever believe we should have done.

Makes you wonder: is this stuff written in the stars?

Listen, good luck to Tyrone. They dug it out, that's what they do. They were tough and hard-nosed and extremely well organized, and they knew how to ride their luck. And it didn't interest them whether the world liked them or not. That was the day Justin and Joe McMahon could be seen roaring into the faces of Donaghy and Tommy Walsh as if trying to communicate the impression they were a little deranged. If you got in that Tyrone team's way, they would fuck you around all day and make no apologies. Their attitude was summed up at half-time when our chairman, Patrick O'Sullivan, got knocked over heading down the tunnel.

'The Bag' was just in the wrong place at the wrong time and got run over.

There'd been a hop-ball just on the stroke of half-time, and when tempers are already high, a hop-ball can be like tossing petrol on a fire. This one made no sense. The ref hopped the ball, then blew his whistle almost instantly. The aggro needed an outlet and found it in bodies colliding as we all went pouring down the tunnel.

Anyway, history is uninterested in could-a-been stories and Tyrone won their third All-Ireland in six years that day. When the final whistle blew, their supporters came piling on to the pitch and one of them gave me a nice dig across the back of the head. 'Fuck off Gooch!' he said as I was trying to get to the tunnel. A few beers and emotion probably had him feeling a bit of a hero I suppose. He didn't hang around for a response, of course, but then what was I going to do?

The fallout was nearly harder to take than the game itself. All we were hearing now was that Tyrone were inside our heads. And, it's true, they were now. No question. How could it be any other way when all around us we were hearing the same noise: the sound of people telling us that whatever it was Harte's players had about them, Kerry just couldn't handle it. That we couldn't cope with Northern intensity. We had Joe Brolly, the national media, everyone in Kerry now singing off pretty much the same hymn sheet.

We'd just been going for three-in-a-row, had now played in five successive All-Ireland finals, but apparently we were soft!

What could we do but pull the collars up and brace ourselves for a long winter?

13

Front-page News

Jack's back for 2009, but things are different now.

The atmosphere feels skewed. He knows it, we know it. He's written a book and there's stuff in those pages that some feel flew just a little too close to the bone. He's been tiptoeing around some of the boys like someone who's just not sure what bad weather might be rolling around inside their heads. We win our nine-teenth League title, beating Derry in the final, but the truth? I remember none of it.

Sometimes we win Leagues without even stopping to admire the view. I won't say it means nothing, but it's just not what we're after. Tyrone are still on our clothes, still in our heads. There's a contrariness in the group, and I'm just not sure it's a healthy one.

Keys to the Kingdom – The Story of the Outsider Who Led Kerry Back to Glory has been more than a year on the shelves now so every smidgen of it has been dissected and analysed. Some lads probably read more than they wanted.

So was Jack ever going to be accepted by the group the way he was the first time? Questionable.

I wouldn't call it a stand-off as such, but there's definitely a sense that the chemistry here needs a bucket and some suds. Everything feels forced. Are fellas buying totally into what the manager's now telling us? Not sure.

I suspect when Jack did the book he didn't imagine he'd be walking back into a Kerry dressing-room so soon again. Probably reckoned he had a bit of licence. Now he's carrying it around in his body language. 'Fuck it, we're sound, lads, aren't we? Lads?'

In June we draw the Munster semi-final with Cork in Killarney. My town and we nearly stink the place out. How we got away with it I'll never know. Some boys must have been running around with rabbits' feet in their pockets. Cork were better than us, but in the same way people seem to think we've got a bit of a psychological issue with Northern teams, I'm beginning to wonder if Cork have that with us. The closer they get to the finish line, the more blinkered they seem to become.

I remember standing there in the Park at one point wondering 'Are we fucking gone here?'

Funny, people have been telling us we have no heart, but heart is the only thing that got us out of Fitzgerald Stadium that day. We dogged out the draw. Pure Kerry stubbornness.

But it feels like we're just rearranging deckchairs on a ship that's going down here. One week later, Cork hand us our arses in a bag. Hammer us. Galvin and Noel O'Leary go at it like rutting stags and both see red. Lord Jesus we're in trouble here. We don't seem to know what we're doing and the management don't seem to know how they want us to do it. Now we're down the qualifier road with all its sneaky mines and cul-de-sacs and lads looking for a big fish to fry.

We play Longford in Longford and struggle. Then we take Sligo by a point in Tralee. Sligo by a point? They miss a penalty with about five minutes to go. Jesus wept, we're all over the place. We look like a team with no game-plan, no idea of who or what we want to be. Worse, there's not a shred of hunger in what we're doing. I'm sitting there in the dressing-room afterwards and I can't believe how bad things feel. And if I feel it, others have to feel it. One Kerry player feeling out of sorts and not playing well isn't going to be enough for Sligo to nearly beat us in Tralee. But we're all walking around like ghosts.

I'd love to see a shred of direction in terms of where we're going, but I can't.

Jack's brought Mike McCarthy back into the panel, and your first thought at seeing that is 'Well fuck it, management definitely doesn't trust these players.' Mike hasn't played for Kerry in three years. He's got no training done, no strength and conditioning. He's got no League behind him. For me, the sight of Mike coming in the gate to training just compounds the sense of things being all over the place.

Don't get me wrong. Mike Mac is a different animal, I know that. So much ability, he could play anywhere. I'm not sure what Jack had in mind when he rang, but he probably thought 'I just need to do something, anything, to change the feel of things here'. So Mike is a toss of a dice.

But if I'm a Kerry defender and I see the SOS going out in July for a man who hasn't played county football since '06, I have to be thinking 'Hang on, what the fuck am I doing here? I've been killing myself since January, doing all the weights, and Jack seems to think nothing of bringing in a lad who's done none of that stuff.'

Still, maybe we're just forgetting who Mike Mac is.

Anyway, we're absolutely haunted to get out of Tralee. Now I'm a closed enough person, and, if I'm honest, I'm just bottling up all the bad stuff in my head now. I get back to my house in Killarney and I've cabin fever. No way can I just sit here tonight, staring at the walls. I'm depressed with this and I just know I need to switch off. Things just feel all over the place.

'Fuck this,' I say. 'I'm going for a few pints.'

Just me and a high stool. That's the only relationship I want now. No talk, no bullshit. I don't ring anyone. I don't want to be getting anyone else in trouble, but my head is like a ticking bomb here. And if I don't switch off, I know I'll have a sleepless night. So I take myself in to Jade's on New Street. Find a spot where I can watch the golf from America on TV. I've always been quite happy with my own company in a pub and now that's the only company that appeals to me.

Now and again, someone sidles over. 'What happened ye?' This kind of line.

'Yerrah look, we didn't play well,' I say.

I've no interest in going any deeper. Only people inside the bubble understand what we're going through now and I've certainly no interest in opening up to anyone here in the pub. The golf gets my attention. I'm polite, but pointedly distant.

I sit there till closing time, head home and slip away into a welcome sleep.

I know the rules, of course. No pints. We have Antrim in a week and, well, Jack wouldn't need to be Sherlock Holmes to hear about one of his better-known players supping Guinness on a Saturday night in Killarney.

We've training the following Tuesday and the call I'm half expecting comes that morning.

'Gooch, I want you to come into training early.'

Fuck, bad news travels fast.

Next thing, Darragh Ó Sé is on the line. 'Just to mark your card, my man knows that yourself and Tomás had pints at the weekend.'

Darragh might think he's just made my heart sink, but all I'm thinking is 'Hallelujah. Tomás was on the beer too? There might be safety in numbers here.'

Still, I'm bolshy on the phone with him. All I'm feeling is frustration.

'I don't give a fuck,' I say. 'I have to go in and talk to him this evening anyway.'

'I don't know,' says Darragh, 'but there's talk about him not playing ye at the weekend.'

'Darragh, does it fucking matter who he plays? We're all over the fucking shop!'

'Look, I'm just marking your card.'

'Yeah, sound!'

I thought Tomás and I would be called before the court together, but Jack decides to deal with us individually. We're clearly going to be the hot topic of the evening. So I arrive into Fitzgerald Stadium, toss my bag in a corner, and because there are other lads in there early too, doing their stretches, Jack calls me outside. 'Come out here, I want to talk to you.'

Now what follows is fairly one-sided because I put up no defence.

'Were you drinking at the weekend?'

'I was, yeah.'

'Well fuck it, Gooch, we're finding things hard enough.'

'I know.'

'I'd expect you to show some example.'

'I know.'

'I need you to be a fucking leader in this group and—'

'I know, Jack, I know.'

Then he finishes up by saying we're going to have a meeting and 'I don't fucking know if you're going to be playing at the weekend now'. Call it stubborn or whatever, that'd be Jack's way. I was all right with it. I'd been in the wrong, end of story.

But next thing the meeting is called upstairs and Jack's nowhere to be seen. None of the management are. Jack's called the meeting, sent up Declan O'Sullivan and Micheál Quirke to chair it, and decided to leave us at it. Ah Jesus. I'm fit to be tied now. To me, he had to be chairing that meeting. Had to be. If we were going to be talking about leadership and why things were going so bad, should management not have been part of that conversation?

But the meeting is only about Tomás and me. About drink and the bold boys we are. Nothing else on the agenda. Lord Christ, we've come clean. We haven't lied about it. We're taking whatever punishment comes our way on the chin. The dogs in the street can see Kerry are all over the shop, but it's as if Jack and the management have decided that Tomás and I are the only problem.

He should have been there in that room and he should have given it to the two of us between the eyes. 'Lads, ye were fucking out of line and the two of ye have been around long enough to know better. We're all really fucking disappointed in ye. Ye're not starting at the weekend!'

Bang. Done and dusted.

Trouble is, he's still tiptoeing. So Declan and Mike are in the chair. Tomás and myself apologize. We know we're wrong but, fuck, we're not schoolchildren here. Nobody discusses a punishment and then the two boys go back down to report to Jack. Fuck sake, treat us like adults! Two fellas who've been playing for Kerry for years – this is just fucking bananas.

Even now, thinking back on it just drives me bonkers. Crazy stuff.

Next thing we hear a story's going to the media that the two of us are being 'rested' against Antrim. Like the media are going to swallow that. Kerry are stinking the place out and they're 'resting' two of their most experienced players. A load of bollocks. Do management honestly think that thirty players will leave the Park that night and not say anything to their girlfriend, father, brother, sister or mother?

What happens?

Next day, it's front page on a national newspaper. Front page. My mother's looking at this, my family's looking at this. Jesus Christ, we drank a few pints. Professional rugby players will do that after a Six Nations game. Premier League soccer players? No problem. And here we are, two amateur Gaelic footballers, and the idea that we drank a few pints after a game is *front page* on a national newspaper.

To this day I'm convinced it was because of the way it was handled. Because Jack and the management weren't willing to tell anyone the truth. Everyone knew we'd been drinking, so how were you going to sell that 'rested' story to anyone?

Jack and I are stubborn enough characters and we laugh about it now. My relationship with him has always been good since. He'd say to me, 'If yourself and Tomás fucked off, sure I'd have had to walk!'

Looking back, I'd say he had bigger worries at the time. I'd say he was half afraid that Darragh and Marc might have taken issue with him nailing Tomás. And if the Ó Sés were unhappy, Jack was in trouble. Believe me, this wasn't our first meeting about breaches of discipline. Boys will be boys!

From day one he didn't believe the Ó Sés were buying into him. Just felt he could never be close to them. He always felt friction, I suppose, because of the Páidí thing in '03 and any impression that he might have had a role in getting rid of him. Now he had no hand, act or part in getting rid of Páidí, I can say that for absolute certain. But blood is thicker than water. He obviously wanted the job. And the three boys obviously had a loyalty to their uncle.

So Jack felt under that pressure. But he should have come in to the meeting, dropped us for the weekend. Job done. Myself and Tomás would be fairly cold about these things. We weren't going to bear any grudges, didn't have time for them. If anything, I'd say both of us were thinking 'If we don't win this All-Ireland, we'll be the ones blamed!'

And, trust me, we were a long way away from an All-Ireland as we left Fitzgerald Stadium that night. A million miles away to be honest.

Nothing had been resolved. No mention of tactics or a game-plan for the weekend in all the hysteria about pints. I was thick as anything heading home that Jack hadn't fronted up. Still am to this very day. Because that wasn't the way to do it, and I'll always stand over that opinion. That said, knowing what came later, I don't doubt Jack will stand over his.

Anyway, we play Antrim in Tullamore in the last qualifying round, and the engine is still pinking. Tomás and I are both sent in early and Galvin gets a late goal to give us a five-point win. Flatters us. We're still diseased. Cat again. The train journey home takes us on some kind of grim safari through the Irish midlands. Portlaoise. Portarlington. Lads have headphones on and eyes on the floor. Then word comes through of the quarter-final draw.

Dublin.

The gloom lifts immediately. There's an energy in us all of a sudden. Thanks be to fuck, a game to find out if we're made of steel or straw. Lads start talking almost immediately. It's as if we've all been plugged into the mains. As I'm getting off the train, I send Tomás a jokey text: 'Are you going for a jar?'

Everything feels lighter.

The Dubs were playing well, and we knew they didn't fear us. But we didn't fear them either because they'd never beaten this Kerry team. For us, a side barely able to put one foot in front of the other, they were perfect for our mood now. Maybe they gave us a little inner viciousness back. Because we knew they'd think we were there for the taking.

And a whole pile of frustration would come pouring out of us that day.

For me, particularly. I got a goal at the Hill End after just forty seconds and I think you can see in the fistpump afterwards that I was there for business. What was I thinking? 'No more Mister Fucking Nice Guy', that's what. I think I'd scored the grand total of 0-5 from play in our five Championship games until then. I wasn't leading. Then the pints thing blew up and, if I'm honest, I felt under ridiculous pressure.

But I also felt that this was the game that could change everything.

Mike Mac was now centre-back, Tommy Griffin back on the edge of the square, and, defensively, things felt more solid. And next thing, this man who hadn't played inter-county football for three years comes floating up the field, the blue sea opening up in front of him. One of Mike Mac's solos goes so high he actually nods the ball with his head. But still he's coming.

I'm no more than half in his eyeline, but maybe he knows the bad mood I'm in. Maybe he's thinking 'If I get to this fella inside, there's every chance he'll stick it'. David Henry is marking me but I've found a yard, and as the ball arrives I know I need to get the shot away quickly because Stephen Cluxton is advancing. When it hits the net, I roar like a fucking bear. Nothing intelligible, just a roar.

But one that says 'We're back!'

The Dubs don't know what's hit them. As we get well on top, I'm going around almost boiling up with anger. Just before half-time we're awarded a free about 5 yards outside the 45. Darragh has the ball in his hands.

'Give it to me,' I say.

'What are you going to do with it?'

'What the fuck do you think I'm going to do with it? I'm going to kick it over.'

He sees a look in my eyes I'd say he hasn't seen before. Hands me the ball. And I drill this kick, no higher than 15 metres at any point, straight over the bar. Like a fucking Exocet. BOOM. And that's me making a statement. A statement about being treated like a school kid. About people trying to put me under pressure.

They'd poked the bear. That's how I felt. Fuck the lot of them.

We won pulling up. Seventeen points. A slaughter. Jack didn't see that performance coming. None of us did. How could we? We'd been operating under a cloud, all kind of gloomy stories leaking from the camp, most of them untrue. Going absolutely nowhere and, next thing, something about the sight of Dublin gave us a pulse.

Anyway, Croke Park was our playground. People should have known it.

We beat Meath then in a nondescript semi-final on a greasy late August day. Navy jerseys. I had to come off after fifty minutes with a hip injury I'd picked up in training. Probably shouldn't have played. Put it this way, it was the closest I'd come yet to missing a Championship game. I was touch and go until the Friday.

Meath stayed close to us, but never close enough.

So we leave Croker looking ahead to the perfect last chapter of a ridiculous season. Another All-Ireland final against Cork. The boys that gave us such a licking in July.

They're swallowing hard now and we know it.

Funny, all of a sudden we've shape and direction and balance. Donaghy's finding his fitness at last after an injury-troubled summer and, credit to Jack, Mike Mac's a revelation. Athletic, able to read the game and make a pass, never gives the ball away. Just the all-round player. You know, if he'd never come back, people would just have remembered Mike as a sticky corner-back. Now they know he's a lot more than that. But the strength and conditioning gurus will have to explain themselves when they come in with their list of Commandments next winter.

Cork start like a whirlwind, and at that moment when Colm O'Neill's early shot explodes high into the Canal End net I'm worried. They race into a five-point lead, but they're like a prize-fighter who's put too much into the early rounds. Jack gets his match-ups spot on. Tom Sullivan on Goulding. Griffin, eventually, on O'Neill. At the far end, Tommy Walsh on Shields.

I'd say we win nearly twelve of the fifteen individual battles and manage a nine-point turnaround, winning by four. We're Cork's worst nightmare. This is our fifth consecutive Croke Park win over them and we just know they don't believe they can beat us there.

There'll be a bit of controversy some months later when Tadhg Kennelly admits in his autobiography that a heavy hit on Nicholas Murphy at the throw-in was actually pre-planned. Like the rest of us, it had taken him a long time to get going that year and, I suppose, justify a decision to come home from Sydney to try to emulate his father, Tim. In the book, Kennelly describes himself as so driven to make an impact that day the eyes were 'almost rolling around in the back of my head. I was like a raging bull.'

Maybe those words captured how a lot of us felt that season. There was an anger coming out of us that just needed to be harnessed right.

Logically, Tadhg should have seen red for that challenge on Murphy, but it would have been a massive call so early in an All-Ireland final. Instead, he stayed on and got to do that little Irish jig next to Sam Maguire in the Hogan Stand.

It was Darragh's last game and, suddenly, everything looked like a poem that rhymed in every sentence. We'd come through so much adversity to bring the canister home. Half the year, people telling us we had no fight, no stomach. People seeing the drinking story and thinking some of us were just some kind of rabble.

I enjoyed the homecoming on Monday night, but with the cup going to Glenbeigh that Tuesday to honour captain Darran O'Sullivan, I decided to get out of Dodge. Took a flight to Malaga out of Shannon with a good buddy of mine, Edmund O'Sullivan. Just wanted to be invisible. I could sense there was going to be a lot of noise around Kerry now and I didn't want any part in it. Just wanted to be anonymous.

Yeah, fuck that. Shorts, T-shirt, the sun on my back, chilling with someone of my own choosing. Nobody giving me a second glance.

Heaven.

14

Low in the Cage

'Oh fuck, fuck, fuck, someone come in here quick . . .'

My 2010 National League campaign summed up in nine panicked words. Well, the first four maybe, to be more precise.

Ten minutes into our game on 11 April with Monaghan in Killarney I got a ball over by the terrace and, bending low, tried to jink past my marker. His hand caught me in the face, something I'd experienced a hundred times before. But this felt different. Instantly my vision was gone in one eye and I could see blood with the other. Lads began gathering around me and I could tell from their voices that they didn't like what they saw. Someone started calling for Mike Finnerty, our doctor.

'Oh fuck, fuck, fuck . . .'

To this day, I'm not sure if it was a sharp fingernail or the ridge of a glove that tore my eyelid. I'm pretty sure it was unintentional, but the outcome was quite terrifying. Usually when you get a poke in the eye, any loss of vision tends to last only for a few minutes. But mine wasn't coming back. All I had was blackness now and the urgency in Mike's voice as he started making phone calls from the dressing-room left me in no doubt that he was worried.

Basically, we've two tear ducts in each eye and my top one had just been pulled out in a freakish incident.

They brought me to 'The Bons' in Tralee that evening where Dr David Wallace was good enough to come in from home, concluding straight away that I needed to go to Dublin, most probably for surgery.

You tear a muscle or break a bone even and there's at least some comfort in having a rough understanding of the implications. Usually you have a timetable for recovery. Here, to begin with, I had none. Here I just needed reassurance that my vision would come back again.

My sister Geraldine drove me to the Eye and Ear Clinic on Adelaide Road that Monday where Professor Lorraine Cassidy quickly confirmed the need for an operation. Essentially, she had to fit this tiny pipe around which a new tear duct could then form. The operation was performed under general anaesthetic and passed off relatively painlessly. All well and good then – except that pipe would have to be removed. And that would prove by far the worst part of the ordeal.

I returned to Dr Wallace maybe a month later in Tralee and had my head wedged into this vice. It brought me right back to our woodwork classes in The Sem. Everything had to be done under local anaesthetic this time because I had to move the eye on instruction.

Even thinking about it today almost brings me out in a cold sweat.

He had to give me multiple injections around the eye so I wouldn't feel the incision of the scalpel. Honestly, the procedure is one of the worst things I've ever gone through. Afterwards, Dr Wallace handed me this tiny pipe, no wider than a strip of spaghetti. 'That's what's done the job here,' he said with a smile.

Lord Jesus, never again.

Anyway, we'd already lost three League games before that clash with Monaghan and the competition just passed us by. And guess who? Cork were crowned champions for the first of what would be three years in a row. The Earth kept turning.

Two months later, 'Bomber' Liston came loping into the Hayfield Manor bar, sold on an idea that the world was singing to our tune.

'Ye're hard bastards all the same,' he laughed, that famous beard creased with happiness. He'd got 'Ogie' Moran by his side, and to see these two Kerry greats so swept up in the jubilation of another Championship victory over Cork offered all kinds of psychological temptation. Bomber was convinced that he'd seen the bite of a dog in us, but I had my doubts. You see, we'd just 'done' Cork in a Munster semi-final replay.

That's the best way I can describe it because we had no right to win. Maybe that's the mark of a proper team, but I couldn't avoid the view that we'd got away with something. And, despite successive years of nailing us in the Munster Championship, I suspected Cork still felt we had something over them. What did those Munster titles really mean to them when they couldn't subsequently back it up against us in Croke Park?

Darragh was retired now; Tommy Walsh was in Australia; Tadhg Kennelly had gone back down under too. That's a fifth of our All-Ireland starting fifteen gone off the page, yet we were still rolling here. When we looked down and out, Marc Ó Sé came in along the end-line to nail us a reprieve just on the stroke of seventy minutes. And everything Cork saw in us to hate was probably written all over the way we celebrated scraping home by a point in extra-time at Páirc Uí Chaoimh.

So I could tell what Bomber thought he was seeing. I just needed convincing that it was real.

We broke Limerick's hearts again in the Munster final, winning by a goal, doing just enough to keep them at bay and probably scarring the careers of some of their best players for life.

Over a period of four or five years, that Limerick team was definitely good enough to win a Munster Championship. They should have beaten us in '04, and they might easily have beaten us in Killarney this time too. I sometimes wonder what confidence a provincial championship win could have given men like Stephen Lucey and John Galvin.

You know GAA tradition is tangled up in a certain cruelty here. Winning that Munster title, our first since '07, would have been just the ticking of a box in Kerry. Once Cork were out of the way it would have been unthinkable to our supporters that we could lose to Limerick, especially in Killarney. I often think a Munster win would have made those Limerick players massive heroes within their county.

But they always seemed just inches short of getting there.

The Sunday evening the All-Ireland quarter-final draw was made, I was playing nine holes with Eoin Brosnan in Killarney. Eoin had taken time out from the inter-county scene so I suppose felt a little detached from everything when the draw came up on my phone. We'd got Down.

'Well,' said Eoin, 'that's probably as good as ye could have got.'

If I'm honest, that's pretty much how I felt too. The media would subsequently go into overdrive about how Kerry had never beaten Down in the Championship, but to us, they might as well have been talking about our rivalry with the planet Jupiter. Because we had no history with Down. None. What happened in the sixties had no relevance to our team.

And Eoin's assessment pretty much encapsulated what we were thinking as a group now. Looking back, it almost certainly reflected a sense of ambivalence in how we would approach the game, because I don't believe we saw danger in Down. Putting it bluntly, we presumed we'd beat them. Our supporters did too, all but the diehards deciding they'd hold fire on a trip to Dublin until the semi-finals.

My memories of the game are a kind of universal grey.

A Saturday evening throw-in in a cold, dreary Croke Park that must have been two-thirds empty, the Dubs supporters yet to come through the turnstiles for their quarter-final with Tyrone. No real Championship heat then, no atmosphere. Kerry almost sleepwalking. To us, it was just another day out, another routine step to get to where we wanted to be. Essentially, we went in on automatic pilot and forgot to perform.

During my career with Kerry, quarter-finals tended to be where we were most vulnerable. Our record in them is nothing to write home about. It's as if we reckoned the time to come alive was in late August, early September. We were so used to getting ourselves up for Cork, usually in a Munster final, that we'd always hit a bit of a flat spot after. The key was to dog our way through that flat spot, which we might have done if the Kerry team Bomber thought he saw in June actually existed.

Down would prove emphatically that it didn't.

We were well beaten on the day, maybe the experience of having played in six consecutive All-Ireland finals making us a little self-satisfied and soft. But Down had a little swagger to them too that you didn't tend to associate with other Ulster teams. And once they smelled blood, they did not hesitate.

I'd still have issues with some of Joe McQuillan's refereeing decisions that day, most especially one where he disallowed a Kerry goal on the basis of a perfectly legitimate hand-pass from Killian Young being declared a thrown ball. It wasn't even close. Joe was never our favourite ref in Kerry, but we had only ourselves to blame that day.

I remember a general sense of disbelief in the dressing-room after. Lads just staring at the floor, their expressions saying 'How the fuck did this happen?' A few of us decided there and then that the last place we wanted to be that evening was back in Kerry. So Darran, Galvin and myself gave the night in Dublin. Stayed in The Berkeley Court, skulled a few beers in non-GAA bars. Drowned our sorrows, I suppose.

And I gave it a few more days on the beer back in Killarney after that with David Moran. Just keeping our heads down in back bars, minding our own business. We stayed away from our usual haunt, The Tatler, because traditionally that's where GAA people gathered. All we wanted was our own company.

We didn't want to face reality just now, so pints seemed the only answer.

In Kerry especially, people are all too quick to give an opinion when we lose and I just wasn't in the humour for it. I do remember a couple of people approaching us, ready to lay down the law. My quick response was 'Were ye above, lads?'

If the answer was 'yes', fair enough, you'd no choice but to give a lad some airplay, take it on the chin. But more often than not it was 'no'. And if they hadn't travelled, I wasn't going to sit there listening to them tell me what we should have done or what Jack O'Connor should have done. I wasn't having that.

And I'd say with the look on my face I didn't have to tell them.

I went back to work that Thursday in Tralee and Donaghy, who was based across the street in another bank, came over in the afternoon for a chat.

He could read fairly quickly that I was in a bad place. Defeat had left me questioning things. I was nine years on the go now and beginning to wonder if there might be more to life than endlessly flogging ourselves in the hope of finishing the year with a piece of metal. Actually, a part of me had begun wondering were we fucking crackers.

'How are you feeling, man?' Star asked.

'Fucking low enough in the cage,' I told him. 'Fed up of it now.'

Truth was we were all down, but my way was to go deeper than most others. I couldn't help myself. I could tell from Donaghy's face leaving me that day he was half worried I might pack it in. Because that would definitely have been my vibe that week. I would be talking to myself.

I don't cut corners; I do things by the book.

So how the fuck does this happen?

Should I have seen signs?

Were lads complacent in training? Taking it for granted?

I thought you were fucking smarter than this!

The defeat just left me second-guessing everything and my morale hit an all-time low. We'd more than enough quality to beat that Down team, but it was obvious we just didn't have the drive or the intensity. They shouldn't have been beating us, but they did. And that was unforgivable.

As we chatted, I remember saying to Star, 'I don't know, Kieran . . . fuck it . . . what's this all about? I honestly feel I can't fucking deal with it.'

At the time I genuinely thought that it wouldn't be the hardest thing in the world just to walk away from it for good. I can see now that that was never going to happen. I'd only just turned twenty-seven, still at the peak of my powers. I'd actually played quite well in the Down game. But this is how I always get after a big Championship defeat. If I had a pair of boots in my hand, I'd fuck them in the bin.

I needed time now, at least that's what I thought. Luckily, the club meant I didn't have any.

*

I stepped back into Crokes business like a bear with a sore head.

The boys could see it in me, hear it in me. I remember giving a bit of a spiel in the dressing-room before we played South Kerry in the county semi-final. 'Is this team going to finally grow a pair of balls?' I asked. 'Because I'm sick and tired of the sight of South Kerry. Are we fucking going to win this thing for once and for all?'

'No fucking hard luck stories' – that was my message. 'No "I should have done this" or "I should have done that". Start that and it's too late. Everyone's to stand up now, no fucking crying!'

It wasn't just me. We all knew the general view of us within Kerry football. We were seen as nice footballers, but ultimately soft. *Get stuck into them and they'll turn their arses to it. They don't have the balls!*

That might as well have been burned into our name with a branding iron. And we resented it.

We'd been such a young team when we got to the 2007 All-Ireland Club final, we basically hadn't been given the space to grow. When I think back to the likes of Kieran O'Leary and myself, we were just kids at the time. But because of our success that year, expectation and presumption went through the roof. It was considered just a matter of time before we'd win a county title.

Trouble was, we'd got to that All-Ireland final on pure talent. We weren't yet fully battle-hardened. Three years on, we still hadn't ticked that box and a lot of hurt was building up inside us.

I remember thinking that the anger I was carrying over from Kerry's defeat to Down needed to be properly channelled now. Asking myself, 'What are you going to do with it?'

For all of us, it felt as if you could almost hear a ticking sound in our dressing-room before that semi-final with South Kerry. We were like a bomb ready to go off. And that's pretty much what happened, with us scoring two goals in the opening four minutes.

Brian Looney got the first; then I was fouled for a penalty, which I scored. It was a big call by the ref who was a long way away from the incident and I have a vivid memory of Declan O'Sullivan storming down the field to have it out with him.

To be fair, we were the better team that day and fuelled with just enough obstinacy not to give South Kerry a way back into the game. And that victory was career defining for us as a Crokes team. It was something we absolutely needed to do.

After that it was an all 'townie' county final against Austin Stacks, a game the media was inclined to build up into some kind of shoot-out between myself and Donaghy, carrying the bonus prize of the Kerry captaincy in 2011. To be honest, that was the least of my worries. Although, over time, I did become conscious of the talk.

I remember meeting Jack O'Connor for a bowl of soup in The Europe Hotel not long before the game. He was a little uncertain of his own intentions at the time and I suppose was just trying to see how the land lay with a few of Kerry's senior players. He wanted to be sure he'd have the dressing-room if he stayed another year and, personally, I could see no reason why he wouldn't.

'Yerrah maybe it's time to step away,' he was saying, clearly hoping for a counterargument.

He was fishing for reassurance, I suppose. Were we not responding to his training? Had his voice become a little old? Was the hunger still in Kerry's big men to chase down another canister?

As we finished up, Jack turned to me in that familiarly gruff way of his and said, 'Anyway, go on and win the county championship. You'll be a good captain now, go and win the fucking thing!'

I remember getting into my car and, maybe for the first time, really starting to think of the implications of me being a Kerry captain. And I started trying to list off in my head the different Kerry captains I had played under. I couldn't do it, not instantly at least. And that reminded me that winning the county had to be my first priority. Anything after didn't matter for now.

The day before the final I agreed to do a radio interview for Robbie Irwin in RTÉ. As it happened, he had Donaghy on the line too. And I'm standing there on the putting green at Killarney Golf Club thinking how wrong it felt that the county final was being brought to a national audience now as just this battle between two county players. Fair play to Robbie, getting the two of us on just twenty-four hours before throw-in was probably a bit of a coup. But it wasn't really the conversation I wanted to be having.

The big thing for me now was showing that I could back up my status as a leader in the Crokes dressing-room. 'Go fucking lead now!' I kept saying to myself, over and over. That was the pressure I was putting on myself. When we won in 2000, I was just a child, hitching a ride in a team of men. This was a different story.

In my head, I *had* to take charge of this county final. That was my challenge.

So Crokes winning and me getting Man of the Match lifted a huge weight off my shoulders. That was written all over my mother's embrace on the field at the end. How herself and my two sisters got on the field so quickly I just don't know. But it was as if every Crokes person alive wanted to be there at that moment.

Pretty quickly I was swamped by supporters, most of them repeating something similar: 'Good man, fucking captain next year!'

It had been a momentous year of growing up for me. A year when I'd asked different questions of myself. And now that I finally allowed myself to think about the Kerry captaincy, I felt absolutely certain that I was ready. I was at a good age for it and I was in a good place in my life. I'd studied and absorbed so many leadership skills from men like Moynihan and Darragh and Declan O'Sullivan, go-to guys whether they had the captain's armband at the time or not. Guys who understood the hurt of losing in a Kerry jersey and knew when fellas were taking shortcuts. Just watching how they conducted themselves and monitoring the passion they brought on an everyday basis, I considered it all an education.

Because, to begin with, I didn't understand their hurt. I had no real personal experience of it. I didn't have their passion. It took me time to realize where they were coming from and, maybe more importantly, why.

Like I earned the right to be a Kerry footballer through my talent. Not through a willingness to hurt. Not through selflessness. Not through an absolute bloody-mindedness. When you think about it, I won an All-Star in my first year of inter-county football. And I did it without even having to do the hard, dirty slog of January and February. Just breezed in when everyone else had already been run into the ground.

Everything came fast and easy to me in those early years. If training was at six p.m., I'd come into the park at 5.45. Boots on and out we go. I couldn't understand why other lads would be in at 4.30, up on exercise bikes, stretching, getting themselves ready.

Jack has this good expression about being a Kerry footballer. 'You have to live the life,' he'd say.

To begin with, that was just a sentence I never paid much attention to. It didn't seem all that relevant to me. Maybe part of the problem was that a lot of things came too easily to me. I found unbelievable personal strength in the fact that I could play at numbers 15, 14, 13, 11 or 12 and just go one-on-one with my marker, fully expecting to win. I could go in the corner, play top of the square, slip out to the 'forty'. I had so much belief in my ability, I never had a sense of panic when things were slow to happen for me. If the first thing I tried didn't work, it never mattered. I honestly felt I had five or six different ways of skinning my man.

Even though I wasn't very strong physically at first, I was good over my head. I could win ball. And once I had it in my possession, I felt I could nearly do what I liked. Peel off the back; dummy solo; get him to overcommit. Because I had so much ability, I started my Kerry career believing different rules applied to me. But '02 and '03 taught me that I needed to get stronger, and I think that by '04 I was a 25 per cent better player having heeded that lesson. Because the physical strength made me mentally stronger too.

At times that year I felt almost unmarkable. Certainly in the All-Ireland final. I just knew that if I got even a half chance in that game, I wasn't going to miss. But the experiences of '05, '08 and '10, those Croke Park losses to Ulster opposition, exposed me to a very different feeling. The sense that opponents might have been more willing to hurt than we were. Likewise those Cork defeats in Munster in '02, '06, '08 and '09.

As Kerry captain, I was now determined that nobody beat us by dint of hunger on my watch. But to do that, first up I needed to make sure that I was ready to lead by example.

15

When Bull Becomes Gospel

Six minutes changed everything. Barely the time it takes a kettle to boil took us from a looming coronation to a wake.

'Retirements Expected' ran a back-page headline in *The Kerryman* the week after our 2011 All-Ireland final loss to Dublin. That's how football life works in the Kingdom. Winning is the only acceptable language. A different last six minutes to that final and the headline might just as easily have read 'Heroes All'. But you suck it up. You don't take it personally.

We live in a climate of extremes in Kerry and the best thing, always, is not to overanalyse.

Was I a good or bad Kerry captain that year? Well, history will say I didn't deliver, and I'm not in a position to argue. But up until Kevin McManamon's sixty-fourth-minute goal in that final, I would have said that we were headed for the perfect season. True we hadn't pulled up any trees in the National League, but seeing Cork win their seventh spring title hadn't unduly bothered us; nor, we can now safely say, did it bother their final opponents, Dublin.

Everything we wanted seemed to be within our reach that

September Sunday as we stretched four points clear in a game that looked under control.

Needless to say, I've looked at the video a few times since. The clock reads 63.37 when McManamon's shot hits the Hill End net. That's the moment that killed us. The team completely lost its shape after and, while it took Stephen Cluxton's injury-time free to win it for the Dubs, I don't think we'll ever be able to forgive ourselves for how completely we unravelled.

It was incredibly naive for an experienced team like ours to allow that to happen. Because we'd have felt we were pretty good at seeing tight games out. In that kind of scenario we'd probably even expect to ease away to win by seven or eight.

Maybe there's a touch of arrogance in that. I mean, would Tyrone have allowed McManamon to waltz in on their goal in such circumstances? I doubt it very much. But we were Kerry. We were comfortable. I suppose fellas didn't feel the need to be unscrupulous at that moment.

And the regret is something we may well carry to our graves.

Jack had shaken up his back-room team earlier that year and the biggest change was his introduction of Donie Buckley as coach.

A Castleisland man, he'd spent three seasons working with Mickey 'Ned' O'Sullivan in Limerick, and we knew from personal experience the steel that had been added to their game in that time. I didn't know him personally but the Monday after we'd beaten Limerick in the 2010 Munster final I met him in Adare. A few of us had clearance to attend the J. P. McManus Pro-Am that Tiger Woods was playing in and we were having a few pints in the village before heading for the hills when I bumped into Donie, a keen golf fan.

It was a fairly brief, superficial conversation really. Little more than 'Hard luck yesterday Donie, ye gave us a right rattle . . .' But you get a sense of insightful people pretty quickly. I liked him immediately. And I remember thinking as we parted 'Fuck it, if he's getting so much out of those Limerick lads and he's a Kerryman . . .'

I thought little more of it until Jack announced that autumn that he was coming on board. Alan O'Connor was now into his third year as our physical trainer, but Donie would be sharing the coaching with Jack, placing a particular emphasis on tackling with intensity.

He was a real student of all sport and couldn't start work with us until the following February as he was heading to Australia to spend time studying the training methods of AFL side Carlton. That was kind of typical of the life Donie leads. He is a sponge for information and a regular traveller to the US, picking up information from how football, basketball and ice hockey teams train.

Another new addition to the back room was our former number one Diarmuid Murphy, who'd been goalkeeping coach to the Kerry minors in 2010.

First impressions were all positive. I think Jack felt we needed to have more physical bite in how we played the game and that, for opponents, maybe the experience of playing Kerry simply had to become more uncomfortable. But just getting fellas to tackle properly isn't quite as simple as it sounds. After all, no point hitting hard if it just keeps costing you frees.

One thing was becoming crystal clear. The way the game was going, the best teams invariably had the best tacklers.

Funny, talking to the likes of Darragh and Moynihan, they'd always say that some of the best tacklers they came across in their careers were the forwards on the Galway team that reached three All-Ireland finals in four years (winning two) between '98 and '01. Lads like Pádraig Joyce, Michael Donnellan, Paul Clancy and Derek Savage were brilliant at it apparently. And if your marquee players are doing that, just imagine what it must be adding to the overall strength of a team.

I suspect Jack knew we had all the talent in the world up front but maybe we were too passive when we didn't have the ball. Against Down especially in 2010 we'd barely laid a glove on any of their defenders coming out with possession. In the modern game, that meant we were giving the opposition easy transfer of delivery out of their own half. Maybe we'd have worked harder in a semi-final or a final, but against Down in a quarter-final we were just trying to play within ourselves. That attitude couldn't be repeated.

The message from Jack in 2011 was that everybody had to be willing almost to sacrifice themselves physically to win possession, no matter what area of the field. He believed that we could ratchet things up higher in the physical stakes; that a corner-back coming away with the ball unchallenged, despite someone being near enough to make a hit, could be the losing of a game. Even if we were only talking small percentages here, he wanted them all closed off.

To that end, Donie was his enforcer. Jack wanted him for a very specific role – and I suspect that the only reason Donie stayed just one season with Kerry was he became a little frustrated with the narrowness of that role. Personally, I liked him from day one. I found him an interesting speaker. Sport is such a passion to him and he's a firm believer that the GAA can profitably learn from how others do their business.

That said, if I'm honest, there was nothing especially revolutionary about what he was doing with us in training. Essentially, he just wanted everything done with more intensity. There was a lot more physical contact in training and, for the first time, we were actually studying the science of tackling, the physics of it. The difference between expending good energy and bad, I suppose.

As captain, I didn't feel any great need to be delivering big orations. Most lads see through you immediately the moment you end up talking just for the sake of it. I do remember putting it out there that I wanted anyone who had issues in their personal or work lives that might be interfering with the football to feel free to come to me privately for a chat. I knew only too well the importance of taking an interest in the players as people.

But beyond that? Fuck it. I reckoned things were pretty self-evident.

'Look I don't have to tell you what the goal is,' I remember saying on our first night in. 'We're going to work like Trojans. Ye all understand what's required.'

Maybe people imagine what gets said at these moments is something more stirring, more profound. But it seldom is. When you're at the start of a hard slog, most players need empathy not noise. They just want an understanding of everyone being in the thing together and making the same sacrifices.

My feeling was that the more sparing I was with words and the more obvious my physical input, the better I would be as captain.

As reigning All-Ireland champions, it was clear Cork were arriving into the Championship with a bit of a chip on their shoulders. Their allocation of just four All-Stars the previous November was a record low and the fact they did not get a single forward position seemed to be interpreted within the county as an extraordinary slight on their achievement in winning the Sam Maguire. As a forward who did get selected on that All-Star team, despite Kerry having a fairly brutal 2010, I suppose I was especially conscious of how it must have looked from their point of view.

But if Cork had a bee in their bonnet about the All-Stars, we had a bee in ours about the fact that they'd won the All-Ireland without beating Kerry.

So when it became clear that they'd be coming to Killarney on 3 July for the Munster final, we were determined to give them a reception they wouldn't forget. We'd been eleven points better than both Tipperary and Limerick to get there and, as a Killarney man captaining Kerry in that provincial final, I felt a huge responsibility on my shoulders to make sure we did not lose that day.

Losing to Cork was always bad enough. Losing to Cork in Killarney would have been horrible. Losing to Cork in Killarney while Kerry captain? That would have cut me in two.

To that end, I played on the history of the fixture at our team-meeting the night before. Cork had not won in Killarney since '95 (and still haven't) and we were actually defending a twenty-two-game unbeaten home Championship record in that game. Sometimes players get so wrapped up in the tactical side of stuff they need to be reminded of other fundamentals. Stuff like history and tradition are hugely important in the GAA, and in my speech to the team I made a big play on both.

I didn't want us treating this as just another game against Cork. I wanted us on a war footing. I remember saying, 'Fucking hell, do we want that record lost on our watch? Not a chance!'

Maybe I put myself under too much pressure that day. I never got into that side of things too deeply with Jack, but he's a clever guy. I'm sure he could sense that energy rolling off me. Like even going back to that meeting we'd had in The Europe Hotel, I can see now that he was already pulling my strings. He knew I'd be a hungry Kerry captain, that I'd demand standards of people. He knew that I'd be hard on myself and expect everyone else to be likewise.

And if I could make that hunger mandatory in the group, that would make his job of coaching so much easier.

Maybe it helped that day that Cork were strong favourites coming to Killarney because we tore into them like buzzards swooping down on a carcass. Just after half-time we had stretched into a nine-point lead and it looked as if we might even humiliate the All-Ireland champions. Declan O'Sullivan was absolutely outstanding. But, over the next half hour, we lost our way. Cork actually scored an unanswered 1-5, and then a John Miskella shot cannoned off one of Brendan Kealy's uprights. We were living dangerously.

In the end, injury-time points from Eoin Brosnan (who had returned to the Kerry squad that year) and James O'Donoghue gave us a 1-15 to 1-12 win.

Michael Shields had done a tight marking job on me in the game and I failed to register a score from play. In those circumstances, losing would have been a bit of a personal nightmare. But the opposite now applied, and I have a lovely memory of walking down the town from Fitzgerald Stadium with Patrick O'Sullivan – a beautiful, sunny July evening and silverware in my hand on Lewis Road. I just loved the sense that we'd looked after business here.

That I was bringing the cup back to my people.

The expectation that we'd most likely meet again in the All-Ireland semi-final came undone on the last day of July when we beat a Limerick team now surely hating the very sight of us by thirteen points in a Croke Park quarter-final.

Because that day Mayo put an end to Cork's title defence in the second game of a double-header, setting up a reprise of a rivalry that had fallen so heavily our way in the finals of '04 and '06.

I was increasingly conscious that my form remained under-whelming and I went into that Mayo semi-final mindful, in a scoring sense at least, that others were contributing far more to Kerry's season than their captain. Thankfully that now changed as I managed 1-7 (1-3 from play) in a contest we eventually won by nine points.

There was a proper intensity to that game for a while too, especially so when Cillian O'Connor's fifty-second-minute goal brought Mayo right back into things after Kerry had scored a bucket of points without reply. Thankfully our response was almost instant, and when I put one past Robert Hennelly at the other end, Mayo's resistance was gone.

The Dubs squeezed past Donegal in the other semi-final, a game made famous by Jim McGuinness's controversial tactic of flooding defence in the hope of frustrating them into meltdown. It looked absolutely horrible to play against, but this was a Dublin team beginning to find new ways of digging deep in games that threatened not to go their way.

And that's pretty much all they had to do three weeks later. In his victory speech, Bryan Cullen would describe Dublin as having been 'to hell and back' en route to winning the city's first senior All-Ireland in sixteen years. Maybe I shouldn't have begrudged it to them, but I couldn't help myself. I was just sickened by our carelessness. By the time of McManamon's goal, we'd outscored Dublin 0-8 to 0-3 in the second half. It had felt like we were cruising.

Earlier I'd scored a nineteenth-minute goal, yet Dublin led 0-6 to 1-2 at the interval. Imagine, Kerry scoring just two points in thirty-five minutes of Championship football. Not good enough. And Dublin stretched their lead to four not long after the resumption only for us to confine them to a return of 0-1 over the next twenty-two minutes.

Then it was as if a bomb went off.

Donaghy looked to have rescued a replay for us with a wonder point in the seventieth minute, but the next thing I remember is protesting furiously against the award of that Hill End free, from which Stephen Cluxton would kick a famous winning point. It felt like an eternity between the free actually being awarded and

Cluxton sending it over the bar. And I remember thinking we'd definitely get one last chance, that Joe McQuillan would at least give us an opportunity to work the ball back up towards the Canal End goal.

He didn't, though. The kick-out was never taken.

The fallout in Kerry was nothing I wouldn't have expected. Suddenly, media focus was on the fact that five of our starting defenders were over thirty. That maybe having played in seven of the last eight All-Ireland finals, the need for an infusion of new blood was now overwhelming. That we were a busted flush and the team that beat us by a single point was football's future.

To me, it was all just noise.

People draw conclusions because it's what they get paid to do but, often, those conclusions aren't worth the paper they're printed on.

Yet the public latch on to them. They're influenced by them. Bullshit becomes gospel. When people wonder why players are so guarded with the media, I'd suggest that the fallout to Kerry's defeat in that All-Ireland final should go some way towards explaining it. Put it this way: I know what's a fair assessment of a game and what's not fair. It's probably why I've been so guarded right through my career.

Because you have to keep some kind of realism in your life. If I allowed media to get to me with what's been written or said, I'd have retired from the game a long time ago. The trouble is, everything gets presented in black and white. There's no room for grey. I hate that.

And that's why, if it has to be me against the world and I end up being so closed about things that even my own family become frustrated, so be it. A siege mentality is no harm at times. It can help you focus and shut out the stuff that doesn't matter.

For months after that Dublin game I was hounded by the thought 'How the fuck did we lose it?'

A few weeks afterwards, Crokes beat Mid-Kerry in the county final to give us back-to-back titles, and with Brossie back and in cracking form on the inter-county scene I couldn't have had any complaints with him being nominated for the Kerry captaincy in 2012. But the club and Brossie decided to give me another shot at it.

And, much as I'd hate to admit it, it might well have been a vote of sympathy.

16

Everything Coming Out Garbled

In the end, Kerry might as well have been stuffing gypsies' heather in our pockets and packing our minds with *piseoga*.

At a certain point in 2012 I suspect we all realized we were waiting in vain for some kind of magical energy that kept eluding us. Jack had run out of ideas and the slow drain of marquee figures from our dressing-room was beginning, finally, to exact a heavy toll. Trouble was, our supporters could not see that and, if I'm honest, those of us inside the team bubble weren't exactly quick to acknowledge it either.

In a sense, I suspect that what we'd done in '09 fooled us into believing that one big performance might be in us and that, if so, it would somehow transform everything. We were waiting for another Dublin moment, a condition maybe best described as 'denial'. Because when I look back now we weren't at the races for a lot of 2012. Nowhere even close. Yet the general vibe among the Kerry public was that we had enough quality to trouble anyone.

We didn't though.

We couldn't.

Maybe there might have been a little bit of feeling sorry for our-selves too. There was definitely a psychological hangover from the 2011 All-Ireland final defeat. We should have won the game, we knew that. And on some level our response to not winning was a form of self-pity when a little bit of anger or disgust with ourselves would have been far more appropriate and constructive. The invitation to look anywhere bar the mirror for that defeat seemed ever-present. And we allowed ourselves to be blinded by it.

I've learned the hard way that when you lose an All-Ireland final, there's only one attitude that offers any salvation. The one that says 'Tough shit, move on, grow up'.

But we didn't grow up for a long time after losing to Dublin in that final.

As captain, I'd have to accept some degree of responsibility for that. Trouble is, hindsight offers a clarity that isn't always available at the time. I look back now and remember a Kerry team suddenly finding fault with referees and feeding on the idea that, basically, we weren't really being given a fair crack of the whip. It was bullshit, but highly seductive bullshit.

Cork won their third League in a row and then beat us easily in a Munster semi-final. It was after this game that Jack brought Eamonn Fitzmaurice on board as a selector – a tacit enough admission, I suppose, that things needed some kind of different energy.

To me, Eamonn's arrival just signalled the addition of a solid voice to the back room. I'd always have regarded him as an exceptional reader of the game when playing, a very sharp, astute guy. And, although he'd done a stint as manager of Kerry's under-21s, I had no idea at the time that he'd any long-term interest in the senior job.

The defeat to Cork bounced us into a mid-July qualifier against Westmeath in Mullingar, and it was a game in which we should have been beaten. We just seemed second best to everything all day until I found Darran with a quick free and he scored a bullet of a goal at the Dunnes' Stores end to get us out of jail. It was a shocking performance. I remember thinking at one point that if we lost, we'd never be able to show our faces again in Kerry.

Jack was trying different things to find a spark, but nothing seemed to work.

He switched me to full-forward and Donaghy to the corner at one point, presumably on the basis that Star would get more room away from the edge of the square where he was almost always being double-teamed. I think the view was that it was easier to foul him in a crowded space and get away with it than it might be outside. Truth was, I could see a certain logic.

With someone of Donaghy's size and aerial strength inside, maybe it was too easy an option to just lamp ball in on top of him too. Maybe to some degree we stopped playing any real football on the basis that the big man made such an obvious target.

With me at full-forward, that had to change. I was decent in the air, but I was no Donaghy. People would now have to be a bit more thoughtful in what they did. A bit more circumspect. But it didn't work. Nothing was working.

Early in the second half we were 1-3 to 1-9 down and headed for one of Kerry's most humiliating Championship exits ever. So Darran's goal was vital. He'd come on as a half-time substitute and began running at the Westmeath defence in a way they were never entirely comfortable with.

But it had taken us over half an hour to register our first score from play. Against Westmeath! It felt as if we were going nowhere.

The strange thing is that James O'Donoghue had broken into the team now and it was obvious he was a special talent. Yet our play remained stuck in neutral. On paper, we had a forward line that should have been terrorizing the opposition, but everything kept coming out garbled.

What was I honestly thinking? I was probably clinging to that condition of denial. Waiting for the game that would electrify our season.

Six days later, in round three of the qualifiers, we thought we'd found it. Tyrone came to Killarney and the build-up felt like getting ready for a highwire act without a safety net. The tension was almost suffocating. And the amount of individual soul-searching that went on that week was huge. Because of our history with them, we knew it was a game we simply couldn't afford to lose. They'd had it over us three times in succession in Croke Park. To make it a fourth in Killarney would have humiliated us.

So you're trying to talk that into the group mindset. The idea that under no circumstances could we let that happen in front of 40,000 people in Fitzgerald Stadium. Against our arch-rivals, a team the media kept telling us we couldn't beat. Everywhere we turned, our lousy Championship record against Tyrone was being pushed into our faces. We were tarnished as footballers with this unbending accusation. 'Ye can't beat them in Championship . . .'

Tyrone were everything we seemingly couldn't make ourselves become.

Hard-nosed.

Resilient.

Ruthless.

Winners.

They had simply inflicted so much hurt on us that this game felt like a Munster final in Killarney with added VAT. From the moment the draw was made, fellas were going to whatever psychological place they needed to go to in order to be right for the day. Because of Tyrone, we'd become the butt of jokes. There was a lot of smart-arse stuff out there and we weren't deaf to it. If ever there was a day we needed to take care of business, this was it.

Yet, hand on heart, this wasn't the Tyrone team that the

propaganda painted. No more than ourselves maybe, they were slipping. They hadn't made the Ulster final and arrived down to Killarney on the back of a big win in Roscommon that nobody was interpreting as anything too seismic.

So we beat a bit of a ghost that day and, deep down, I suspect everybody knew it. Because the great Tyrone team lost to nobody by ten points. They wouldn't countenance it.

Still, the relief we felt was indifferent to any small print now. Paul Galvin was grabbed for a TV interview at the final whistle and pretty much broke down live on air. That's not Paul's form, and it's not ours. But this just felt like a huge monkey lifted off our backs.

But there was, of course, a deeper context to that game that had everyone's emotions a little frazzled.

Michaela Harte's shocking murder in Mauritius eighteen months earlier was still a matter of disbelief in the broader GAA community. On one of my first All-Stars trips, to Hong Kong in '05, I'd sat beside her on the outward flight; Mickey Harte and John Maughan were the two managers on that tour and both brought their daughters. As footballers I suppose we all felt young and unbreakable back then, and I sometimes wondered after what the two girls made of us from a distance.

I remember Michaela as a real lady. Warm and friendly and utterly passionate when she talked about Tyrone and her father's involvement with them.

So none of us could even fathom what Mickey was going through now. Maybe football was a help to him at the time, maybe it wasn't. I haven't a clue. I've done some media work with him and we've always got on well. A few years after, he'd even come down to my mother's funeral, which was a lovely gesture. He's a man I have massive respect for. But that day in Killarney everything had to be still so raw for him, thinking about football the way the rest of us were thinking must have been impossible.

It's a huge and important thing in our lives, but I think people were sensitive enough that July Saturday to appreciate that, win or lose, we needed to communicate a sense of care to the Harte family too.

Which is pretty much what the Kerry supporters did, applauding Mickey and his team on to the bus after, that applause following them all the way down Lewis Road into the town.

It felt an important gesture given the tension that had built up between us as football teams. Again, maybe hate is too strong a word, but there was definite needle. We had little choice but to grow to dislike them. How could it be any other way when they were the reason for us being ridiculed by the media and, in some cases, even our own supporters?

But something broke in the rivalry that day in Killarney. Maybe it was the removal of bile. Maybe it was a common acceptance that stuff like judgement and priorities and the simple sense of who we are sometimes get skewed in the pressure cooker of serious sport.

I think that's what Galvin's emotion was about. A good few of us went to Mickey at the end just to articulate whatever emotional support we could. I'm not even sure what it was I said. I've never liked overdoing the talk with a beaten opponent for fear they'd ever think I'm milking it. So sometimes I might even seem a little curt, a little unfeeling. My instinct is always just to get out of there. To move on.

One week later, we beat Clare by nineteen points in the Gaelic Grounds. We were into the last eight and beginning to get notions again.

The day after one of Kerry's greatest men, Con Houlihan, passed away in a Dublin hospital we were knocked out of the Championship by Donegal.

It was a result that signed all the cheques being written in the media about football's new guard. Jim McGuinness's team would go on to claim the Sam Maguire and establish themselves in the minds of many as having rewritten football's terms of engagement. They were modern, cutting-edge, innovative, smart. We were old school. Tired. Obsolete.

When I think of the reasons why I've largely taken pundits with a pinch of salt during my Kerry career, the way that loss to Donegal was presented pretty much explains why.

As bad as we were in 2012 (and we *were* bad), we lost that quarter-final by two points. Less than ten minutes in, Donegal fluked a goal when Colm McFadden's line ball from the Cusack Stand side eluded both Michael Murphy and Aidan O'Mahony, ricocheting into Brendan Kealy's net off the crossbar. In a low-scoring game, that goal was huge.

Near the end we had a chance to level the game but Paddy Curtin pulled his effort wide. (Paddy was from Moyvane, a serious talent, but he worked all over the world and would die tragically in a car accident in Guatemala just over three years later.) Seconds after Paddy's effort drifted wide, Karl Lacey kicked a score at the other end for Donegal.

It was, literally, that fine a line between winning and losing that day. But we went home to Kerry, tails between our legs again, everyone telling us that we'd just been beaten by Gaelic football's future.

And I remember thinking 'Fucking hell, if we'd only half got our act together, history could have been written differently . . .'

17

Behind Closed Doors

I used to envy Darragh Ó Sé's gift for *ráiméis* and convincing people that he was taking them into confidence.

If I'd run a mile from fellas asking me about Kerry training, Darragh would almost invite them to pull up a stool. 'C'mere, don't say anything now . . .' he'd say before drenching them with a bucket of bull. 'Tomás isn't moving well at all, he won't be on at the weekend. But don't say it to anyone now!'

It might be just someone he'd met in the street, now walking away with what they regarded as confidential information.

Of course, Tomás would play the following Sunday, and most probably a blinder too. And if the chap he'd just confided in ever pulled up Darragh on giving him a bum steer, the standard wide-eyed response would always be 'But sure you surely didn't tell anyone? I told you not to . . .'

Gossip has always been gold dust in Kerry. Having a fresh line about what might be going on in training gives a man status. He knows his stuff, in other words. It might just be a simple 'David Moran was moving much better last night' and he'll have people's attention instantly.

But one of the first decisions Eamonn Fitzmaurice made when he replaced Jack O'Connor as Kerry manager was to close the gates of Fitzgerald Stadium to the public. And that went down like a lead balloon. In Killarney especially, where there'd been a long tradition on warm summer evenings of people walking up the hill to Kerry training.

In hindsight, it was a huge, ballsy thing for Eamonn to do.

Attending training nights had nearly become an institution for people (even tourists) and I remember, personally, feeling a little sympathy at the time for diehards like Jimmy O'Brien and Johnny Culloty, men who'd have been up there every night without fail. But the flow of people in and out of training meant a commensurate flow of information. Eamonn just felt that if he was trying anything different, we'd hardly be out of the showers by the time people were hearing about it in Cork or Tyrone or Dublin.

He tried to explain his position, but not many were inclined to listen. And he took an awful lot of flak on Radio Kerry particularly. I remember listening in one night and the gist of what people were saying was that access to county training was essentially a part of Kerry culture. In other words, in closing the gates, Eamonn was betraying his own.

He'd known that was coming and, to be fair to him, never flinched.

His message to us was simple: 'If anyone's giving it to ye in the neck over this, just tell them it was my decision. I'll take whatever shite is coming.'

Eamonn's point was that you wouldn't get into Carrington to watch Manchester United train or Melwood to watch Liverpool. With the gates open, there was nothing to stop someone coming into Fitzgerald Stadium and videoing an entire session. And with the game becoming increasingly tactical, it just didn't make any sense for us to be an open book.

So there were ructions for a while, people stopping players in the street, maybe saying they had relatives coming down with children from Tipperary or Galway just hoping to meet Donaghy or get a signature from Darragh and, now, even that small privilege was being denied. And I'd be there all 'I know, I know, 'tis hard on people all right. But sure that's Eamonn!'

One year later, roughly a week before Kerry's All-Ireland final against Donegal, someone would be spotted perched in a tree in the grounds of St Finian's Hospital, which overlooks Fitzgerald Stadium. They scarpered the moment they were seen and we heard little else about it, apart from rumours that the culprit turned out to be Kerry based but with Donegal connections.

What's that I said about Kerry and gossip?

I was late back to the 2013 National League and it was only when myself and Paul Galvin were introduced as a double substitution with maybe twenty minutes to go against Cork in Tralee at the end of March that I got an inkling of what Eamonn had in mind for me.

'Paul, you go to ten,' he said. 'Colm, you go to eleven.'

We were under real pressure in that League and would only avoid relegation by winning our last three games.

The Tuesday after beating Cork, we flew to Portugal for a week's training. And from the moment we touched down I just felt ridiculously sharp. My eye was in, my handling was on the money. My fitness wasn't as far behind the others as I had imagined it would be. In camp we'd do two or three sessions a day that would really test you.

Early on we played a full fifteen v. fifteen game and, in my head, I was on what would have been perceived as the B team. That didn't surprise me at all. The way I read it, the other fifteen would almost certainly be the starting team for our next League game against Tyrone in Omagh. The challenge for the rest of us was to try to make the subs.

Anyway, I started at 11 again, played really well and just felt myself moving with a different energy. I'd played centre-forward for Crokes before and, if I'm honest, felt excited at the idea of being reinvented in a Kerry jersey now. If I'd been playing at 13, I'm not sure that same energy would have been in my body.

It came to the last game of the camp and again I felt incredibly sharp, scoring, setting up plays, winning breaks, tracking back, turning over ball, just ticking all the boxes. As we finished up and lads were heading to the showers, Eamonn told me to hang back.

'How are you feeling?' he asks.

'Fine. A little bit tired after the week, but happy enough.'

And he grins at me. 'Happy enough?'

Then he tells me that on the basis of what they've seen, they feel there's no option but to start me in Omagh.

I mount an unconvincing protest. 'Right, right . . . I haven't played or trained much though—'

'Never mind that,' Eamonn interrupts, 'you've done enough over here for me to see that you're ready.'

So we went to Omagh for a game both teams needed to win and my form stayed with me. I was on Joe McMahon, a good player, but someone who'd have much preferred marking me in the more confined spaces of the full-back line. I was just too nimble for him at centre-forward, making darts out left and right, getting balls off Donaghy, stepping back, picking passes.

I'd say when Tyrone saw me listed at 11, their view would have been that it was only bullshit. But now our secret was out.

We won by a point, preserving our Division One status and, essentially, bouncing into the Championship in high spirits. Tipperary (seventeen points) and Waterford (twenty-six points) were then overcome in Munster almost without breaking sweat, and next up, on 7 July, we had Cork on the ropes in a Killarney Munster final only to let them back into it.

We should have been out the gate at half-time but, I don't know, was it carelessness? In the end we pretty much just fell over the line. A roasting-hot day, the tar melting on the roads, and we seemed to run out of gas.

Cork had pulled a few familiar stunts like bringing in Noel O'Leary to yank Galvin's tail, and with me now out the field, Graham Canty picked up Donnchadh Walsh. My marker for the day was James Loughrey. A good, energetic, athletic player, but I was named Man of the Match (pretty fortuitously I'd have to say). So this experiment at 11 was gathering steam.

Our tradition of sloppy All-Ireland quarter-final performances was then suitably honoured with a laboured, unspectacular 0-15 to 0-9 victory over Cavan. And that was when Dublin came back into our lives.

There's a lot made of my first-half performance in that All-Ireland semi-final. We played brilliantly as a team, scored three goals and went in at the half-time break leading 3-5 to 1-9. Our first goal, netted in the seventh minute by James O'Donoghue, still draws a lot of compliments to this day. Personally, I don't regard it as anything quite as spectacular as it is generally conveyed.

Basically I took possession in the centre-forward position and, seeing two Dublin players advance towards me, took a step back, just to buy myself half a second. When two defenders are rushing forward it has to mean there's someone free inside. And, if that someone caught my eyeline, I felt sure that I could make the pass.

In this instance, Donnchadh Walsh did. I picked him out and his pass put James in for a classy finish into Stephen Cluxton's left corner. I'd later pick out Donnchadh with a similar pass for another goal, and he was pulled down for the penalty that brought our third. Looking back, I don't think he ever quite got the credit he deserved that day for the intelligence of his running between the lines.

So we played really well against the Dubs, looked extremely dangerous going forward. But then they hit us with a sickening sucker-punch.

The sides were level with two minutes to go when a ball fell into Kevin McManamon's hands and, miskicking for a point, it looped in over Brendan Kealy's head for a Dublin goal. We were still trying to shake the shock from our system when Eoghan O'Gara blasted another one in off the underside of the crossbar to send Hill 16 into raptures.

We were shattered. Pundits waxed lyrical afterwards about it being one of the greatest games of the modern age and everywhere we turned people were telling us the final seven-point winning margin didn't even go close to telling the truth. They were trying to make us feel better, to humour us in the face of desperate frustration.

And they were failing. We'd given a massive performance, but that performance hadn't been good enough.

And, for Kerry, there's never been any consolation in failure.

18

'We Can Fix You, But . . .'

I'm lying on the ground in Portlaoise and Kieran O'Leary reckons he knows how to get me straight back up on my feet.

He goes appealing to my vanity. 'It went over the bar, Gooch!' he says, leaning low.

Kieran doesn't realize that a bomb has just exploded in my body, that every last molecule of me feels cold in a way I've never experienced before. Not just my knee, everything. It's as if the circulation has stopped, and I'm hanging on to our physio, Jana, like a drowning man clinging to a lifebelt.

'Just give me a second,' I plead.

'Yeah, give him a second,' repeats Vince Casey, our manager. Vince reckons I might be winded, that I'm just looking to catch a breath. Like Kieran, he's never seen me down for any longer than it takes to tie a bootlace.

But my whole system feels as if it's gone into shock here, into complete shutdown. And the knee? I'd swear I heard a little pop as Tom Cunniffe and me collided. Then there was this sudden shock wave of pain.

Oh sweet Jesus.

The medics are fussing without yet being certain, but they can see I'm white as a bed sheet. Kieran's still standing there.

'No, I'm fucked here, Kieran. I'm in trouble.' Even my vanity won't get me up on my feet.

It's the middle of February 2014, we're a quarter of the way through Dr Crokes' All-Ireland Club semi-final against Castlebar Mitchels, and a whole host of little presumptions I've always made about myself now lie in the grass like a spilled jigsaw. Technically, I've just ruptured a cruciate, the impact – I'll later learn – fracturing my knee cap as if it had been hit by rifle fire.

But before the misery comes the foolishness.

I walk to the dressing-room, thinking something miraculous might come my way here if I hedge my bets long enough. No need for a stretcher, boys. This is me, remember. I'm not some-one made of flesh and bone. I'm unbreakable. But in that room, the self-delusion fairly quickly runs out of road.

I look over at Dr Donal Kavanagh as they sit me up on a table.

'Donal, you're going to have to give me something here for the pain.'

Fuck, fuck, *fuck*.

Deep down I'm every bit as conceited as the next man and there's more than a ligament in my knee just after rupturing here. There's a badge of honour gone. Since making my debut with Kerry in '02 I've never missed a Championship game. Seventy-odd days on duty without a sick note.

I've never spoken about this to anyone, but that record meant nearly as much to me as an All-Ireland medal. I was supposed to be too small, too weak to play for Kerry, remember. Maybe not fast enough. You look at what the game has become today, all the gym work, the protein shakes, the winters spent bulking up for a summer bull-run, and all the negatives thrown at me from the start should have become multiplied a thousand times.

And yet I'd become the indestructible one. The one who kept togging out.

Here's the thing. I'd overtaken Mike Sheehy's Kerry scoring record the year before and enjoyed the banter that that watershed brought my way. But the distinction that really meant something to me was this largely invisible one. Nobody knew how proud I was of that record. My brothers didn't know, my best friends didn't know, the Dr Crokes lads didn't know. I just internalized it.

I kept thinking 'Imagine if I could go through my whole county career without missing a single Championship game. I'll be forever defined as a tough Kerry fucker!'

There'd been a bit of an adductor tear at the end of '03, but no big deal. I went to Gerry McEntee in the off-season and got back playing without much fuss. There'd been that League game against Monaghan in 2010 and a finger accidentally going in my eye. Nasty, but just a few weeks out of action.

Medals, All-Stars, scoring records – all these things are brilliant. But, trust me, when you've grown up to the sound of tongues clucking about how you might get killed out there, being considered a tough Kerry fucker would feel like a very personal kind of triumph. I started playing for Kerry the same time as Marc Ó Sé but passed him out in Championship appearances when he was struck down for a couple of games with glandular fever.

We'd be tossing the numbers over and back in the dressing-room.

'How many are you on now?'

'Seventy-five.'

'Yeah, I'm on seventy-one.'

Marc hadn't a clue what that record meant to me. Nobody had. Maybe I hadn't even fully understood it myself. Until now.

That day in Portlaoise, I went back out to watch the second half, Castlebar easing away to win by eight points. Devastating. We'd reckoned we were the best Dr Crokes team ever to leave Killarney. Would we ever see that stage again? I sat on my own the whole way home. First time I'd ever boarded a bus with crutches. Usual seat. Second last, left side, window. Always the same with Crokes, same with Kerry. Nobody said much, most lads taking refuge behind headphones.

FUCK, FUCK, FUCK.

Ed Harnett, the Kerry physio, rang while bags were still being tossed in underneath.

'What's the story?'

I wasn't in much of a mood to talk and gave him the bare facts. I'd say he could tell from my lack of chat that I was in trouble here.

'OK,' he said. 'Regardless of how you feel, you've to be in Santry Monday morning, nine a.m.'

Back in Killarney, there was nothing that made any sense now other than slipping away for a quiet pint. It's not ideal mixing alcohol with strong painkillers, but the alternative was going home and spending a night just staring at the walls. So I headed down the street to McSweeney's where myself and our chairman, Ger 'Granny' O'Shea, settled down wordlessly on two high stools.

And there we sat like ghosts, staring at our pints of Guinness.

A few people came over asking about the knee, but I suppose our body language didn't encourage them to linger. The arse had fallen out of our world here.

Darran O'Sullivan drove me to Santry that Monday. We lived in the same Killarney estate, would be close buddies, and the six a.m. departure didn't faze him. The whole way up we just tip-toed around the story brewing. He's Manchester United, I'm Liverpool. That made it easy to fill the spaces.

But I have this vivid memory just as we left the M7, swinging left towards the airport, and this feeling of sudden panic coming over me. As if the gravity of my predicament was beginning to hit home. Somehow, Darran seemed to sense it too. He started giving me this positive spin about how a little break could be the best thing in the world. That I could just take the League off and be totally fresh for Championship.

'Right now, I'd take your hand off for six to eight weeks,' I told him. 'A medial ligament I could cope with.'

What I didn't realize was that Eamonn Fitzmaurice happened to be in Dublin that day and, as I sat in Ray Moran's office waiting for the news of the scan just taken, he'd be outside with Darran in the waiting area. Pretty quickly I could sense I wouldn't be going out to them with good news. Just something in Ray's expression as he was looking at the screen.

Eventually, the silence broke.

'Look Colm, I can't really dress this up any other way, you've done your cruciate. But, unfortunately, there's another few bits. We can fix you, but . . .' He stopped in mid-sentence, excused himself and said he'd be back in a minute.

And I sat there, trying to decode the language.

Another few bits . . .

Then he returned and became specific. 'Look, it's a little more complicated now because there's also a fracture.'

The blood clearly drained from my face because Ray asked me if I was OK. I lied that I was. He said they'd operate on the fracture first, the cruciate maybe six weeks later. Any questions? I had.

'Can we bring Eamonn in now and tell him exactly what you've told me?'

Now Eamonn Fitz is a master at keeping his emotions in check but I'd noticed some time ago that he had this habit of touching his nose when something was bothering him. And, sure enough, up the hand went to his face now. I could tell he was rattled. I mean he'd just lost the likes of Paul Galvin, Tomás Ó Sé and Eoin Brosnan to retirement, now I was gone for the year.

He must have been sitting there thinking 'What more fucking bad luck can be coming my way?'

But, of course, nobody really says what they're actually thinking at that kind of moment. Ray assured me that they'd take care of me and, as if on reflex, Eamonn replied, 'Yeah, whatever it takes, just get this man right.'

Bad news doesn't drag its heels, and we hadn't reached Newlands Cross when the story of my cruciate was already breaking on national radio.

Darran tried recycling it as a small blessing. 'Fuck it, you can relax and enjoy your summer for once.' But I was having none of that. My way is always to cling on to the percentages. If the theory was that I'd be out of commission for six months, who was to say I wouldn't make it back in four? If I'd been Mr Indestructible for the previous twelve years, mightn't I have better healing qualities than most now?

I was being naive, but I had nothing else to cling to here.

And then I thought that, of all the busted cruciates Ray Moran must have seen in his life, there can't have been many X-rays that sent him off in search of a radiographer for a second opinion. Fuck, this had to be bad.

That Friday my sister Geraldine brought me back to Dublin, and before being administered the third general anaesthetic of my life, Ray got me to sign the requisite waiver. He said that they wouldn't be certain how much they could get done until the knee had actually been cut open. 'So if we do find something else . . .'

And I'm lying there, saying, 'Of course, just do whatever ye have to do.'

I was under the knife for about three hours in the end for a procedure that should, normally, take about fifty minutes. Geraldine and Karen were beginning to fret in the waiting room. Apparently, the anaesthetist had to give me an extra dose while I was on the table as I'd started to come round.

I felt absolutely rotten when I did wake up and remember thinking 'How the fuck am I going to do this again in six weeks' time?'

Ray left it till the following morning to see me, while doing his daily rounds. I was still half groggy as he was talking. 'It was great to get it all done in one go,' he said. Turns out he'd done the cruciate too.

The relief on hearing that was huge, but there was a flip side. They kept me in for seven nights, determined to keep a close eye on me because some of the surgery had been so complex. Ray just didn't want me putting any kind of stress on the knee and, I suppose, worried I couldn't be trusted if left to my own devices at home.

So I had a week of just lying on a bed in Santry, doing little else but watching Sky Sports.

For a time, the room almost became my very own bachelor pad, visitors just sitting watching matches with me, conversation drifting to just about anything but the obvious. On the surface, I was fine. Underneath, I was struggling.

For the first couple of days I couldn't lift myself out of bed because the knee was held in a rigid brace. Couldn't even manoeuvre myself over to get my hands on a crutch. The nights felt endless and, with my stomach struggling to handle the medication, I became more and more frustrated. The staff couldn't have done enough for me, but I just wasn't comfortable pressing the button so often for assistance.

This girl's going to get so sick of me . . .

Eventually all I wanted to do was get back to my own house. To pull the front door behind me and get on with rehab. But getting home would be just the beginning of my problems.

I think it was my third day back in Killarney when I finally hit rock bottom.

The assumption had been that, given my compromised condition, I'd settle back in under my mother's roof and be waited on hand and foot. But I wanted my own space. I wanted independence. Once I was able to get up and down the stairs on crutches there was no real need for me to be anywhere but my own place. I could still go to Mam's to be fed.

It might sound strange, but there's a kind of euphoria that kicks in when you go home initially. Unfortunately, it doesn't linger. My memory of that third morning is of nobody being around, and I'm sitting on the couch, my leg up. I lift the blanket, have a look down, and what I see is like the leg of a grand piano.

Everything is so swollen it's just unimaginable that I'll ever play football again. And I'm thinking 'You can't turn this around. Dress it up whatever way you want, Gooch, there's no way you're going to get back playing football from this.' The possibility of being able to do a simple exercise like jumping on to a coffee table and off again seemed a million miles away.

This would be the toughest time. An incredible loneliness set in. There seemed no light, no future. It was the first time I remember thinking 'Maybe I'm never going to play again'. All the best wishes in the world counted for nothing at that moment.

Tears began streaming down my face, and that's just not me. Generally, I just don't get overemotional about things. But this injury was pitching me into a place I just wasn't sure I had the tools to cope with. All I could think at that moment was that I was in deep, deep trouble now. My body was being physically tested, but I was slowly beginning to understand that, if anything, my mind was being tested even more. I couldn't see the light.

Now I know that, in hindsight especially, those words probably seem a little melodramatic and self-important. When you think of the burdens some people carry in their lives, a footballer coping with a knee injury is pretty small beer. Trust me, I understand that.

But it was beginning to dawn on me that I'd become completely defined as a person by my ability to play football. Nobody ever identified me as 'Colm Cooper'. It was always 'the Kerry footballer Colm "Gooch" Cooper'. And that day at home alone I just became completely swamped by self-pity.

It wasn't bitterness, as such. It wasn't a case of 'Why me?' This stuff happens to people, I understood that. You see it every day on television, in the newspapers.

But my sense of invincibility had suddenly been stolen. My record of never missing a Championship for Kerry was about to go. And the word that kept echoing in my head was 'Fuck, fuck, fuck . . .'

To begin with I couldn't drive, of course. The leg had to stay in that rigid brace for six to eight weeks because of the fracture, so any work on rehabbing the cruciate had to wait. Psychologically, that was really difficult. It meant two months of doing nothing and, inevitably, wastage in the leg. I'd be starting from a desperately low base when the time came to build up flexibility again. Just bending the knee would prove a major ordeal.

Eamonn was determined to keep my spirits up and encouraged me to start doing my rehab work at Kerry training sessions just so I'd still feel part of the scene. I said no. I just didn't want to be a distraction. 'I can be of absolutely no help to ye,' I told him. 'There's no point in me being there until that changes.'

What I did ask was to go in the occasional night to use the

physios while the lads were out on the field. One of those physios, Ger Keane, should have got an award for the amount of work he did with me. Early morning gym and pool sessions in The Europe Hotel became the norm. He'd also come to my house in the evenings, maybe three times a week, to manipulate the knee. The World Cup was on during that time. It might be ten when he'd arrive and we'd be watching the late kick-off from Brazil as he went to work.

Once the brace came off, I had a problem straight away. You see, my legs have always been the strongest part of my body. People always saw me as small but it was often a joke in the dressing-room about how my legs looked so strong they were almost out of proportion with the rest of my body. 'Fuck lads, look at the size of his quads!'

Now, straight away, I could see the wastage.

But that wasn't the real challenge. The real challenge was trying to get it to bend again. The more I tried, the less progress I seemed to make. And the pain was unrelenting.

Gradually, I began to wonder if something had gone wrong with the surgery. Or maybe I had done something to it since that I shouldn't have. Ed Harnett and Ger seemed to be working overtime for absolutely minimal gains. For the whole of May it felt as if we were getting nowhere.

By the first week of June we were all agreed that something just wasn't quite right. It was decided that I needed to go back to Santry again for another procedure under Ray Moran. To this day, only Eamonn and the physios know that this happened. I especially didn't want the news to get out in Kerry where, straight away, I knew people would start writing my retirement story.

Ray was extremely reassuring, saying he knew exactly what needed to be done. The problem was simply that to do it without an anaesthetic would be excruciating. Until then I'd been telling the physios to stop, that I simply couldn't cope with the pain. Other lads would be waiting in line to get a rub and, deep down, I knew they were looking at me thinking the worst. 'Poor Gooch is fucked, he's getting nowhere. The surgery hasn't worked.' I suspected even the physios themselves had begun feeling awkward around me. We'd be in Fitzgerald Stadium and I'd be almost crying with the pain, getting nowhere. The lads would be measuring the flexibility and, almost always, the figures were deflating. After a while I just didn't want anyone else around while we were working. Didn't want my struggles in full view.

So I headed back to Dublin hugely apprehensive about the implications of being knocked out again. And I was especially wary of the visit getting out, thinking of the gloomy headlines it would trigger.

But everything was done discreetly and, immediately, there was a massive improvement. There wasn't even any pain when I came round, which was simply unbelievable. I was kept there for two days because Ray wanted to get me in the gym, and by the following Tuesday I was a different person heading into physio in Fitzgerald Stadium.

The leg was stiff, but we'd gained maybe another thirty degrees of flexibility. Massive. Now the boys were able to manipulate away without me screaming. Ray Moran had somehow worked the miracle that he'd promised.

19

'Go Home, Dude'

The All-Ireland about to come Kerry's way was nowhere to be seen (or even imagined) in the early summer of 2014.

On 22 June I travelled up to our Munster Championship opener against Clare in Ennis with Brian McMahon, a Crokes lad and a good friend of mine, stopping off in Garvey's in Newcastlewest for tea and a bar of chocolate. I felt a little awkward meeting Kerry supporters there, with their polo shirts and coloured ribbons, most of them inclined to tell me how strange it was seeing me in jeans on match day.

All the customary questions began spilling my way.

Will they do it?

How are they moving?

Is there a big summer in them?

The assumption that I'd have the inside track was understandable, but unfounded. I'd been going into training all right, but still just doing my own thing. That said, after the second surgery in Santry, I could see some of the lads were taken aback by the scale of my improvement now. From not being able to bend the knee one week, I was now doing trampoline jumps, stepping on and off boxes, doing the ladder shuttle, kicking balls even. They'd be having their training matches while I was doing all of this on the line or behind a goal. Every night they trained, I was there. Pushing. Suddenly, I'd say my progress made no sense to them. From almost not wanting to be even in their vicinity, I could now see light at the end of the tunnel. I was feeling far less of an impostor.

But I hadn't been asking too many questions of Darran or the others. To some degree, the training ground is sacred to me in that regard. A private place. My own family would often get frustrated with my reflex secrecy whenever they'd ask me stuff about training. Eventually, one of the brothers might become exasperated.

'Fuck sake Colm, we're not asking you for the third shaggin' Secret of Fatima here!'

In the car now, Brian did most of the talking. It felt more comfortable that way. Easier for him to speculate that so-and-so might struggle than for me to say it. That's just me, I suppose. Still closed, even to those I would actually trust the most.

We had to drive two laps of the town to find a parking spot that would facilitate a quick exit and, of course, all of this was new to me. The complications of civilian life. The logistics of it. Parking on the day of a Kerry match hadn't been an issue for me in over twelve years. I felt like a fish out of water.

My hope was to remain as anonymous as possible, slipping around the back of the stand in Cusack Park and picking a perch up against the back wall. A few people recognized me. But it was all good stuff. Well intentioned.

How are ya Gooch?
Look after yourself!
The lads will miss ya!
Whatever is in me, I didn't really want to engage. I suppose you

just get tired of having the same conversation, over and over. Saying the same things. Just wanted to watch the game and point the car for home again as quickly as possible. Just leave myself and Brian do what we'd call our 'forensic analysis' on the way home.

Anyway, Kerry won, but were poor. There was much to ponder.

I remember the week before the Munster final watching an As v. Bs game in Killarney and thinking that Eamonn's jigsaw was a long way from completion. Nothing looked settled. Nobody seemed to be nailing their place down. Usually at that time of year there might be one or two positions up for grabs in the Kerry team. In this case, it seemed there could be six or seven.

I was sitting there with Patrick O'Sullivan, the gates around us closed. The more football being played, the cloudier the picture. And I turned to him: 'Jesus, Patrick, I can't see the team they're going to pick here, can you?'

He couldn't.

The only positive I could see in Kerry that evening was that the players were in great physical shape. But there was no team and, worse, I couldn't detect any chemistry or balance. It seemed to me that the more Eamonn searched for solutions, the further away from them he was getting.

Then they went down to Páirc Uí Chaoimh and pulled a performance out of nowhere.

The build-up to that game had been all about Cork. It would be their last Munster final before the old stadium was bulldozed and all the indications were that they wanted to sign off in the best way imaginable, by giving Kerry a good hiding. The view nationwide would have been that they had a decent chance of doing just that. The consensus was that, with so many of Kerry's older heads now gone, we just wouldn't have the toughness to get out of Cork with a victory.

So pretty much nobody saw it coming. Kerry 0-24, Cork 0-12, James O'Donoghue scoring 0-8 from play.

I had a few pints in Killarney that night with some of the players and you could sense a profound mood change. From being all over the shop, from nobody giving them a prayer of being at the business end of things, now they were contenders. I could read it in them. That's how things work in Kerry. One good day can transform the county mindset. Why? Because we always believe that, given momentum, anything becomes possible for a Kerry team.

The next week, Eamonn suggested I rejoin the group. He's a clever guy and reads situations really well. 'Look, we see you in there every night, you've taken huge strides. It will be good for us to have you back and I think it will benefit you too.'

He knew the situation with my mother, of course. We'd never spoken about it but, by now, things were getting pretty desperate at home. Mam would actually pass away a couple of weeks after that conversation.

So I probably needed Kerry more than Kerry needed me. Because I was doing exactly what I tend to do in those situations: going into a shell.

Mam was buried on a Saturday morning and, of course, cousins descended upon Killarney from every corner of the country for her funeral. There was a meal afterwards and I stayed for an hour, but that was as much as I could manage. I remember thinking 'No, this just isn't for me now . . .'

It wouldn't be my form to leave people like that. In different circumstances, with family around, I'd always like to stay and have a couple of pints. But this time I couldn't. I'd only been just about able to do it when Dad died; this time I needed to be in my own bubble. I didn't want to be in an environment where it was expected that I be open to people. Because I couldn't be.

I needed the space to be alone with my thoughts now.

So I went home and took myself off for a long walk. I remember sitting down that evening to watch the Donegal–Armagh All-Ireland quarter-final on the TV. Next thing, Darran rang, just checking in to see my form.

'Jesus, I thought you'd be out with the lads for a few beers.'

'No, didn't have any interest, had to come away.'

The two of us have the kind of relationship where we can call in on each other at any time of day. So he invited himself over for a cup of tea and we sat there watching the game, little enough conversation flowing back or forth. In many ways, I had tuned out.

'Is there training tomorrow?' I asked him almost absent-mindedly out of the blue.

Darran nearly choked on his tea. 'Fuck it, you've no business up there tomorrow!'

What he didn't know was that I had every business. Right there, right then, just about the only thoughts keeping me sane were football thoughts.

'Do you know what?' I said. 'I might shoot away up. The bit of training might be good for my mind.'

And that's what I did.

I remember coming in the tunnel of Fitzgerald Stadium the following morning, bag over my shoulder, everyone's eyebrows arched at the sight of me. And I'm all 'How ye doin' lads?' Trying to feign normality. Business as usual. I could feel the room staring back at me as I put on the boots. Lads wondering where my head was.

True, I didn't re-engage fully to begin with. I still had my individual programme to follow. But then one or two lads came over for a bit of kicking. And that was it. Without any formalities, I just slipped back into it. Back in the group again, a squad member, albeit a million miles from playing.

When I look back now, one man I owe a huge debt of gratitude to is Denis O'Callaghan, my manager in AIB at the time. Through all the ups and downs of rehab, he gave me tremendous support, without which the ordeal I faced would have been so much tougher.

We'd beaten Galway comfortably in our All-Ireland quarter-final, and that was the evening Martin McHugh went on *The Sunday Game*, branding me a 'two-trick pony'. I didn't see it myself. I was having a pint with a few of the players in Killarney when, next thing, the phone started buzzing in my pocket. Twitter, it seemed, was in meltdown.

We had just arrived into Scotts when somebody announced McHugh had had 'a pop' and was able to show us the segment on their phones.

I think Martin had been extolling the virtues of James O'Donoghue when, seemingly to stress how much more he was bringing to the Kerry table than I ever did, he came out with that description.

Maybe he just didn't express himself properly, but I thought it was a cheap shot. I'd no problem him saying James was better than me – everybody's entitled to their opinion. But to call me the one thing that I've never been, to suggest I had only two ways of beating an opponent – well, to be honest, I thought it was absolute nonsense.

Actually, I didn't think much of the comment on any level.

Firstly, knowing I was sidelined for a year through injury, I'd have thought he'd have had a little more consideration for what I was going through. Secondly, the description was clearly ignorant.

Why did he say it?

I can't honestly say. It strikes me that some people almost

overstretch themselves when they sit in front of a TV camera, that their intention is – above all – just to get themselves noticed. They seek controversy because, if they can generate that, they're more likely to be asked back.

My abiding memory of the Galway victory is a really frustrated Kieran Donaghy back in the Croke Park Jurys hotel after. Star was flogging himself, but just not getting a look-in. And I'm there, telling him to 'hang tough' even though I'd no real idea if he was even figuring in Eamonn's thoughts.

You'd have got some odds of him winning his third All-Star at that point and I've often thought since that I couldn't really have blamed him that evening if he'd told me where to stuff my fucking coaching manual positivity.

But Donaghy and I are tight.

People talked about him and me having an almost telepathic relationship on the field, but I've always loved his company off the field too.

We kept the same ritual on the team bus, sitting down the back, opposite sides, maybe Barry John Keane playing the rogue. There's actually a bit of Donaghy himself in Barry John, which is probably why he could wind him up so mercilessly.

A wink at me, then the pin removed from the hand grenade.

'Donaghy?' he'd ask, with the big wide eyes of an altar boy. 'LeBron is the best player ever in the NBA, isn't he?'

Knowing Kieran was a worshipper of Michael Jordan, this was paraffin on a bonfire.

Donaghy would even know he was being wound up, but just couldn't help himself. He'd enter the debate.

'No, just look at the numbers.'

'Look at the amount of rings Jordan has won.'

'There's no comparison, man.'

And that's when Barry John would go back for more paraffin.

Might leave it for a minute, but only for theatrical effect. Then he'd throw again.

'Ah he is, Donaghy, LeBron's better than them all.'

And Donaghy, half laughing, nearly ready to pull Barry John's hair out by the roots, would be reduced to an exasperated 'Barry, what the fuck do you know about basketball?'

Another day it might be Kieran O'Leary doing the wind-up. Wouldn't have a clue about basketball.

'Donaghy,' he'd say, 'is Larry Bird still playing?'

And that's when you'd almost see the smoke coming out of Star's ears. 'Would you just shut up to fuck!'

You know, I could always chat sincerely to him about the game, but then I was genuinely interested. Like when I was a teenager, those Saturday nights down in Presentation Gym when maybe Liam McHale and Ballina were in town or some cool black cat like Deora Marsh, they were nights I'll always treasure.

There was such a buzz around the game back then. Every club had two Americans and those Americans, almost always black, would have hero status in provincial towns. The pre-season speculation about what Americans might be coming was almost as thrilling as the season itself.

Niall 'Botty' O'Callaghan, a current selector with Dr Crokes, was a big part of St Paul's at the time and always seemed to have the inside story. 'Oh there's this fella coming from the University of Phoenix . . .'

But you could just toss out a basketball name to Donaghy and he'd give you an instant spiel. A pocket biography. His knowledge of the game is almost encyclopaedic. I might actually have played a bit against him in First Year, but basketball was never my dream. For people like himself and Micheál Quirke, it unequivocally was.

Around Christmas of '07, Kerry went on a team holiday to San

Francisco, Hawaii and Los Angeles. We were in San Fran one night, drinking late, when, with the bar closing, we were asking directions to another watering hole. And down this street we were sent in not the most salubrious of districts.

At some point I began drifting away from the others and ended coming upon a few locals sitting on a wall, a basketball court directly opposite and a ball at their feet. It's around two a.m. now, but all I can see is the court. So I'm there, giving it socks.

'C'mon,' I say, 'I'll take on any of ye!'

I make no reference to the court across the street, just keep delivering the same challenge: 'C'mon, c'mon, any of ye up to it?'

This goes on for a couple of minutes, their expressions growing more hostile all the time. They're telling me to 'go home, dude'. Next thing, Donaghy spots me down this side street, comes loping over and, just like I did, sees the basketball hoop before he says anything.

'Right boys, two on two, let's go,' he says with that Donaghy smile.

The penny drops.

And suddenly they're all cool-cat smiles, telling this big beanpole to take his crazy red-haired friend out of this neighbourhood before someone else falls under the impression that he's squaring for a fight.

Of course, the following day, I'm the story that keeps on giving.

'Did ya hear about Gooch, trying to start a riot last night? Only for Donaghy, he'd have been roadkill!'

Six minutes of action from Kieran would transform a 2014 All-Ireland semi-final against Mayo that looked to be slipping away from us. There's probably not another footballer in the country who could change the terms of engagement so dramatically in a contest of that intensity by simply standing on the edge of the square and inviting team-mates to lamp ball in on top of him. But that's what Donaghy did.

And Mayo's heads almost melted at the impact.

We came from five points down to draw the game, and the night before the replay in the Gaelic Grounds on 30 August (Croke Park had been pre-booked for an American football game) we stayed in The Brehon Hotel, Killarney. It was a five p.m. Saturday throw-in and Eamonn just didn't want us hanging around Limerick for the whole day.

The next morning we had our team-meeting. The bags were being put on the bus and Eamonn came across to me.

'I want you to tog off today,' he said and, without another word, climbed on board.

I stood there speechless. I knew the man was under pressure, but was he losing the plot here? I was obviously not ready to play – he knew it, I knew it. Then I'm thinking 'He just wants me to participate in the warm-up. To be seen to be getting close. That's what he meant, right?'

Out on the pitch in Limerick before that warm-up I bumped into Mayo manager James Horan.

'How's the knee?' he asked.

'Yerrah, getting better James, but obviously taking a lot of time, and it'll take a lot more,' I said.

Next thing, he'll see me striding out, a jersey on my back, and I'm sure he's wondering am I acting the bollix here? Are Kerry pulling a stroke?

We went back in after that warm-up, and I was sitting next to Declan O'Sullivan. Thinking that that was my day done now. Eamonn had said nothing. Not a word. And I started taking off the boots.

'What are you fucking at?' asks Declan.

'That's me done,' I say.

'Oh fucking no way boy,' says Declan, 'that's not you done. Your thing is here!'

'What thing?'

'There's your jersey, number twenty-eight. Put it on now and fucking shape up a small bit!'

People might find this far-fetched, but that's exactly how the day unspooled for me. With Declan O'Sullivan, a tough, tough Kerryman, a brilliant footballer, a guy I'd been playing with in Kerry colours since the age of fourteen, giving me this look that pretty much said, 'Grow a pair now and get on with it!'

Next thing, Eamonn said his last few words and we were galloping out into the August sun.

And still, I knew nothing. Well, that's not strictly true. I knew I wasn't a listed substitute because the playing squad had to be submitted in midweek. My name wasn't on the match programme. But, still, there was only uncertainty in my head.

He's not thinking of springing me here surely? I'm a million miles from ready.

What I did know was that I couldn't go to him and ask. How could I? An All-Ireland semi-final, everything on the line for Kerry, and I'm asking questions about myself? No, just couldn't happen. So I felt a back-seat passenger in all of this. But just being there, just being a part of things again . . . it felt fantastic. I could sense a buzz in the crowd at seeing me togged too. It was a very warm evening and none of us were wearing tracksuit tops. So we're in the blue jerseys and I'm out there, kicking frees in front of nearly 50,000 people. And it's as if all anybody can see are those two digits on my back. Number 28.

He'd never chance him, would he?

He didn't.

It took extra-time to separate the teams and the emotion of

Kerry people at the end told you everything about what it meant to us. Players and supporters were euphoric. From a season that looked to be promising nothing, we were back in the All-Ireland final. And I don't know why, but something persuaded me to sprint across to Eamonn and have a quiet word in his ear.

'There's a final to be won here!' I said. 'Make sure fellas remember that!'

And, with that, I took myself away into the relative quiet of the dressing-room.

We love our gossip in Kerry and, after edging out Mayo, the rumours went into overdrive about me having a chance of figuring against Donegal in the final.

The truth?

Three days after the Mayo win, I went to Santry for a scan on the knee, Ray Moran telling me that everything looked 'fantastic'. Even better than he'd anticipated. He'd been getting reports throughout the previous weeks from Kerry's medical team and those reports seemed universally positive.

You won't believe what he did last night . . .

Everything Kerry asked me to do, I was doing now. And more. I was pushing every boundary. Strangely enough, even my kicking was on the money from the moment I'd started back. And, unknown to me, Eamonn and Ray had already had a conversation about me, potentially, having some kind of cameo involvement in the final. Given where I'd come from, that just seemed off the charts.

Looking back, I'm not sure how much was real and how much was designed just to keep my spirits up.

The Tuesday after the Mayo game, Eamonn rang me. 'Look, what you've been doing in the last few weeks is incredible,' he said. 'We've watched you and we don't really understand it. Who

Top: On the naughty step: Tomás and me, briefly looking in from the outside at the All-Ireland qualifier against Antrim, 26 July 2009.

Above: Bouncing back: getting to the ball ahead of Anthony Lynch as we avenge our defeat by Cork in the '09 Munster final by beating them in the All-Ireland final later that year.

Left: Redemption!

Above: 'That's my boy!' One of my favourite photos – celebrating with my mother after Dr Crokes won the County Final in 2010.

Below: Cavalry arriving: Séamus Scanlon and Bryan Sheehan coming to the rescue as things get heated with Cork's Derek Kavanagh and Noel O'Leary in the 2010 Munster semi-final.

Above left: No holds barred against Graham Canty in the 2011 Munster final, Killarney.

Above right: Taking care of business: captaining Kerry to Munster glory in my hometown, 2011.

Left: Suited and booted: All-Star evening, 21 October 2011, National Convention Centre, Dublin; *from left*: Darran O'Sullivan, myself, Marc Ó Sé and Bryan Sheehan.

Left: Eyes on the prize: rising high with Stephen Cluxton, National Football League Division 1, 26 February 2011, Dublin v. Kerry.

Below: Rush-hour traffic in Croker: surviving the press of Dublin's James McCarthy, Michael Fitzsimons and Cian O'Sullivan in the 2011 All-Ireland final.

Bottom: Perfect start: an early goal, just a pity we couldn't close the deal.

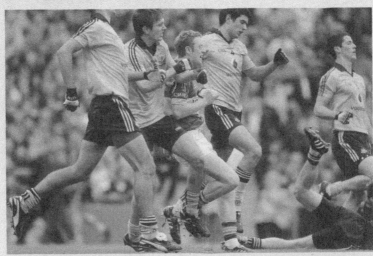

Above: Finally, a Championship win over Tyrone: in conversation with Jack O'Connor after the All-Ireland qualifier in Killarney, 21 July 2012.

Below: Broken: down and out with a cruciate injury; AIB All-Ireland Club Championship semi-final, Castlebar Mitchels, Mayo v. Dr Crokes in Portlaoise, 15 February 2014.

Above: Well done, big man: celebrating with Kieran Donaghy and physio Ger Keane after our victory over Donegal in the 2014 All-Ireland final.

Below left: Didn't think I'd see this day: getting my hands on Sam, 2014.

Below right: Pointing the way: in conversation with Eamonn Fitzmaurice during squad training, Killarney, 2015.

Left: Close encounters with Philly McMahon of Dublin, 2015 All-Ireland final.

Below: Whatever it takes: battling with Dublin's James McCarthy, Philly McMahon and Rory O'Carroll, 2015 All-Ireland final.

Below: A picture tells a thousand words: at the end of the 2015 All-Ireland final.

Top: We did it: Pat O'Shea and me at journey's end as Dr Crokes are crowned 2017 All-Ireland Club champions.

Above: Heaven on Earth – champions!

Left: Worth waiting for: lifting the Andy Merrigan Cup after the AIB All-Ireland Club final against Slaughtneil.

Right: Céitílís and me, 17 March 2017.

knows what could happen here? All I'll say is that I'm going to give you every opportunity between here and the final.'

Talk about giving a man a lift.

But I was nowhere near the pitch of what was going on. Maybe in my own head I was. I mean, I was doing things now that six months previously I feared I'd never be able to do again. And, maybe, this was becoming the fairytale in people's eyes. Mine especially. That if Kerry were five points up in the dying seconds, the idea of throwing me into the mix might carry some kind of symbolic meaning, given the rotten year I'd had.

I'll admit that that became the idea splashing around my head now. Thinking of Mam. Thinking of the tears on the couch. Jesus, what a way it would be to draw a line under the year.

We told nobody, though. The only ones privy to the conversation were Ray Moran, Eamonn and our physio, Ed Harnett. I didn't even tell any of the players. But from that Tuesday on my mindset was that of someone who'd be playing against Donegal. That's the way I prepared, ate, rested. In some ways it was hard to keep my emotions in check, to keep everything bottled up.

Because people were asking questions. They'd seen me out on the pitch in Limerick and wanted some kind of clarity on where I stood. And I just fobbed everybody off. Family included. 'Ah no, I'm just being brought along for the day . . .' That was my party line. Nobody outside the bubble knew what was going on in Kerry training now, so they'd no idea just how far I had progressed, that I was doing all the drills, albeit not involved in full physical contact.

Even that changed the Tuesday before the final. I played in the As v. Bs game, no holds barred, Pa Kilkenny marking me. I was centre-forward on the Bs. Now maybe Pa was told not to kill me, but I got through it intact. Scored a point. And, Jesus, it felt good. Eamonn had more or less said to me that if I got through that

Tuesday night OK and woke up Wednesday to a morning free of any repercussions, I'd have a chance of being in the twenty-six for Croke Park.

So, the session over, he came across to me.

'How was that?'

'Felt great!'

'That's good enough for me!'

At that moment, incredibly, I knew I could be – rightly or wrongly – in the Kerry match-day squad. And I'll admit, my thoughts were 100 per cent selfish. Someone else was obviously going to be missing out as a consequence. I could pretend here that that bothered me. But it didn't. I remember thinking 'Fuck it, I don't care. I just want to be in the middle of this.'

To this day I actually don't know who was omitted from the twenty-six because of my return. And I don't want to know. It's not a question I would ever put to Eamonn, and on the day I was given the number 28 shirt, so it was something that – largely – passed without people noticing.

In hindsight, the situation was pretty strange, pretty odd. But Lord God it gave me some lift spiritually.

Was it all just some kind of complex mind game from Eamonn? Was it his way of getting me to buy into the dynamic around the group? Was he possibly just trying to communicate something to the group itself? I can't answer any of those questions.

It's been said to me since that, above all, maybe he was just trying to spook Donegal. The week of the final I was driving somewhere and Jim McGuinness was being interviewed on the radio. Ordinarily I'd immediately switch channels in these circumstances, but for some reason I left it on. And the interviewer asked McGuinness if he thought that 'Colm Cooper might play'.

His response was 'I don't know, but it's something we'll have to plan for.'

When I heard that, I was thinking 'Jesus, maybe I'm going to get a run here. And if I am, I'd better make sure I'm fucking ready to go.'

We stayed in Dunboyne that weekend and I was rooming with Alan Fitzgerald, number 27. His first year on the squad and, no more than me, he didn't really know if he was going to be involved. And I remember saying to him, 'Whatever else we do this weekend, we'll prepare for this All-Ireland final as if we're fucking playing.'

And Alan's response was exactly what I wanted to hear: 'Damn right we will!'

So the two of us were wired to play. No messin', no fuckin' around. In my head I'd have a role to play against Donegal. It might be ten minutes, it might only be five, but I was on a war footing now. My attitude was 'This is fucking business!'

I'd seen members of extended panels before pretty much zone out of what needed to be done and treating the match like a week-end away. Or lads who might have been injured or suspended swanning around, acting the comedian, their brains locked into neutral. I didn't want that. So for Alan and myself there was no staying up, watching TV into the early hours. No acting the bollix down in the physios' room. There were medals to be won here and, irrespective of whether we saw game-time, we were going to be in the zone.

Looking back, I pretty much knew I was never in Eamonn's thoughts as a serious option. There was an understanding anyway that throwing me on as some kind of symbolic gesture mightn't be the wisest course given Dr Crokes might then put pressure on me to get stuck back into action with the club when in reality I simply wasn't ready. *You fuckin' played in the All-Ireland final, you can tog out for us now* . . . From a medical point of view it could have been disastrous for me to be pressured into a heavy Club Championship campaign when my body just wasn't ready.

So the deal was that if I did get on, it was to be seen simply as a one-off. But it was a deal that never needed signing.

The final was dour and tactical, a bruising game of chess, and certainly not one Heaven-sent for my kind of skill set. Eamonn knew we couldn't play our natural game against Donegal because we'd seen what they did to Dublin in the semi-final. They'd have liked nothing better than to invite us forward, then tear us asunder on the break.

Maybe there's an inherent arrogance in me saying this, but I always think we probably have greater tactical adaptability than any other team in the country. Why? Because we've such natural footballers. And if you've really natural footballers, you can tweak things tactically in just a matter of days.

It's true we'd never previously had to do it to quite the same extent, but we were really confident in our match-ups.

And Donaghy was now a key factor in everything we did. He'd started the replay against Mayo, causing havoc again on the edge of the square. And having transformed our season now, we knew Donegal were going to find him a major headache. Because Donaghy's a unique kind of presence. When he's hot, he's unplayable. Not just in size, but in the cleverness of his movement, the quickness of his hands. And when he's going well, his personality becomes infectious. Put it this way: whenever that man's smiling, it's as if the whole dressing-room is smiling with him.

But we knew too that with David Moran and Anthony Maher we were strong in midfield, where Donegal did so much damage to Dublin with clever flick-ons to the likes of Ryan McHugh running an overlap.

Our analysis of Donegal was extremely strong, extremely thorough. And Eamonn got just about every match-up on the money. To a man, fellas did everything that was asked of them, carrying out the game-plan selflessly. Maybe nobody more so than Aidan

O'Mahony on Michael Murphy. But Marc Ó Sé too. He'd been dropped for the replay with Mayo, come in as a sub, played a blinder, and now produced a great All-Ireland final performance on one of Donegal's real danger men, Colm McFadden.

To me, that's the definition of a real Championship player.

I was so proud of the group when the final whistle sounded. Rather than celebrate, I just made a point of walking around the pitch, having quick one-to-ones with every player, telling them how proud they made me feel to be a Kerryman. I meant every word of it too. What a title it was for us to win. A real Kerry All-Ireland. Just when nobody thought you could do it, you gritted your teeth and reminded them of who you were and what you represented.

At the end of a rotten year for me, the journey to that All-Ireland had kept my spirits off the floor. We were heading south with the canister again.

And all I could think was that, more than anything else in my life now, I wanted to be a central figure for Kerry again.

20

Systems Failure

Fast-forward a year, and Philly McMahon wants a hug.

Maybe it's just a game he's playing for the cameras, a snapshot declaring us some kind of spiritual brothers, friends even. But I've shaken his hand, congratulated him on the win and would quite like him to disappear now and give my head some space. Dublin are worthy All-Ireland champions. They've been too smart, too strong physically for us, just better all round in the September rain – and, from where I'm standing, there's not much more to say.

Trouble is, I know few enough others will see it that way.

I've spent the day chasing Philly up and down the field, and if anyone's looking for a handy synopsis of why Dublin have the cup, the fact that he's scored and I haven't . . . well, that's probably too good to turn down now. I know it. Eamonn Fitzmaurice knows it. We allowed Dublin to set the terms of engagement. When we needed them worrying about us, we made it clear that the shoe was actually on the other foot. We went to battle programmed, above all, for containment.

To this day I haven't discussed it with Eamonn.

But we were just so concerned about Dublin's running power, we became preoccupied with putting up roadblocks. The way their wing-backs James McCarthy and Jack McCaffrey could come bombing in off the wings or young Brian Fenton surging through the middle, the Dubs just had a way of outnumbering opposition defences within a matter of seconds.

And Philly? He'd been scoring in virtually every game from corner-back. We were hoping that Dublin concerns about me might mean he wouldn't bomb forward quite as much this time. But they obviously reckoned I was no longer the force of old, deciding to test me physically by running me all over the place.

So Philly kept on bombing out and I kept on chasing.

That meant I virtually became a corner-back's chaperone for the day. Chasing him the length of Croke Park, over and over again, poacher and gamekeeper wearing each other's clothes. I hated every fucking second of it, but what could I do?

Take a chance and let him go?

Would it have been worth someone on the line giving me that licence? *Gooch, next time he goes, you stay!* Maybe. It's not exactly a revolutionary thought, is it? I just feel we were all a little brittle that day. Me, for sure. Conditioning-wise and physically, I was fine. But confidence-wise I was still a long way from where I needed to be. Because of the injury I'd become reactive rather than proactive. I was waiting for Eamonn to make decisions for me – decisions that, in my prime, I'd have comfortably made for myself.

I was questioning myself a lot more, second-guessing things.

And maybe the biggest problem of all was that, most of the day, we just couldn't get our hands on the ball. You can make all the bold decisions you like if you're dominating possession. If you're not, you've just got to play what's in front of you. And that's a hard thing to do. You just end up running and chasing, using up all your energy. Do that for seventy minutes in Croke Park against a top team and you'll find it very hard to manufacture a win.

So I was a greyhound chasing a grinning hare that day. And at the end, the hare wanted us to be friends.

Long-term rehab is as much about a state of mind as it is about physical recovery, and for me, the adrenalin high of Kerry's All-Ireland win in 2014 would disappear with a shuddering jolt.

The end of the inter-county season meant the end of any structured access for me to three- or four-times-weekly physio. Remember, I still wasn't back playing with Crokes and wouldn't be before the end of the year. So, essentially, the onus fell on me now to take control of my ongoing recovery, and I found that a bit of a struggle.

Part of the problem was psychological. If I'd been ready to tog out in September 2014 (which I suppose I had been on some notional level), it stood to reason that I'd be a million miles advanced on that position by January 2015. But I wasn't. With the end of Kerry training, everything just fell off the radar. I needed to prioritize stuff myself now but, left to my own devices, I didn't.

You see, I've never had a problem doing work, but I need to be doing it as part of a group. That applies to every aspect of my life. I just work better in a team environment. What I needed to be doing now was taking myself to the gym on a relentless, almost regimented, basis and keeping up the momentum that had been built through August and September. But I didn't. I got sloppy. I stopped prioritizing it.

On some level too I suspect I still didn't fully understand the extent of the damage that I'd done.

So if I fully expected to be flying by January, instead I came across a huge psychological barrier that began testing me in so many ways. I'd see the boys playing or doing runs, yet couldn't join in. I was still working in virtual isolation and hating it. Trying to dance around a cone or step over a hurdle, knowing the knee was still not right.

And the whole thing began to close in on me.

Every other injury I'd ever had, I almost made it a badge of honour to get back quicker than anybody predicted. This was different. This was my body becoming contrary.

So I didn't get back until the last League game, against Tyrone in Omagh on 5 April. Got through it, nothing spectacular. We went to Portugal for a week's training then and, little by little, I just felt I was getting closer to the pitch of things. Not to the pitch of what I used to be, but to the pitch of what I reckoned might justify selection.

Eamonn thought so too, starting me against Tipperary in the Munster semi-final. But I was poor. We were poor. We won by six points, but the scoreline flattered us hugely. Next up was Cork in Killarney, and I knew what was coming.

It didn't sit well with me being dropped, but I knew too that I could have no real complaints. My form just wasn't there.

Eamonn's a quiet man in these situations, but anyone who knows him recognizes the steel within. He was much the same as a player. I remember one trip to Portugal when we were on the same team in this intense seven-a-side practice game and I was trying to manufacture a goal. I didn't quite pull it off and made the mistake of not killing the ball. Next thing, the other team breaks, we're suddenly outnumbered, and they get the goal. And Eamonn is incandescent.

'Will you kill that fucking ball!' he roars.

Of course I'm all 'You shut your mouth, the goal was fucking on . . .'

But even in mid-sentence I knew the point he was making. He

was setting standards. Now, as a manager, he wouldn't be afraid to cut someone in two if need be. But any cutting will stay between the four dressing-room walls. He'll call a fella out at the video analysis.

'Did we not establish on Tuesday night what position you were supposed to be in for the kick-out?'

More a statement than a question.

Or, 'Did I not explain it clearly enough?'

If you're on the end of that, it's tough going I can tell you. Your ears will be ringing. Because what gets measured, gets done. If you don't have the ability to learn pretty quickly in that environment, you just won't survive. Or, if you do survive, you certainly won't win.

There was no need for a big chat with me before the game with Cork. He knew I'd be hurting but he knew, too, that I wasn't stupid. Anyway, we got out of jail the first day with the combination of a dubious penalty that James O'Donoghue slotted and a late equalizer from Fionn Fitzgerald. And, with Páirc Uí Chaoimh now a building site, it was back to Killarney two weeks later for us to win easily in the replay.

I came on in both games, felt OK without really feeling strong.

I remember saying in an interview once that my knee was probably fine at the time, but I just wasn't sure it had yet communicated that message to my brain. Looking back now, I'm not so sure it was fine. In training I'd occasionally experience stiffness just trying to turn quickly around cones. But the biggest problem was psychological.

I was chatting to David Moran once, picking his brain about how his own recuperation from a similar injury had evolved.

'Are you getting any soreness?' he asked.

I wasn't. That was the problem. If I had soreness, I could maybe have identified some lingering physical issue not yet resolved. But I couldn't. And it was then he said something that really got me thinking.

'When I was coming back, people would be telling me that I was running with a limp,' he recalled. 'I didn't think I was but, in hindsight, there might have been some truth in it. Over time, I think I just ran the limp away.'

That registered with me. When I was running now, the best way I could describe it was I felt like a fella pedalling a bike with the back tyre flat. I just couldn't go at full speed. I was pumping my arms, pumping my quads, but nothing was flowing.

And with frustration, I suppose, came a small element of self-pity too.

Like I remember the very first time Ed Harnett had me doing basic stuff above in the stadium, this exercise of stepping on and off a stool no more than a couple of feet high. And I was hesitating. I was afraid. 'Are you sure man?' I was asking. Then I'd be trying to pick my way around a cone rather than whipping around it. You're looking to take an extra step to avoid stressing the knee. Instinctively, you don't want to pivot. You don't want to even try.

People kept telling me that I had to stop worrying, but the connection between my brain and my knee just wouldn't process that. I couldn't convince myself that the knee was back to normal. My brain was still worried and I couldn't override that.

Ray Moran's mantra was still 'baby steps, baby steps', but a year into the process of recovery there was probably a distinction between hearing him and listening.

All of those worries had stayed with me through the first half of 2015. Yes, by the time of that Munster final replay I was beginning to feel better about things. I was lively in training again and edging that confidence back up. Trouble was, I knew I was chasing my form too.

I wasn't selected for our All-Ireland quarter-final with Kildare in early August, but when Donaghy, our captain, didn't pass a fitness test the night before, I was in. Maybe I should have been buzzing, but I wasn't. Knowing I was only getting the nod because someone else wasn't available just made me feel that there still wasn't massive faith or trust in me on management's part. Eamonn kept reassuring me that that was not the case of course, but I didn't really believe it.

I knew, deep down, they didn't see me as being anywhere close to my pomp yet.

Still, I was buzzing later that evening, leaving Croke Park after scoring 2-3. Only problem was, when you score seven goals against a team inside thirty-five minutes of Championship football it's hard to know if that has any real significance. Kildare were truly awful. And as happy as we were heading south again that evening, there was probably more talk about the shoulder injury picked up by James O'Donoghue that day than any serious chat about us being in a good place to retain our All-Ireland crown.

Next up I was decent in a semi-final against Tyrone that never really flowed. They did what they do well, getting bodies behind the ball, frustrating opposition forwards by sheer density of traffic. For all that, we coped pretty well, even if Conor McAliskey blazed a great Tyrone goal chance over the bar before half-time.

Immediately after that we scored a quick pocket of points and looked to be easing home in the second half until Peter Harte scored a penalty with ten minutes remaining. In the end I was thrilled to get through the full seventy minutes, particularly against a side not known for taking too many prisoners.

But was I ready for the Dubs? Were *we*?

The only wonder is that, had a late Kieran Donaghy penalty appeal gone our way, we could have scavenged a second chance.

We could actually have caught them. Had that penalty come our way or had Killian Young not slipped when in behind their full-back line, we could have got out of jail.

If I'm honest, it would have been a travesty. Because Dublin were so much better than us. And, yes, Philly McMahon was better than me. I suspect I overvalued how I'd gone in the semi-final against Tyrone. I thought I was coming, but I'd played so little of the League I ended up trying to cram like a student who's left things late for his exams. Apart from that ten minutes above in Omagh, my preparation for the Championship had been a few club games.

You can't build your confidence properly on crumbs, and that's what I'd been trying to do.

And every time I found myself chasing Philly down the field now, what confidence I did have dwindled. Every opportunity he got he just went haring forward and, well, my instruction was to follow.

I suspect that if we were having this conversation with Eamonn now, he'd say that was a mistake. I was using up all my energy in a role that never involved me getting my hands on the ball. But Kerry had systems failures right through the field so, in fairness to him, he had more to worry about than my struggles to hold a corner-back.

I've always felt that the biggest danger when you play this Dublin team is that you end up getting flustered. They're so strong across the field and play with such a high intensity, you find yourself working so hard against them that the slightest of lapses in concentration can be hugely costly. It just takes one player to switch off and they'll punish you severely.

The great teams don't switch off, of course. They see games out, even when not playing well.

But, that day, we weren't a great team. Dublin were.

They won a lot more match-ups than we did and, as I said, it would have been a travesty if we'd caught them. Still, it probably says something about our collective resilience that we were within a single score of them at the end. Because the whole day had been a struggle, but we just never downed arms. We never stopped trying to rescue what often felt like a hopeless situation.

When Philly came to shake my hand, I was happy to accept. I'll always do that. I mightn't think much of an opponent's antics over the previous seventy minutes, but you park that at the final whistle. You swallow it and move on. If you're a forward in the game, you get used to being blackguarded. It isn't personal. They'll tell you it's just business, and fair enough.

I just didn't want a conversation now.

So I'm standing there, waiting for him to finish, thinking 'What do you want? Well done, go and enjoy it with your teammates. That's the fucking end of it.'

But he's telling me, 'That's just the way I play . . .'

And you know something? I didn't give a fuck. The game was over. Dublin won. I didn't need this now. I didn't need an apology. I didn't need 'You'll be back next year . . .'

I've no problem lads knocking lumps out of one another. No problem with teams wanting to sow it into you. Humiliate you even. But don't come to me at the end looking for a hug. Don't come to me wanting to be my friend.

You're not. You're an opponent. Move on. Live in the real world.

Listen, Philly's far from the worst I've faced. More and more teams are willing to cross boundaries now and there's no point giving out about them. You just need to find a hard enough edge to cope. If I'm honest, maybe to some extent even reciprocate.

But it can be especially hard for a forward when you feel as if your marker's getting away with murder. Like, for the life of me,

I don't know where the current pinching culture came from. You're standing there, sizing up what's happening out on the field, and next thing this fella is grabbing you and twisting skin. Nobody can see it happen but, fuck, it's sore.

Trust me, you'll get levelled laying off a ball in a Munster final just as quickly as you will anywhere else. Lads will go through you.

But I can never remember a marker pinching me in Kerry football. You might get all sorts of clipping, but most of it's up front. And, to begin with, I think Kerry didn't handle the more cynical stuff too well, especially against Northern teams. We suffered because of that.

Playing against Tyrone, McMenamin and the McMahons were always big talkers. Likewise Dessie Mone in Monaghan. Likewise Philly with the Dubs. They'd be just trying to upset you, get inside your head. Clearly hoping you might take a swing back and they could hit the deck. They'd be just trying to knock you off your game, testing you out, stopping you doing what you normally do. Because you're a threat to them. They're thinking 'If I leave this fella off, he could take me to the cleaners!'

In my experience, you get over the efforts at physical intimidation quicker than the other stuff. When you're a forward, you'd be naive not to be expecting to ship the odd belt. But some of the stuff you hear these days is crazy.

Like, I've never experienced it myself, but I have heard of some pretty rotten verbal abuse doing the rounds. Of a back having the phone number of his opponent's girlfriend written on his forearm. Or, worse, of someone slagging off their marker's family.

I just think, if you're at that kind of poison, there's got to be some kind of karma coming down the line. How can you expect to have any luck if you're doing that? If that's how you behave, I've not an ounce of sympathy for you if your life turns sour after.

I'm just convinced that what goes around, comes around. If you're at that stuff, it'll catch up on you.

And I genuinely wonder, when they finish up playing will they not find themselves asking, 'Jesus Christ, what was I at? How will I ever be able to look that man in the face ten years from now?'

It strikes me that these players either haven't thought it through or have already reconciled that in their heads and, basically, don't care. If the latter is the case, all I can say is that they're a different type of person to me. I just don't get it.

And I have to ask the question, is it being openly promoted by certain management teams? If you're acting the pup, mouthing off at people non-stop, and nobody on the management side shouts stop, well, is that management not actively endorsing what you're doing?

Look, Kerry players are hardly whiter than white. I'm not implying that they are. We can be unscrupulous with the best of them, but – unless I'm mistaken – there are certain lines we've yet to cross. I don't think we go pinching. I don't think we go trash-talking. We'll hit you hard, and sometimes we'll hit you late. But that's about the size of it.

Put it this way. How would you ever be able to show your face at, say, an All-Stars night if you met someone you'd been pinching and trash-talking to that summer? How could you hope to have an adult conversation with them? Are you kidding me?

Imagine, say in ten years' time, meeting the player you abused at a National League game. I'd be ashamed to show my face. I'd walk out of there thinking 'I can't face that man after what I did to him'.

Anyway, Philly seemed to take exception now to the fact that I wasn't in the mood for a lengthy conversation. And the TV camera picked up on the fact that there was some kind of tension in our little exchange. To me, it was irrelevant. There was nothing to it.

I've never wanted to be friends with my opponents. Never. Maybe I'm just cold like that, but it holds no interest for me. I'll mix with anyone on an All-Stars trip, but I wouldn't dream of texting during the Championship season, even if I had their number. To me, that would almost be a sign of weakness.

I remember playing a match in Croke Park once, we were hammering this team, and with about ten minutes to go my marker says to me, 'Can I have your jersey when it's over?' An inter-county footballer, playing in Croke Park! I couldn't believe it. All I could think was that if I overheard one of my own team-mates doing that, I'd be fit to be tied. So I kind of brushed it off, mumbled something along the lines of 'What? Look, I can't talk to you now . . .' In my head was that I had ten more minutes of business to attend to.

I mean, I just haven't swapped jerseys in recent years. Some of what I see really pisses me off in that respect, players coming in and swapping training tops and shorts and socks. What is that all about? It drives me over the edge. I'll be sitting there watching it, thinking 'If you want their gear so bad, go fucking play for them!'

It's weakness to me. You're putting that opponent up on a ped-estal. Almost saying 'He's better than me, I want his jersey'. That cracks me up. Always has done, always will.

21

Ten Days of Madness

Kerry went on a team holiday to Miami and Orlando that December, but it just wasn't for me.

I had too many questions in my head now to be off skulling beer and, maybe, pushing away reality. I'd been getting pains in my left shoulder and, after what I regarded as a pretty lousy year with club and county, I just felt I was at a major crossroads. If I was going to go another season with Kerry, there were serious issues that would have to be addressed.

So I booked myself in to Santry for minor surgery under Ms Ruth Delaney, just a little chiselling of bone that needed to be smoothed, and immediately threw myself into aggressive rehab while the boys were abroad on the lash. Late December, then, and I started doing daily work above in the gym in Fitzgerald Stadium with Daniel Murphy, one of Kerry's strength and conditioning team, followed by swims in The Europe Hotel.

In my head, I had to get my body right again. Maybe, above all, hard.

Only with a hard body could I go to war, and that was the nature of what I needed to be ready for now. I knew that. People might have been giving out about the role Eamonn had given me against Dublin, but I was more preoccupied with my own unquestioning acceptance. With the confidence of old, I'd probably have challenged his decision. But that confidence simply was not there. I needed, somehow, to become proactive in my football again.

I've always taken a view that the first point of reference when facing any problems with my football has to be the mirror.

My way was to self-analyse and self-motivate. Sports psychologists were never my thing. Jack O'Connor went down that road one year, and I'd say he regretted it afterwards. Not because there was anything particularly wrong with the thoroughly decent man he brought into the dressing-room. It was more the virtual impossibility he faced of trying to get into the heads of thirty yahoos, most of whom just weren't into that kind of thing.

It certainly wasn't for me or boys like Darragh or Declan. We'd see him strolling towards us and immediately redirect him away over to the far side of the room.

Maybe I'm old-school, a traditionalist. Maybe it's because I believe I've always been my own harshest critic. But my view was always 'I'll get myself right, I'll find a way'.

Look, I'm not knocking it. If someone like Brian O'Driscoll felt he was getting value from it towards the end of his rugby career (which he clearly did), then who am I to argue? But I just hear all these stock phrases, the 'control the controllables', from people who I know have never been out there in the bear pit. And you know something? I'm really not sure they understand what's coming towards me in that bear pit, let alone know how to help me deal with it any better.

Criticism is in your face every step of the way as a county footballer. Look at Declan O'Sullivan in '06, one of our greatest men, a hard bastard and our captain that year, taken off in Páirc Uí Chaoimh and jeered by Kerry supporters as he walked. Fucking terrible stuff. I could just as easily have been in the same boat that day as nearly every one of us stank the place out.

What did Declan do? Gritted his teeth, that's what. He went to ground and trained like a mad dog. Did extra work without being asked. There was no sports psychologist going to get him out of the hole he found himself in that year. His hardness got him out. His hardness and his talent. He knew himself better than anyone else.

So what career coach or sports psychologist was going to go down to fucking Dromid and tell that man where he could find his inches or a couple of per cent?

He just vowed to himself that he was going to get his place back on the team, and that's exactly what he did.

Well I'm in Declan's school of dealing with shit. The school that says 'Thanks very much, but I can find whatever it is that's missing myself'.

Listen, every day you go out in this game, someone's trying to take the head off you. Teams are watching video clips of what you do and what your attitude is like under pressure. It's gone past the forensic point at this stage. I'd say the opposition practically know which side of the bed a man sleeps on now. Mental toughness is vital.

I'd like to think that one of my biggest strengths as a footballer was an ability to learn from my mistakes. I knew that everyone could have a bad game, but I would not countenance having two in a row. So I learned very quickly from a bad game. I was hard on myself. Ruthless.

And, if I'm honest, I was intolerant of fellas who did not share that ruthlessness. Who maybe couldn't. Team-mates would probably tell you I was the crankiest bollix most of them ever played with. If someone made a mistake, they'd get the stare from me.

Why the fuck did you do that?

I understand now that that's not in everyone. But it took me thirty-three years to figure it out.

So that was the mindset I was taking into Christmas and New Year 2015/16. That if I had to go to another level in my preparation, that's exactly what I would do. And even in a matter of weeks I could feel the difference, see the difference. In my legs especially. The Kerry physio, Ed Harnett, took one look at me when they came back from the holiday and said, 'What the fuck have you been up to, Gooch?'

It was *that* noticeable.

No coincidence, then, that I played six games in the National League. We got to the final, it didn't work out. Dublin hammered us by eleven points. But I still felt I was going into the Championship in infinitely better physical condition than I had in 2015.

You know, this might sound perverse, but I think we all felt a little better about the Dublin thing after that game too. Yes, we had collapsed in the end. Yes, we took an awful kicking from some quarters where the impression was gaining traction that we just couldn't handle Dublin's athleticism and physicality. But the truth was, coming away from Croke Park, we reckoned we could have a right cut off them if we got another chance. The only question was, would we get that chance?

We beat Clare comfortably in Munster, and Tipperary took out Cork. So we had a Killarney provincial final then against Tipp, a game I just could not see us losing. I was happy with my form and with how I was moving in training. In my head, lads were looking at me thinking 'This fella's back close to his best'. So I was pumped for it. Couldn't wait.

And that's when my world began to unravel again.

I look back on it now as ten days of madness. Just bad news coming in short, sharp gun blasts. BANG. BANG. BANG.

The week before the Munster final started with me lying on the couch at home, feeling emptied of energy, shivering. Flu-like symptoms. I rang Eamonn. 'Don't know why, but I'm just not feeling the best . . .'

So down I went to my GP, Mike Moloney.

'Not feeling the best, Mike, my energy's gone.'

Mike's instant diagnosis was that I had contracted cellulitis. Just a small cut on my foot, near one of my toes. A virus had infected the cut, sucking all the energy out of me. Ransacking all the good. Mike reassured me that I'd be fine for the game but that, in the meantime, the only medicine was rest.

It wasn't ideal having to ring Eamonn to tell him I wouldn't be able to play in our customary As v. Bs game one week out from showtime. I could tell he had concerns, but if I was moving well in our final training session, he'd give me the benefit of the doubt.

Then, midweek the following week, my right knee just didn't feel right. The one I'd pretty much crucified in 2014. I could actually see the build-up of fluid, squeeze it like a small balloon. John Rice, one of the doctors with Kerry, reassured me that it just needed draining. Not ideal in the week of a big match, but manageable.

So the knee was drained and I arrived into the game thinking 'Surely I'm due a bit of luck now!'

Then, about twenty minutes in, I was coming out of defence with the ball and took a dunt off a Tipp lad, then a second one from behind. As I landed hard, my AC joint just went. Dislocated shoulder.

Ah fuck this.

The clown that I can be, I tried playing on for another couple of minutes. Couldn't raise my hand above shoulder height, but Jesus Christ I couldn't bear the thought of being injured again. Of people fucking nursing me. Of more doctors, more physios, more tables. Luckily, I didn't take another dunt before accepting the inevitable, but I was gutted leaving the field.

The boys, mind, were just fine without me. We beat Tipp by ten points, setting up an All-Ireland quarter-final against, God help them, Clare. Probably their worst nightmare. I could have played in it at a push, but that would have been an unncessary risk. We were confident of beating them again.

And we did.

So Dublin had our attention again, and during the build-up I could see that Eamonn and the management team were thinking in terms of an inside forward line of myself, Donaghy and Paul Geaney. James O'Donoghue still wasn't quite at the pitch of things after a shoulder injury, so he was being held in reserve.

I'd been playing at 11 up to then and I still wonder, if I had been physically right all through that season, would they have left me there against the Dubs? Something that was always in my head was that Cian O'Sullivan was inclined to stand off a centre-forward. Would he have done the same with me? I mean, I knew I didn't have the fitness to play there in 2015, but 2016? Maybe, maybe not.

Early on in the semi-final I had an easy chance of a score but sickened myself by becoming flustered. I caught a ball over Jonny Cooper's head, maybe 20 yards out, and remember thinking 'If I get away here, there's a goal on'.

But as I caught the ball, I had to stumble backwards to get my balance. And, I don't know, that stumble just suddenly clouded my thinking. The one thing I usually have in abundance for that kind of scenario is composure, but at that moment it deserted me. I snatched at the ball, kicking it wide over my shoulder.

Another time, in the second half, I dummy-soloed Cooper, sending him diving at thin air, only to drop my kick short into Stephen Cluxton's hands. Fucking madness. That wasn't a 99 per cent kick for me. That was a 100 per cent kick in my head, and to drop it short was unforgivable.

And those were the margins.

Hand on heart, I should have kicked 0-4 from play that day. If I'd been there for a week in 2015, I wouldn't have had that many opportunities. That's how much better I'd become physically in a year, but my return from play was just 0-1. And I'll carry that frustration with me into retirement because the Dubs were there for the taking.

We'd been slow out of the blocks, taking fourteen minutes just to get our first score on the board. So they led 0-9 to 0-4 after twenty-four minutes; but then we hit an unanswered 2-4 approaching half-time to go in at the break leading by five. You could tell it was almost as if Croke Park had witnessed some kind of earthquake. The hum of conversation as we went down the tunnel was that of a crowd suddenly keyed into something dramatic unfolding.

Our first goal had come when Paul Geaney intercepted a Cluxton kick-out and Donnchadh Walsh set up Darran. The goal brought us level. Almost immediately, another Cluxton kick-out went over the sideline and, soon, Geaney was goaling from a high Anthony Maher delivery. Dublin got on top again just after the resumption, but we rallied and the sides were actually level after seventy-two minutes, only for stoppage-time points from Eoghan O'Gara and Diarmuid Connolly to pull them over the line.

When I look back, half-time just came at the wrong time for us that day. Because we were bombing. We had them completely on the rack for the seven minutes leading up to the interval. During that time I felt Cluxton could direct his kick-outs anywhere he liked, we were still going to get them. We had pressed up high on every line and he seemed reluctant to go long because of the strength we had in Maher and David Moran at midfield.

For that seven minutes, they were more or less in meltdown.

Look, I've no problem saying we were well beaten by the Dubs in 2015. But 2016? And 2013? And 2011? Fair play to them, they won all those games, but there was little enough between us. History gets written by a final score, and that's fine too. Dublin beat us in four Championships on the bounce (something they'd never previously done) and for that generation of Dublin players it's a fair boast to have. But, for me, three of those games were virtual tosses of a coin.

Of course, the usual suspects will always paint that type of statistic as proof of one team being 'made of the right stuff', the other being a bit flaky. Horse manure.

But, look, there's never any consolation in being close. Not an ounce of it.

And I was angry after. Angry with myself. If I'd been up to the standard I'd generally demand of myself, we'd probably have won that game. And I found that head-wrecking. I also found it a reason to start questioning, immediately, if my race with Kerry was now run.

To go again, I felt I'd have to be better. Would that be possible in my thirty-fourth year? 'Better' meant converting those four chances and being clinical in the white heat. It meant maybe a personal 10 per cent improvement in 2017. Where would I even start looking for that 10 per cent, let alone find it?

The more I thought about that, the more it felt as if there was another storm brewing in my head.

22

'You'll Have to Make Your Decision Soon'

January 2017

I buy an *Irish Independent* in Cork Airport and feel the pressure build.

Eamonn Fitzmaurice has given an interview, suggesting that anyone intent on being part of Kerry's plans this year must decide by the end of the month. Right now, I honestly don't know if that includes me. My head only has room for Dr Crokes and surely he understands that.

But a part of me wonders if Eamonn's sending a message too, trying to put a gun to my head. I'm headed to London with a mate, Eoghan Cronin, and tomorrow we fly to Thailand for a ten-day break. The idea of the trip is that I clear my head of exactly this kind of stuff.

So, not a great start then.

Eoghan lives in Ruislip, but has been home for Kieran O'Leary's wedding. That night, we go for a pint in an Irish bar, Hennessys, and across the way there's an elderly man reading the same newspaper. He looks over at me with a gentle nod of recognition.

'You'll have to make your decision soon,' he says.

'Suppose I will,' I smile.

Gut instinct? I think I'm done. All the certainties I once felt wearing the green and gold of Kerry have been under attack these last few years and the last thing I want to become is some kind of sentimental squad selection who ends up as a glorified cheer-leader. If I can't be an important player for Eamonn, I'm not sure I can be anything. Your body might weaken over time, but my experience is that pride doesn't.

Anyway, that article has set me wondering. Is Eamonn now looking for an earlier answer than I'm comfortable giving?

The last conversation I had with him finished with me saying that I'd like to train away with Crokes and just see wherever that took me. Then if I reckoned there was anything left in the tank . . .

Nothing he said at the time suggested there was a deadline. Now I'm wondering if that's changed.

Maybe people imagine communication in this kind of situation is far more open than is the case in reality. I go back a long way with Eamonn and we've always been good. But the last thing I'd feel comfortable doing now is picking up a phone and asking, 'What's the story?'

Anyway, Thailand is meant to be all about escape. I've had a long year with Kerry, ending in disappointment, and we're still working flat out with Crokes. Sixteen sessions in twenty-one days through the Christmas period, and my logic is that, if Crokes make it to the All-Ireland final, I want to get there in a good place mentally. I don't want to arrive there knackered.

And who knows, if Crokes end up All-Ireland champions, I might just bounce into another season with Kerry on the crest of a wave.

Our manager Pat O'Shea wasn't thrilled when I told him about the trip, but I reckon he knows me well enough to trust that I won't be out there doing the dog on it. Trouble is, a week after winning the Munster Club, we got caught in the East Kerry final. I think that shook Pat a little bit. He has an ingrained dread of complacency in players and, right now, he just wants the group to hang tight together, to stay hard.

All well and good for the lads who were able to get away in the summer, but I couldn't do that. And that's my point to Pat.

'Look, I just need a break here . . .'

'Ah fuck it, Colm, it's not the time to be going on the piss.'

'Jesus Pat, I'm not twenty-three any more. I'm thirty-three!'

'I know, but . . . fuck it . . . go handy.'

My plan is to train at least five times on the holiday and go easy on the sauce. I'm going to eat well and maybe use the trip as a kind of psychological spa. And Eoghan's the perfect company. He knows better than to ask the questions I can't answer and I know he'll leave it up to me to initiate any talk about Kerry.

Most nights we just have a nice dinner – Eoghan's big into his food and every evening we dine like kings – and chat about anything and everything. He's a big Manchester United supporter, I'm a massive Liverpool fan. There's enough material there to get us through the entire holiday.

We're staying in a beautiful hotel on Karon Beach in Phuket. I'm in the sea every day, going handy on the beer, behaving myself. We've been trying to make contact on WhatsApp with Kieran O'Leary who's out here on his honeymoon and said he'd be coming down to Karon, but the Wi-Fi is up and down and it looks like we're going to miss each other.

Then one afternoon Eoghan and I are sitting in this shop window, our bare feet immersed in water tanks being nibbled on by these lucky fish, and who comes striding down the street with an

O'Neills ball under his arm? Kieran and new wife Andrea. And that turns into just the kind of night Pat O'Shea's probably envisaged in his worst nightmare. Put it this way: I'm blowing a lot of smoke out the back on my next beach run.

Still, it's just a one-off.

A friend of ours, John Feeney – a Mayo man living in London – is on his way back from a Christmas in New Zealand and links up with us as our personal tour guide. He knows Thailand like the back of his hand, rents a car for a couple of days and brings us to all these beautiful small beaches and coves that are off the beaten track.

The trip is heavenly. Nice lunches, afternoon swims, some early nights.

John tells us the only proper way to get around these islands is on scooters, and I'm sure he's right, but this time I don't bite. I can just imagine ringing Pat from a hospital bed in Thailand.

'Pat, fuck it, sorry, I fell off a scooter.'

Then, one night, Eoghan and I are having dinner at The Cliff restaurant in Koh Samui when, somehow, we end up stumbling into the very territory I've been determined to avoid. We're sipping bottles of Chang in this absolute paradise and, out of the blue, I end up talking about Kerry.

'Sure if the body is good, why wouldn't you give it another go?' he wonders.

Immediately I'm defensive. 'Eoghan, by the time I play another Championship game I'll be thirty-four. Am I going to be better than I was last year?'

'Sure who fucking knows?' he answers, chewing on a breadstick.

'You watch a lot of soccer,' I say. 'Do you think Wayne Rooney is getting better?'

'Yeah, but fuck it, you got Man of the Match in the county final.'

'That's different!'

'Maybe, but if you're winning a county championship and Munster Club, you can't be motoring too bad!'

And then I say exactly what I'm thinking.

'I don't know, but right now I'm ninety per cent clear in my head that I'm retiring.'

Eoghan's taken aback because he can see that I'm not bluffing here. I get the impression everyone's been assuming I'll go with Kerry again, and sometimes it feels as if my head is about to explode because of that. Now, finally, I've said what's really in my head. And Eoghan is sitting across the table looking like a man who's had the wind taken from his sails.

We're not home long when, out of the blue, I get about ten Whats-App messages just after seven one Monday morning. Donnchadh Walsh has done a newspaper interview, saying myself and Don-aghy are expected to be back for Kerry. Thanks, Donnchadh.

The following day, Donaghy rings. Sussing me out.

I recycle all my doubts to him. I haven't made a decision, but I know the way I'm leaning. I don't think I can do the volume of work Eamonn wants the group to do. Can I follow a separate training plan to everyone else? I've yet to see that arrangement brought in for anyone in Kerry.

When I said that to Eamonn, his response was that it would be up to them to manage my workload. He wanted me back, he made that clear. But let's face it, he's not going to give me any guaran-tees about what role he has in mind for me. How could he? Does he see me as just an option coming off the bench? Has he the same idea for Donaghy?

I don't know, and neither does Kieran.

The man whose face I see every time I think about this is Marc Ó Sé. One of the best players I've ever played with and unquestionably one of Kerry's greatest ever corner-backs. Marc's career just petered out a little in the end. I don't want that. I've had too much fun with Kerry to allow things to finish that way now.

Put it this way: I always wonder how Marc feels about how it ended. He was playing great stuff in the League but had a poor final, and after that he never quite regained his form. That's hard. I look at something like that and can't help think 'Fuck it, after fifteen years of giving it everything, great days and memories, I wouldn't like that to be the way I go now.'

The ideal scenario?

An All-Ireland Club win gives me the energy to commit to one more year with Kerry. But that feels a million miles away right now.

All I'm thinking about is club, but I know too that people outside Dr Crokes basically don't care a damn about Dr Crokes. I can sense an impatience in people that I'm not making my intentions clear. I can detect too a feeling in some that I shouldn't play any more. That they reckon my legs are gone, that Eamonn's better off now going with a younger breed.

No one would ever communicate that to your face, of course, but in Kerry people say a lot of stuff from behind pulled curtains.

I know in my heart the supporters are split about the idea of me continuing. And that's fair enough. I'm conflicted too. My comment to Eoghan of leaning 90 per cent towards retirement was sincere. Unless I can deliver two big performances for Crokes now over the next couple of months, the talk about Kerry is superfluous. Because if I can't do it for my club, why in God's name should I ever believe that I can still do it for my county?

Am I getting faster? Am I getting better? I know the answer to both those questions.

And you know something? It mightn't sound great to say it, but right now Kerry are the last thing on my mind. They have to be.

I have tunnel vision for Crokes. That's the very least I owe them.

23

Longest Journey

The madness of Pat O'Shea is that he believes in us more than we believe in ourselves.

He is the club evangelist. Not in a shouty, preachy way, just in lighting fires in people all of the time. In challenging ambivalence. It's a year ago now that he sent out that text inviting anybody with an ambition to play senior football for Crokes in 2016 to a meeting in the clubhouse. Maybe forty of us pitched up that January evening, some of us familiar with Pat's psychological intensity, some not.

I had an inkling of what was coming here, I just wasn't quite sure how he'd package it. People like myself, Kieran O'Leary, Luke Quinn and Mike 'Smiler' Moloney had danced to his baton before, but in '09, after we'd lost a third county final to South Kerry in five years, he stepped away, throwing himself into what might be considered more menial tasks within the club.

And, of course, we somehow catapulted forward to win four titles in a row then, almost in defiance of him.

But the last two years had been poor and a little soulless. We'd drifted off the pace and so a group that had Munster Club titles to its name stopped even reaching the business end of the Kerry Championship. Maybe there were extenuating circumstances. My cruciate. Luke's cruciate. O'Leary's Achilles. Either way, the hunger dropped. Within the county, I'd say people presumed we were a beaten docket.

So Pat called this meeting, I suppose partly to announce his return as senior team manager, partly to fire a few rockets.

And on this January Friday night, standing in front of a decidedly sheepish audience of potential A, B and C players, he opened his address with a question.

'OK lads, what's the ambition?'

I'm not sure if he wanted anyone to put a hand up or to throw out something woolly about restoring lost pride. I suspect he didn't. I suspect he wanted this to play out exactly as it did. A kind of awkward silence followed by a light shuffling of feet. And, in the absence of anyone taking up the baton, Pat choosing to answer his own question.

'I'd say,' he said, 'it has to be the All-Ireland.'

A few of the facial expressions that night suggested men in white coats might be about to come spinning in under the railway arch on Lewis Road with signed forms committing a Mr O'Shea to some mental institution.

I could see it in fellas. Eyes full of 'Fuck sake Pat, we can't win our own championship for the last two years and you're looking to take us on some kind of fucking magic carpet ride?'

Maybe the younger fellas especially didn't quite know what they were dealing with here. We had three lads in that room – Gavin White, Micheal Burns and Jordan Kiely – who'd just won All-Ireland minor titles with Kerry, who'd maybe dabbled with senior in the club and been given zero reason to believe there was any revolution brewing.

Me? I knew Pat well enough to understand that he believed absolutely in the dream he was about to sell here. To say he's an ambitious man would be like describing Ruby Walsh as handy on a horse. The logical thing to an ordinary mind that evening would have been a call for everyone to get back to basics. To target a Kerry title and take anything after that as a bonus.

That's not Pat, though. One way or another, he wanted the room's attention. He knew it was a bugbear with us all that, when we were flying high, winning those four county titles, we hadn't been good enough to kick on and bridge that gap to '92 with an All-Ireland. Now Pat was selling the idea that that dream was still attainable. Better still, he was instantly setting the standards required that might deliver it.

So he began outlining the kind of commitment he had in mind.

He said anyone with an ambition to travel that summer should let him know now, not with boarding passes in their hands at the end of May. 'If you think you're heading away to New York this summer and playing with us in the county championship, forget it,' he said. 'I'll tell you here and now, you're not in my plans.'

I could see, instantly, what was happening here.

Pat brings a bit of a fear factor to this kind of meeting. He's not an attention-seeker, he doesn't bang tables. But he looks people in the eye with an intensity that instantly sets them straight about who is in charge. He knows how to play fellas. Whether it's injuries or missing training, they won't pull the wool over his eyes. They won't bullshit him.

And that's the message he was getting across here. My way or the highway.

Listen, if I'm honest, I felt he might have been selling a pipe-dream that evening. I didn't doubt for a second the sincerity of his belief or the intensity with which he'd pursue it, I just feared he might have been seeing things in us that no longer existed. Or, at least, that had receded with time.

Within a week, though, he had made two calls that I knew were smart ones. He made Johnny Buckley captain and Daithí Casey vice-captain. Now Johnny and Daithí are chalk and cheese, but that's why it made so much sense to me. Johnny's just such a smart, solid guy, very balanced, never a bullshit talker. Daithí? He's naturally shy, tends to be hard on himself. A man with huge power, massive ability, but someone who needed to drag a bit more out from within. Making Daithí vice-captain was Pat's way of saying 'I need more from you now big man. I need you to lead!'

Before lads had a chance to process the new regime, Pat had set out an intensive training plan, so detailed, so structured that I doubt many county regimes would come even close. And I was delighted. Whether or not it got us back to winning ways, I knew at least that fellas who might have been in party mode for the previous two years were being shunted into a new reality here.

He was ready to call lads' bluffs too. 'Oh I work Tuesday evenings, Pat' would be instantly met with 'That's no problem, I'll be up Wednesday night, we'll do another one. Might be difficult with only two or three, but . . .'

Gym sessions were going to be monitored. If a lad didn't play more than ten minutes for the As on any given weekend, Pat expected them to be available for duty elsewhere.

Maybe every club has somebody like Pat O'Shea, but to me, his commitment to Crokes almost sets the standard for others. He's fanatical. There isn't a night goes by you won't find him up at the pitch watching some under-age game, or inside addressing some committee. Three years ago he trained the B team. On Saturday mornings he's there with the under-6s. He's over the under-age structure in Crokes. He served for a time as club vice-chairman.

As I mentioned earlier, his wife Deborah-Ann, daughter of Eddie 'Tatler' O'Sullivan, is equally fanatical, running the club shop and serving on the Ladies' Committee. As a couple, Pat and Deborah-Ann might as well have 'Dr Crokes' tattooed on to their foreheads.

Anyway, the 2016 revolution got up and running with some big county league wins, our new fitness regime beginning to reap quick dividends. Pat's view would always be that if you can't run, you can't play. He wants high-impact, high-intensity football and that's just not possible unless people have the legs.

Now they weren't seeing much of me at this point, but I was expected to be at training if the Kerry schedule allowed, and my attendance on the line was presumed upon at all League games. The same applied to the other county men too, but it was never an issue. We all wanted to be there; we all wanted to feel a part of things even if we weren't, yet, available to play.

By May, everything seemed to be working like clockwork, the boys wiping the floor with some teams. We hammered West Kerry by twenty-two points in the first round of the county championship, then went down to Cordal to play a divisional team, St Kieran's, in the next. And what I saw that evening left me absolutely livid. We fell over the line by a single point, everyone just doing their own thing, playing as individuals, swanning around like a group who'd started believing their own publicity. I got the impression they'd become complacent after the West Kerry win and, walking to the bus that evening, I gave it to Pat with both barrels.

'Pat, that was fucking cat out there. Where are fellas' standards?'

And, suddenly, Pat was the one calling for calm. For patience. For cutting lads a bit of slack.

'It's OK,' he said, 'we're fine. Tonight wasn't hectic, but we're still exactly where we wanted to be.'

I was having none of it. 'Fuck that,' I said. 'This won't be good enough. If these boys think they're at the level they need to be, they're only fooling themselves. Worse, they're trying to fucking fool you.'

I look back on that exchange now and marvel at his calm. He effectively wasn't going to see me or the other county boys again until September or October, when Kerry's Championship story had been written. And here I was, in June, laying down the law. Lecturing him about standards.

But that's the rhythm of business in Kerry. The Championship stalls in mid-summer and, save for a few League games, lads are free to relax until us county boys come back into the picture. For Crokes, that happened with the Club Championship final (a secondary competition) against Austin Stacks in Fitzgerald Stadium a week before our October county quarter-final.

And it's fair to say we were absolutely diabolical. Should have won in a canter, but lost by a point, missing five goal chances and having a man (Ambrose O'Donovan) sent off.

Now this might sound like a contradiction, but I felt the defeat was perfectly timed. It hosed away any dangerous sense of self-regard. It gave Pat a stick to beat us with, reminding us that, without humility, we'd be sitting ducks the following week for a Kerins O'Rahillys team with the likes of David Moran, Tommy Walsh and Barry John Keane in their guard.

And that was when the jigsaw in Pat's head began falling into place.

He's a disciple of the Roy Keane theory about preparation and failure and, basically, reaping what you sow.

I'll give you an example of the environment he created for us in that county championship. We beat Kerins O'Rahillys 1-16 to 0-14, then Dingle – the emerging club in Kerry given the Hogan

Cup successes of Pobalscoil Chorca Dhuibhne, Daingean Uí Chúis – by 1-15 to 0-15 in the semi-final. Just over twenty-four hours after the Dingle win, Pat had us gathered in a room in The Gleneagle Hotel doing video analysis on our final opponents, Kenmare District. That's how meticulous the man is. He likes players to have a full week of programming themselves for the individual challenge ahead. To know who they're going to be picking up.

His view of the final was that we needed to show a bit of mean-ness. To be physical without being dirty. Kenmare had a predominantly young team and we wanted everything to be a battle, a scrap. We wanted to rattle them. We'd watched their semi-final defeat of Rathmore as it was the second game of a Killarney double-header with our game against Dingle, and, almost to a man, we were sitting there in Fitzgerald Stadium thinking we were witnessing something with all the intensity of a backs v. forwards drill.

So we made it a very physical county final and Kenmare just didn't have the street smarts or resolve to handle it. I was named Man of the Match after a six-point win and it struck me that this county medal was the first thing I'd won since suffering that knee injury in 2014. On a personal level, that made it very special.

But I'd be lying if I said there was any great euphoria around Killarney town that evening. After all, this was our fifth county title win in seven years. We enjoyed our Sunday night, but were back training that Tuesday, Pat's vision, suddenly, gathering credibility.

With games coming almost week in, week out now, our football was getting slicker, our unity growing tighter, our physical condi-tioning really well advanced. In fairly quick succession we took care of Munster Club business against Kilmurry Ibrickane, Loughmore-Castleiney and The Nire to be crowned provincial champions.

Typically, the final was played on a filthy late November day in Mallow. Daithí Casey scored three first-half goals to close the door on any suggestion that it might be a serious contest. We were already 3-9 to 0-1 up by half-time, fully on top everywhere. It was my fifth Munster Club final win, easily the softest. Actually, the eventual nineteen-point margin meant it had been too comfortable almost to grant us any great satisfaction.

The following night I remember sitting at home in Ardshanavooly watching a replay of the Connacht Club final in MacHale Park on TG4. Corofin had just done the same kind of number on St Brigid's that we'd done on The Nire. Won by fourteen points. Yet, seeing the quality of the football, the intensity of the hits, the general bite and pace of their play, I couldn't help but feel that their game had been on a different level.

And I was thinking 'Fuck, we've our work cut out for us here!'

I don't know how many times on our journey to the summit that I heard someone describe the man leading us there as 'stone fucking crazy'.

Routinely, lads wondered aloud if Pat had anything else in his life. The more he got, the more he wanted. He just kept squeezing. Time management is an immediate issue when you win a provincial club title because of the two-month gap to the All-Ireland semi-finals. What do you do through Christmas? Cut lads slack or try to get them to take the Matt Talbot Road?

Cutting lads slack has never been Pat's first preference.

One week after The Nire win, five of us went to New York for a short break with Kerry. We hadn't touched back down in Shannon long when Pat's Christmas training schedule landed with us on WhatsApp. Sixteen days out of the next twenty-one would have a session of one form or another. Some might have seen that as the virtual cancellation of Christmas, and it was certainly more intense than anything I had expected.

I do remember wondering at the time how Pat honestly felt he could give lads an appetite for working outside in the cold and dark as December eased towards January.

But he didn't even try. Most of the sessions were indoors, always changing from night to night. Sometimes it might even have been basketball, just all of us doing three-man weaves. Sometimes it would be a gym session. Every night he had something different up his sleeve, the focus just on keeping the lungs open. And there was no mention of a drinks ban. People could do what they liked in that regard, so long as they pitched up at training.

I thought that was really clever. I've often found myself going to the pub over Christmas, almost just for the sake of it. As if there's some kind of silent obligation to go drinking in recognition of the festive season. But knowing you had a session the following day just made lads more choosy about where and when they had their pints.

I even kept to that mindset while on my January break in Thailand. I was never going to be a slave to any schedule out there, but neither was I going to come home in any condition that might justify Pat's reticence about me travelling in the first place. At times I must have sounded like a broken record to my friend Eoghan. But there would be exactly one month to the Corofin game from my return and, if Pat was planning a ball-breaker of a session that Tuesday night, I wanted to be ready.

One thing that struck me throughout this period was how Pat had people eating out of the palm of his hand. As intense as the schedule was, most people were actually doing even more. You'd see it every second day on WhatsApp, someone saying they'd be in the gym at two p.m. and welcoming anybody interested to join them. A couple of times in late December I looked through the glass panel of the gym door to see half a dozen of my team-mates inside, pushing weights. On a rest day!

With me, Pat's way has always been to invest a lot of trust. I wouldn't say we talk a lot, but I know he appreciates my opinion when we do. The only one-on-one I had with him all year was when we met for a quick coffee in The Killarney Park before the Munster final. I just felt there were a few small things that we could tweak in an attacking sense, and I know he's always open to the opinions of his senior players. Pat would often reference me in the speeches he made too. Just a simple 'Remember what Colm said . . .'

Maybe above all, he trusts me on the field. There's never been anything too prescriptive about his instructions to me before a game. He's inclined to give me a licence to make my own decisions. As long as I'm an influence in a game, he's not too bothered what position on the field that's in.

'Don't be looking at me to call it!' he'd often say. 'I don't care what you're doing once you're touching the ball!'

Actually, that's pretty much the essence of what he communicates to most people.

Just get yourself right.

Take responsibility.

Make the correct decisions.

Don't look over to me if you haven't touched the ball after fifteen minutes. It's your job to go and find it!

Make things happen.

I've always liked that about his style of management, because I suspect there's a lot of talking for the sake of it in GAA teams and that becomes just the equivalent of empty noise. Players, particularly club players, don't want an overload of advice or information because their mental computers simply won't break it down.

Some people remarked after the Corofin game in February that I'd been playing very deep. The truth was, I didn't have a set position. It simply made sense to us all for me to be moving constantly, to be linking things, picking passes. From the outset, Kieran O'Leary looked dangerous inside and we stretched into a comfortable lead. Then Corofin came back, only for Gavin O'Shea (Pat's son) to score a goal he had intended as a point.

Again, we played with a lot of physicality, and again, our match-ups were on the money. Their big danger men, Gary Sice and Michael Lundy, didn't have much impact, and when a great Daithí Casey run set up Jordan Kiely for our second goal, the game was as good as done.

About ten minutes from the end I took a heavy jolt to my shoulder and signalled to Pat that I now couldn't raise my arm above shoulder height. And his response was precisely what I should have expected.

'Sure you don't have to!' he said, turning away to more urgent matters.

I'll tell you a story about Crokes and place and lineage that, for me, goes to the heart of what we were now chasing.

Like myself, Pat comes from a big working-class family. He grew up in the middle of town, the O'Sheas' house nestling right behind Fitzgerald Stadium. His parents, Murt and Bridie, were massively passionate Crokes people and it's fair to say his contra-riness isn't something he licked up off the floor. Famously, the team that would win the '92 All-Ireland got an impromptu pep talk along the way one day when Bridie stormed into the dressing-room.

It was the '91 Kerry Championship, the boys struggling half-way through a knockout game against West Kerry in Dingle. Next thing the dressing-room door swings open and a furious

Bridie takes to the floor in a mood that no one could wisely challenge.

'Ye'd all want to effing wake up out there I'll tell ye!' she roared.

And Pat and his brother Seanie were left standing there, mortified, gently trying to dismantle the bomb that was their mother's temper. 'Aah Mam, you can't be in here . . .'

It was out of that dressing-room that our greatest ever team sprang, and that's where Pat is coming from now when he's on Crokes business. The club is in his bones. This isn't a hobby he's pursuing. I sometimes hear that word attached to what people do in a GAA cause and have to stop myself laughing out loud.

I'll say straight out that winning the 2017 All-Ireland Club became an obsession for all of us on Lewis Road. When you want something so badly but you've failed and failed and failed to claim it, I suppose the most natural symptom is it makes you irrational. So, honestly, Slaughtneil weren't facing fully rational creatures in Croke Park on St Patrick's Day.

And that photograph of me at the end, arms outstretched, running to embrace Pat, captured arguably the most perfect moment of my entire football career.

You see, when I was first showing promise as a footballer in Crokes, a line that was recycled pretty often was that I looked like 'a red-head Pat O'Shea'. Did I model myself on his game? Not intentionally. Not consciously. Bear in mind I had four older brothers to follow in that regard. But it's fair to say that Pat and I had pretty similar qualities as footballers, and for a Crokes child of the nineties to be compared to Pat O'Shea never felt anything less than a compliment.

I'd stayed out of any media stuff in the build-up to Slaughtneil, mindful that any interview would, inevitably, arc round to a question about my future with the county. Silence suited me fine. The

last thing I wanted was this story to become about me. This had
to be about everybody.

It had to be about people who will be my friends for life. Like
our chief messer Fionn Fitzgerald, about himself and O'Leary,
the cute hoors robbing laces out of fellas' shoes. It had to be about
Brossie. About Daithí, now, finally, finding the best of himself. It
had to be about Ambrose with that heart of a lion, but a gift for
making Pat apoplectic ('Just mark your fucking man, Ambrose!').
It had to be about Smiler and Buckley and Looney, about Lukey,
about Andrew Kennelly and Shane Murphy. It had to be about
the young fashionistas of the room, O'Shea, Kiely, Burns and
Tony Brosnan, with all their shapes and styling mousse and dis-
dain for those of us inclined to dress for comfort.

It had to be about John Payne, soon to walk off the field as
Man of the Match in an All-Ireland final.

You know, I could go through the full dressing-room here, but
it even had to be about more than us too. It had to be about the
back-room men. About Harry O'Neill, who'd trained Crokes to
win two county titles in a row when Pat took that time-out. About
our captain's dad, Mike, still there more than two decades after
many of us first set eyes on him behind the wheel of that Saturday-
morning bus. It had to be about selector (and Kerry water boy)
Niall 'Botty' O'Callaghan. About Vince Casey, Daithí's uncle,
fundraiser supreme, head of our Organizing Committee and a
man who previously trained us to a county final. About lads like
Seamie Doherty, Matthew Courtney and James Hurley, up on
the pitch every evening doing stuff that in more refined settings
might be categorized as logistics.

It had to be about someone like John Lyne, quietly dipping in
and out of pubs on a Saturday night selling club lotto tickets. It
had to be about the women, more than a dozen of them every
evening, feeding us like kings in the clubhouse after training

(I loved the way Pat made a point of always thanking them before any of us left the table).

It had to be about Eddie 'Tatler' and Patrick 'The Bag', father and son, two men without whom I'm not sure what Crokes would be today. Think about it. Patrick, club chairman, county chairman, played with the juniors. Now his nephew was on the team, his brother-in-law the manager, his father a selector. It had to be about our sponsor, Maurice Regan junior, and his dad, Maurice senior. It had to be about our current President, John Moynihan, ninety-plus years old and sharp as a new shaving blade.

It had to be about our mascots (and I should know), The Bag's son TJ and Noah Sexton, every night up there collecting balls from behind the goals, soaking up the rhythms of our devotion.

And it had to be about Stephen Brosnan, Tony's brother. Stephen is a young lad with Down's syndrome, and to all in Crokes, he is just one of us. Across the years, Stephen became as much a part of our dressing-room as any of the above. At the end of our last training session in Killarney before the final, Pat asked Stephen to say a few words. And there Stephen stood before us, articulating his excitement at heading to Croke Park for this big day. He finished by wishing us luck 'on behalf of Pat, myself and all the management' and, I don't know, I remember thinking that that just felt perfect.

It wasn't the greatest final. I'd say for neutrals it might even have been a bore. We didn't play great. I didn't play great. The day was never about that. We just saw things out, took care of business, dealt with the pressure. Not many All-Irelands are won with just ten scores, but we'd have settled for getting there with one.

My goal was important. Daithí took off from very deep, and once he hit the 45 I started thinking his run might open things up for a goal. We'd seen it in the Munster final and against Corofin. The man just doesn't understand how good he is and the damage he can do. I remember the small number 5 for Slaughtneil running after him and knowing that Daithí would be too strong for him. But, just as he took the hop inside, the ball kind of got away from Daithí and it was only his vision that rescued things. He got a palm away to me, and the only thing in my head at that moment was 'This has to hit the ground!'

It was the first Championship goal Slaughtneil had conceded in seventeen months, and I think psychologically that made it a sickener for them. Daithí kicked a great point afterwards, Looney kicked two more just before half-time, and then the sending-off was an absolute killer for them. True, they were able to block up things pretty well afterwards, but they couldn't really offer anything going forward.

And Jesus we were street-smart.

When we got that last line ball, I remember saying to myself, 'Well there's no one else fucking taking this . . .' I just thought if we lost possession here I could end up regretting it for the rest of my life. So I ran over, not sure if it was Fionn or O'Leary beside me, but I pushed them away. The Crokes management team was all around me, every last one of them wired to the moon. Shouting at the referee, telling him to blow.

And I remember looking up at the big screen. It said sixty-four minutes on the clock.

I went to jab a short kick to Johnny Buckley so he could pass it back and I could, maybe, work my way up the line. But before the ball even got to him the whistle went. And fuck it, elation, joy – what words are there to convey that kind of feeling?

I turned around and there was Pat O'Shea, standing no more than 10 feet away from me. He's not the biggest man in the world and I think I nearly body-slammed him to the ground. Then I picked myself up, and suddenly all these cameras were in my face. And at that moment they're catching a side of me I've never shown. I'm crying. I can't help it. With all the things I'd won with Kerry across the years I'd never let my guard down to this extent. Never.

But I'd felt a pressure here that I'd never felt before. Huge pressure. I'd needed this. *We'd* needed this. And so there I stood, cameras clicking, everything pouring up out of me now. Nothing concealed. Nothing private. I was just so proud of everyone. Maybe proud of myself too. Proud to be a Crokes man. Proud of everything that meant.

Proud that we'd held our nerve and delivered on Pat's vision.

Inevitably I was in immediate demand for interviews after, and between that and meeting family I was more or less last back into the dressing-room. And what I walked into was surreal. Just quietness. Just this image of normality. Lads sitting down, taking off their boots. Smiling, but nearly too tired to talk now. A few exchanging quiet hugs, but no madness here. No bedlam.

And there on a table in the middle sat the cup. I walked straight over, lifted it to my lips and shouted as loud as my lungs would let me 'YOU FUCKING BEAUTY!'

That ignited roars, but soon enough Pat called us into an anteroom. It felt like we'd travelled light years from that January evening fourteen months earlier when he'd started selling this far-fetched dream to a sceptical audience. Now he wanted us to relish the moment rather than lose it in a blur. He'd done no media all year, just kept his head down, pushing us forward with that quiet but furious zeal.

I suppose he has that eccentricity you see in a lot of great coaches. In the Klopps and Mourinhos and Contes and Bill Belichicks of this world. They just see things from another angle. They work things out in a different way.

And now it was just him and us in the big cathedral. He began talking. He was emotional. He spoke of the journey, the hurt, the people we'd just represented. And I thought about that afterwards. His dad, Murt, had died in 2016. His mother, Bridie, the year before. His son was playing. His father-in-law was a selector.

And standing there, listening to that voice that had been such a constant in my life for twenty-odd years, I thought of my own parents and of what and who we were all standing together for here.

And at that moment, maybe for the first time ever in Croke Park, the goosebumps sent a shiver through me.

24

A Ticking Time Bomb

How do you explain the GAA to anyone not familiar with its madness?

I was in New York in December 2016 watching an NFL game over a few beers in Tír na nÓg, just off Times Square. Just myself, Colm Cronin – a guy I went to school with – and some American friends of friends. As often happens, they were trying to get their heads around the fact that I could play in front of as big a crowd as, say, the Giants, then go to work in a bank less than twenty-four hours later.

It's an old conversation, but one that keeps repeating itself.

'Really, you don't get paid?'

'Not a bean?'

'So who does?'

Here's an admission. GAA has been my life, but even now I don't fully understand it. I understand the appeal of trying to be a Kerry footballer. That's simple. We always feel we have a chance. Putting in the effort seems somehow logical because there's always the possibility, maybe likelihood even, that we'll get to the business end of a season and be playing big games in Croke Park.

But what motivates a Wicklow player? What motivates some-one in Longford where in 2016 something like a dozen of their better footballers decided that the county game just wasn't worth the trouble?

From some of the stories I hear, being a county man isn't exactly a badge of honour everywhere you go. In some places it becomes almost the opposite. You lose games badly, end up lambasted in the local media, and the follow-up noise can get ugly. Why bother flogging yourself when the probability is that things will end badly?

I can't begin to tell you the respect I have for players in these counties where any shot at glory is little more than a pipe dream.

Because criticism is given out for free in the GAA. It's every-where. Even in Kerry, losing a National League game can trigger the most ridiculously irrational reaction. Suddenly there'll be a radio phone-in with everything up for argument.

The manager's picked the wrong team.

This fella's legs are gone.

The whole team just waved the white flag.

I'm sure it's much the same everywhere, but in Kerry disappointment isn't ever more than an arm's length away from anger.

If you're a player or manager, you've got to be prepared for that. You've got to know that supporter panic comes with the territory. That, inside the bubble, you've just got to be hard-nosed about what's happening outside.

And there's endless room for gossip, for an 'inside story'. When Tomás and myself were found guilty of supping those few pints in '09, Kerry were going so bad that our predicament cried out for a bit of embellishment. Next thing, the Dr Crokes boys supposedly weren't talking to the South Kerry lads. And the South Kerry lads weren't talking to the Ghaeltacht fellas. None of it true, but why spoil a good yarn with the facts?

Imagine putting up with that in a county where you'd no chance of ever even seeing Croke Park.

And one thing I've learned with experience is that man-management is a complex job. When I became Kerry captain, I began to understand a little better that in a dressing-room of individuals there is no end to the possibility of different people needing a little extra sensitivity or at least awareness of their personal circumstances.

My friend Kieran drowning and my father dying suddenly, all within the space of eight months, pitched me into a place that wasn't nice, but because of my status I had people looking out for me all the time. I had Jack O'Connor treating me with kid gloves. Observing me. Maybe tiptoeing around me even. It's something about the GAA I think that gets lost sometimes. We can be seen as major stars in Irish society, but we have real, ordinary lives outside the game. Everyday troubles.

When something catastrophic happens, the shock of it can fester. I remember back then questioning a lot of things. Wondering was there more to life than just flogging myself to try and win football games. When you're young, it's natural to think you won't die before you reach seventy at the earliest. You feel you have all the time in the world.

Then something like that happens and, well, the brittleness of life pulls a little rug from under you.

But it doesn't even have to be that extreme. A fella could be dealing with a relationship break-up. He might be stressed about trying to get a promotion at work. A parent could be sick. There might be a bill outstanding that's keeping him awake at night. No matter how big your name in the GAA, you don't suddenly become immune to these things. Just because you're put on a pedestal doesn't mean it lifts you above that kind of trouble.

But there's this attitude out there that the only thing you need to worry about is finding your form. That nothing else matters. That you're a totally one-dimensional human being whose only demands in life are the seventy minutes you put in that weekend for the county or the sixty minutes for the club. Sometimes it's as if people almost see you as some kind of product.

That's why I had to get away at the beginning of 2008. I remember thinking 'OK, football is number one in my life, but there's a lot of other things I'd like to do as well'.

There may even have been a small element of just trying to get to know myself. Because I was on this relentlessly moving treadmill, missing weddings, christenings, all kinds of family occasions. All for what? For being handed a little medal? For a night on the beer?

You know within a week of winning an All-Ireland in Kerry, it's on to the next year. No mercy. 'Yerrah, sure what you did in the past is done now . . .' It's already about next season. Always the same mantra in Kerry – one I personally would condense into three words:

Commitment.

Dedication.

Enjoyment.

The last (and probably most important) is the one that I question most. In any walk of life, if you're enjoying doing something, chances are you'll do it well. But I'd question how much of top-level Gaelic football is actually enjoyable for a player now. Put it this way: I don't think you'll see any more Tomás Ó Sés or Aidan O'Mahonys playing beyond the age of thirty-five.

Something needs to be reined in. And I don't really know how you do that.

Because everybody's playing some kind of catch-up on something or somebody else. You feel a constant guilt that you should be training even harder, though the training you're already doing might be brutal. It's not an amateur effort. Not by a million miles.

That's why I mention the lads in the so-called weaker counties, busting their arses to put in the kind of preparation we put in when, deep down, they know they won't get near Croke Park in autumn. Week in, week out now, you read about guys opting out. Who can blame them? Do you really want to horse yourself from November to lose to Dublin by twenty points in June? Where's the dream there?

It's different when you know you have a shot at things. When you know you can have 40,000 for a Munster final in Killarney. You want that kind of day. You need it. Everybody does.

But the gap between the haves and have-nots is getting bigger all the time. If that doesn't worry the GAA, I think their eye is badly off the ball. I mean, good luck to Dublin signing a deal for a million plus with AIG, but what does Leitrim's annual sponsorship bring in? Fifty grand? We're trying to pretend they're chasing the same thing here when, palpably, they just aren't.

I'll admit there are no easy answers. Certainly waving a white flag and going 'Ah sure, fuck it, they're just better than us, there's no point' isn't one of them.

If you don't have self-help, you have nothing. In my early years with Dr Crokes, we weren't getting to county finals. But we had people within the club who committed incredibly towards changing that. We built ourselves into the force that we've become. Nobody does that by just feeling sorry for themselves.

What is needed most of all is people who inspire. And, beyond that, patience with those people. You need a culture of buying into something for the long haul.

I'm often asked if professionalism will ever take over the county game and maybe I'll end up regretting that I wasn't around for it. When you see the Sky deal, it's natural that that question arises. But I'm not so sure. Personally, I can't really see it at the moment. I can't see the structure that makes a professional GAA model sustainable.

But it seems to me that the body that should be directing a true vision of the future, the Gaelic Players' Association, can't now do that because they're effectively in bed with the GAA. I remember having a long chat about this with Tommy Walsh when he finally came home from Australia. He was saying that in the AFL the players' body is at the League's throat the whole time. That sounds like a more natural relationship for a union to have with a governing body. They should have that nuclear weapon threat of members withdrawing their services if they aren't satisfied.

The GPA are nowhere near that headspace. The structured payment system they've agreed just reflects a culture of appeasement. I wouldn't be astonished to see a day down the line when a separate body might be set up to represent county players. I mean, what's happening with team preparation is patently out of control. The effort is going through the roof and counties are spending fortunes.

Look at the figures for Kerry in 2016 and reconcile that with just four Championship games, two of which were against Clare. It doesn't make sense.

Some day soon I can see the players just deciding that enough is enough. And they might have to do that with or without the GPA. I know a lot of people outside the GAA who consider what we do these days as insane. The whole thing is gone way beyond the old days when players were delighted to get a bit of exposure in the newspapers or on television.

Actually, there's something perverse about the concept of amateurism within the GAA as it stands. In my opinion, the Association is just giving token things away. Trying to keep a lid on it. Hoping that everybody will just stay quiet. Yet millions and millions keep rolling in and, more and more, the squeeze is on the players.

I say that as someone who was privileged. But I'll be a volunteer when I'm finished playing. I'll be above in the Crokes field in some shape or form, training some under-age bunch. I'll be that person putting out cones, collecting little Johnny off the estate wall, giving them the investment of time that so many people put into me.

I've never had any big dealings with the GPA. I know they do a lot of good work, particularly in the area of mental health. But that's a societal issue. Don't get me wrong, I'm not trying to trivialize that in any way. But that problem's not exclusive to the GAA and in my view it should be a job for the Government, not the GPA.

I don't quite know what the GPA's long-term ambition is. I'm not sure what it is they want. What would they consider success five years from now? I don't know. I'm not sure they know either.

Right now, if you're in a successful set-up, maybe none of the above really matters too much. I never minded putting in the hours for Kerry. It's natural that you'd question things after a defeat: 'This is fucking heartbreaking. Wouldn't I have been better off playing a fourball in Killarney?' But the golf, hopefully, will always be there. When you felt you could make hay with Kerry, there seemed an obligation to try to take the chance. That chance doesn't present itself in every county though.

Personally, I think the GAA has been clever in keeping professionalism at arm's length for so long. They understand that changing the ethos of the game could be hugely dangerous. But what's happening at the moment might, in the long term, prove just as big a threat. Because the way things are going, it's inevitable there'll be an even bigger divide. The better teams keep going up another notch. The weaker ones slip further down.

And you can watch virtually everything live on TV.

That's the trouble. The GAA wants the best of both worlds. They want the TV money and they want the gate receipts.

I'm not sure they realize it, but that, to me, is a ticking time bomb.

25

The Room

Characters. A GAA dressing-room houses every breed and every shape, and sometimes I find myself wondering if there's any place on earth in which a man could feel more alive.

Over time, you learn to mark your territory. Croke Park? Turn right into the dressing-room, second last seat on the right. Marc Ó Sé one side of me, a doctor or physio on the other. Why there? No idea. But that became my spot. It was where I'd settle into the beat of whatever was coming down the tracks, and there'd be days I'd sit there, the heart nearly jumping out of my chest.

What the fuck am I doing here?

Strange as it might sound, I miss that knot in the stomach, the butterflies, the stress even. I miss that sense of going to war and the glue of big-day comradeship, the feeling that every last ounce of energy inside of us was going to be needed here. I miss going into the warm-up area and just banging a ball off the ground, feeling the strength in my legs and the conviction building: 'Someone's in for a heap of trouble here!'

I miss Moynihan's stare, that cold killer's look in his eyes. No words. Just a stare directed at certain people, challenging them. I miss sitting there, thinking to myself 'This man will kill someone today'.

Seamus's way was to pace the dressing-room, always looking to make eye contact. Looking to remind you that everything was about to get hot and heavy in our world and, fuck it, we'd need to be clued into that fairly quickly now.

Everything about him asking, 'Are you ready?'

And Darragh the same. The teeth gritted, that cold-blooded shine in his eyes. With him, some days were always more personal than others. He'd have that darkness about him, that look of something pulling at his patience. Maybe a sly dig someone took at him six months back, or maybe a year. The memory of an elephant, that man.

And God help whoever it was with the bad weather now coming their way.

You'd have the sunshine boys then, the high-fivers, the likes of Donaghy and Darran, all 'best of luck man' or 'have a big one today bro'. You'd have the silence of Anthony Maher. You'd have the coolness of Tom Sullivan, strolling about, maybe chewing a Jaffa Cake, looking to the world like he might slip away for a sneaky cigarette. Some days I'd look at Moynihan one side, Sullivan the other, and try to reconcile the two. One man almost ready to go up in flames, the other practically on a sun lounger.

I'd look at others, carrying their nerves like bricks in a rucksack. Just sitting there, eyes on the ground, brooding. The more knowledge I collected, the more I would back myself to go to them, offering reassurance. Maybe 'twas something I learned from Moynihan. Pick the moment. Keep it brief.

'Never seen you fly like you've been flying in training, man. You're well ready for this.'

And the payback was when you saw it register in their face.

'Fuck it, I am, aren't I?'

Others might even throw up as part of their routine, just tip off into a cubicle as matter of factly as tying their laces. Empty their stomachs of what they didn't need and straight out the door like fucking stallions.

Funny, I have a memory of the '09 game against Dublin and a dressing-room full of low eyes and dry mouths. Next thing, the lace snapped in my shorts and I needed Vince Linnane to get me a new pair pronto. One thing I never do is wear underpants under shorts, so across the dressing-room I stride, buck naked from the waist down. Wearing the jersey like a mini-skirt that's showing more than any archbishop needed to see.

'Vince, Vince, I need a pair of shorts here.'

Darragh sees me in all my glory and let's out an old heifer's groan. 'Aaragh for fuck sake Gooch, will you put on some clothes.'

And the place explodes with laughter, stood down – all of a sudden – as a dentist's waiting room.

Then there was Munster final day against Cork in 2013. Killarney bursting at the seams and Eamonn getting ready to give it thunder in the dressing-room. His first big Championship day as Kerry manager. 'Right lads, everybody pull in.' We go tight into a huddle, studs clacking on the stone floor, every last one of us ready to march to war.

Eamonn's just opening his mouth when someone enquires, 'Lads, where's Tomás?'

The Bag, who is chairman at the time, answers, 'In the horsebox!'

There and then, Eamonn's moment is lost. He stalls the digger until Tomás comes striding out of the toilet a few seconds later, not a clue about what's just happened.

'Are we right?' says Tomás, nobody knowing where the fuck to look.

Later that evening we'd be below in Tatler's, out the back on a baking-hot evening, sitting on barrels. Cork beaten and, for Eamonn, big pressure now lifted from his shoulders. He's got a pint in his hand. 'Here I was with the speech I'd been working on all week,' he says, laughing, 'looking for the right thing to say, just about ready to go, and The Bag leaves it in smithereens! By announcing Tomás is in the fucking horsebox!'

Maybe people imagine everything has a clinical touch at those moments, but sometimes the best-made plans get torn asunder. You might prefer the schedule working like clockwork but it's often no harm if, intentionally or not, the seriousness goes missing for a few split seconds. Because, trust me, when you're sitting in a stone room, maybe 40,000 people outside, it can feel as if the walls are closing in around you.

At that moment, in that place, football is the most serious thing in your life. It's a warped kind of reality I suppose, so no harm then to be letting off some of the steam.

I'd say that was Jack O'Connor's thinking one training weekend we had in Cork. Staying in the five-star Hayfield Manor, flogging ourselves hard in UCC and The Mardyke. Our last night there and word comes down from on high that we're allowed a glass of wine with dinner. Just a small concession.

I think Jack reckons it might help boys sleep, but he's after pulling the pin out of a hand grenade here.

Next thing, one particular waiter finds himself all but reinvented as Kerry's personal sommelier. The house red is hitting the spot, grins beginning to grow wider. 'Keep it coming my man,' says Tomás regally, handing across a tenner. For one of the few times in my life I have the good sense to stick to water because, before Jack knows it, half his squad is down in Washington Street, skulling pints in Rearden's. Some settle in for the night, only making it back to the hotel in time for breakfast.

The 'light run-out' scheduled for that morning turns into a wheezing parade of bears with sore heads. And Jack gives it to everyone down the banks, even those of us who didn't go.

'A fucking disgrace,' he says. 'Come up here on a serious training weekend and ye go and do that. Ye wouldn't beat a club team with that kind of behaviour!'

At this point, Ger O'Keeffe pipes up. Ger's friendly with the owner of Hayfield Manor and that friendship's got Kerry 'a deal' for the weekend. He's clearly offended. 'Jesus Christ, ye're supposed to be role models, our county's highest-profile people,' he says. 'We come up here to a five-star facility and the way ye conducted yerselves was a holy fucking show! Not only that. Two of ye fucked off with robes from the rooms too!'

The lads with robes in their bags are sheepishly forced to return them.

We're just about to get on the bus when Jack draws a line under the whole sorry episode.

'By the way,' he pipes up, 'just in case anybody's wondering, there'll be no more fucking wine!'

I played under four senior Kerry managers and they all put a personal stamp on how they went about their business.

Páidí was Páidí. A law unto himself, an independent weather system in many ways. He'd walk around the dressing-room, hands behind his back, thinking through whatever speech it was coming towards time for him to deliver. Always wearing that same yellow *bainisteoir* polo top, always the same cream slacks and always a pair of 1970s runners with so many holes in them they looked like they'd been a bulldog's toy.

Piseoga filled Páidí's head.

When he won an All-Ireland, his instinct was to preserve everything like a crime scene so that next time Kerry's preparation would be identical. Same hotel. Same bus. Same grub. Same Mass. Same everything.

The things that stood him well in 1997 and 2000 were always held precious. And he liked to keep a sheet of paper on which to scribble down some bullet points, a bit like Rafa Benítez and José Mourinho. I always had this image of him pacing the strand in Ventry that morning, fine-tuning his pre-game message. Those notes were Páidí's safeguard against losing a little nugget that came into his mind, and also, I'd imagine, protection against a mental block.

When I came in first, he had a habit of walking around the dressing-room in his underpants, the shirt hanging open. Not much left to the imagination as he went around, stopping for short one-on-one chats. One of the physios, Aoife, wouldn't know where to look when he'd stop by the table.

'How's Seamus's hamstring?'

Aoife's one of the most polite people I know and would be the colour of beetroot as she answered that Seamus was 'fine'.

I kind of came to love that about Páidí, though – the sense of someone so wrapped up in the mission that he had no time for thinking about small stuff like wearing his trousers.

And I'll never forget the shock of hearing in December 2012 that he'd died suddenly. Dr Crokes were heading to London to play an All-Ireland Club quarter-final in Ruislip and had just arrived at Farranfore airport when Brossie called me away from the bus.

'You're never going to believe what's after happening,' he said. Then, after a pause, 'PO is gone!'

I couldn't believe what I was hearing. Páidí was simply indestructible to us. Instinctively I began thinking that there were a couple of other Páidí Ó Sés living in the west of the county and this was probably a mix-up. People were surely jumping the gun.

But, soon enough, Brossie got confirmation from Marc, and I

remember sitting on the flight like a zombie, staring into space. None of it made sense. This man couldn't go at fifty-seven. No, I couldn't believe this.

It's hard to describe the sheer scale of his presence in all our lives. Personally, I felt great affection for the man. I never knew him until I became a senior Kerry footballer, but just being in close proximity to Páidí was never anything less than a memorable experience.

I sat on the plane now, thinking of the trip to South Africa when I was just eighteen and this great legend of Kerry football calling us young fellas over. 'Now boys, here's some South African rand for ye, go out and enjoy yourselves.' Just magical stuff.

That was the same trip he kept saying that he'd have to buy a new suit if – as he seemed to expect – Nelson Mandela happened to come calling.

Anyway, we played the match in Ruislip, the occasion completely swallowed up by the news from home. I did some media interviews afterwards and everything was about Páidí, no one really able to make any sense of it.

Even the Crokes lads, who'd never have played for him, would have loved everything about Páidí. When they did that TV documentary *Marooned* about his time in charge of Westmeath, the moment where he challenges one of the players about being 'fucked out over the line like a loaf of bread' would have been recycled over and over again in Crokes training by players who barely knew him.

That was the larger-than-life element to Páidí. He was a hero to people who never even met him, because I suppose everybody claimed some kind of small ownership of him.

When you think of Bertie Ahern coming to Ventry to launch his football tournament every year, it seems barely believable now. The Taoiseach of the country!

One thing that struck me forcibly at his funeral would be the look of heartbreak in the eyes of his old team-mates. They all seemed a little broken by his passing. I remember talking to Ogie Moran especially, the emotion flooding through him. So many were palpably hurt at losing Páidí.

Nobody, of course, more than Máire and the kids, Neasa, Siún and Pádraig Óg. But watching Darragh, Tomás and Marc carry their uncle's coffin that day, I remember trying to imagine what they were going through. Because everything they'd done in their football lives pretty much followed the template Páidí had set for them. If he'd told them to climb Carrauntoohil blindfolded, they'd have done it.

His legacy was enormous. The Ó Sés trained with the same fury Páidí did in his playing days. That's what you did with Kerry. No excuses.

I often think back to the 2002 All-Ireland final, Páidí manager and the three boys playing. Just imagine the number of tickets that must have flown through the Ó Sé hands that September. It must have been hundreds, and, rest assured, they'd still have been looking for more.

Anyway, driving out of Ventry the day they laid Páidí to rest, it felt as if Kerry had lost more than a man. We'd lost a small part of what defines us. Even walk into the pub today – the photographs with Dolly Parton and Tom Cruise, Páidí presenting them with a Kerry jersey or, in Dolly's case, a pair of shorts.

Where would you get it?

I was down there on New Year's Day – the place packed – and you could still feel his spirit. Of course, the statue is up outside too. I'd challenge anybody to look at those photographs and not break out into a smile.

That was Páidí.

Jack, of course, was a much quieter type. He had this kind of all-seeing presence in a dressing-room, just standing with his selectors, observing everyone, monitoring. Watching people. Watching the time. Making sure that whatever schedule had to be followed wouldn't be missed.

And I think Eamonn's cut from the same cloth. Holds his fire a lot. Picks conversations with certain individuals, mainly backs, but no great bombast. 'Everyone happy now, lads, on who they're picking up?' Keeps things short. Always logical. And calm.

Pat O'Shea would probably be the most wound-up of the four. Sometimes in Croke Park he'd take himself away to the Astro-Turf room to kick the ball around by himself, just letting off steam. I don't know a man who thinks more intensely about football when getting his team ready for battle.

Still, it's fair to say none of the Kerry managers I served under were into banging tables or kicking doors. They all knew the distinction between wisdom and noise.

I was grateful for that.

There was a time when Kerry warm-weather training camps always ended with a final-night session, a blow-out to clear the pipes.

Today the trips are dry from start to finish, and I'm almost certainly to blame. There's a story about Vilamoura and a missed flight during Pat's time in charge that has been twisted and bent into a selection of half truths. As that story concerns me, maybe it's high time I came clean.

Our final night took us into The Irish Cabin bar where the appeal of a few ice-cold bottles of Corona was massive after a week of flogging ourselves under the hot Portuguese sun. Soon enough I was feeling no pain, and having bumped into a gang of people, male and female, from Tipperary, I accepted their invitation to keep the night going back at an apartment they were renting.

We were due to depart Browns Sports and Leisure Club for Lisbon airport at six a.m. the following day and, of course, everybody reported down to the bus on time except yours truly.

I was still in the Tipperary apartment, sleeping the sleep of the dead on a sofa and completely non-contactable to Pat and the boys who were now desperate to get on the road to Lisbon. Eventually they'd no choice but to leave without me. Sensibly, my passport and gear were left in the hotel room so that when I did come round – at, say, eleven a.m. – I wasn't going to be stranded.

When I saw the time, I nearly had a heart attack. 'Oh sweet Jesus, you have to be kidding me!'

Then I did the only thing that seems to come naturally to me in a crisis: I phoned The Bag. He was at home and managed to book me a flight to Dublin out of Faro that afternoon. Better still, one of Johnny Buckley's drivers was able to pick me up at the airport and ferry me home to Killarney.

As it happened, this plan worked so smoothly I ended up home in Kerry before the rest of the squad touched down. Brilliant. Problem solved. Wasn't I the smart cookie?

The following day I was doing some kind of Dr Crokes photocall with Pat and decided to get my apology out of the way.

'Sorry about that, just slept in . . . but sure look, we're all home safe and sound now, so no harm done.'

And he looked at me like he was fit to be tied.

'Come over here,' he said, moving out of general earshot. 'I want to talk to you.'

He proceeded to give me an absolute roasting. Called me a disgrace. Told me how I'd held up the whole group, that I'd basically let everybody down. He just had to get all that anger off his chest, but the moment he was finished, that was the end of it. Pat's never been a man for storing grudges or lingering resentments. He just said his piece, and we moved on.

Of course, it became comedy gold dust with the lads. 'Typical Gooch, misses the fucking flight and still lands home before us!'

Well, that last-night blow-out has been a thing of the past ever since. The following year Pat was outlining plans for the same trip, telling people what they'd need to pack. And Tomás pipes up: 'Do we need to bring going-out clothes?'

Going-out clothes? Only Tomás.

'No, Tomás,' said Pat, half exasperated. 'You may leave them at home this year.'

In a strange way I cherish those memories, the little moments of chaos and madness and human panic, now every bit as much as I do my medals. Because we had to have those escapades to keep the competitive intensity up. You're talking about human beings after all, and sometimes maybe we need to be reminded of that.

I mean, I still love hearing the stories of the seventies boys and the craic they had between them. Their era was certainly less abstemious than ours and, if I'm honest, I'd say they got the better deal because of it.

I remember David Moran telling a story about his dad, Ogie, once. He was on the beer with Tim Kennelly at Listowel Races one year, the All-Ireland safely housed. As usual, the Dubs were down too and this particular session was drifting into a second night. So they're in this bar when Ogie notices Tim's eyes closing.

'You all right there Horse?' he asks.

'I am, I am,' says Tim. 'But is it today or tomorrow?'

I was talking to Henry Shefflin about this the evening we appeared together on *The Ray D'Arcy Show*. We were kind of lamenting how in the old days the best craic after a big Championship win was almost always on the Tuesday. Because that was when the rest of the world returned to normal, but you still had a window to leave things hang. And, better still, maybe you now had an element of privacy too.

I look back at those days and think that the old existence for a GAA man effectively encouraged binge drinking. Because fellas would literally be cramming the pints in, knowing that that'd be the end of it for maybe another two months. Madness. The one-line text might go out – 'We're in Dingle!' – and that's where we'd drop anchor.

Now that Tuesday is gone. Now there's such an emphasis on rest and recovery and refuelling the body, some of those old scrapes we got into probably seem reckless in the extreme. The nutritionists, dieticians and strength and conditioning people would come out in a cold sweat if they saw some of the antics we used to get up to.

The way they do things now is more conscientious and more disciplined, no question. Whether or not it builds the same friendships, I'm not so sure.

26

Out of the Bubble

In my head, I've spent all summer looking for a man who is no longer there.

Two days after the 2017 National League final, Niall 'Botty' O'Callaghan rang me at work. I could tell instantly from his voice that this wasn't a social call, that something bad had happened.

'It's Vince Linnane,' he said.

'Vince is dead?'

Now nothing lasts for ever, but in Kerry, I suspect some of us reckoned this man might be the one to break that rule. Because the expression 'larger than life' was coined with someone like Vince Linnane in mind. He was the person who gave me my first Kerry jersey and the one who gave me my last. And through the fifteen seasons in between, he grew from one of the most terrifyingly cranky people I'd ever known into a great and loyal friend.

Maybe every county has someone like Vince keeping some semblance of order on the distribution of gear in a dressing-room. But to us, he was unique. He was a man with a bark far worse than his bite, as Botty especially knew. The two of them could have these 'rows' in front of us that weren't really rows at all. You'd think they'd be at each other's throats sometimes, but then you'd see it was always with the hint of a grin.

My last image of Vince was a glimpse of him on TV at the end of that League final, called into the players' circle, a gear bag – typically – flung over his shoulder. He was eighty-two.

On hearing the news, I rang The Bag for confirmation. He was in bits. They'd been great buddies for about two decades and, like everyone who'd been with them two days earlier, Patrick couldn't believe that someone so swept up in the victory over Dublin had now, without warning, slipped into the next life.

Vince was a Mayo man, Kiltimagh originally, who'd found love with wife Noreen in North Kerry.

Now he was to be buried on Good Friday, and much as I wanted to be part of the guard of honour that the Kerry squad would form for his funeral, I knew that I just couldn't. Johnny Buckley asked me if I'd be joining them, but it simply wasn't my place now. And an ex-player needs to know many things in Kerry, but maybe nothing more so than his place.

So I drove over to Ballyduff that day with Daithí Casey, the journey shortened by stories of our shared experiences with Vince in Kerry senior and under-age dressing-rooms.

A Ballyduff friend of mine, Gerry Rochford, happened to be home from London, visiting his father over the Easter weekend. And he said what many were probably thinking as we followed Vince's coffin to the cemetery: 'Jesus Christ, the biggest funeral ever to hit Ballyduff and all the shaggin' pubs are closed!'

The turnout of players, past and present, was an eloquent reflection of Vince Linnane's place in Kerry football. I remember starting off with Kerry minors and how he'd nearly terrorize any-one trying to take a jersey out of the bag without his permission. Some lads routinely wore his patience, asking for extra shorts and socks every single day. And a look on Vince's face told you exactly where he'd like them to stick the extra gear.

Still, everybody came to love him.

He never travelled on Kerry team holidays, which I always thought was a bit of a shame. Just wasn't his scene, I suspect. But you could tell he loved wearing the official team suit the night of an All-Ireland win. I have fond memories of him looking proud as punch on some of those nights, the only circumstance through which we'd ever meet Vince in a social capacity. And even then he'd stay low-key, unobtrusive. Just as he was in a dressing-room.

I've two stand-out memories of Vince Linnane that I'll always treasure.

The first was a big celebration of Kerry's so-called 'Second Golden Generation' in the INEC in November 2016. More than a thousand people sat to dinner in recognition of the county's seven All-Ireland victories between 1997 and 2014. And I think it was The Bag who decided it might be timely to make a special presentation to Vince. I'm so glad he did now. Because he got a standing ovation that evening from people who would have presumed he'd still be around us for many years to come.

The second memory is also from 2016, of a rough-house National League game with Donegal in Tralee. You see, Vince was groundsman for Austin Stack Park since the 1980s and took massive pride in the redevelopment of that stadium, particularly the improvements made to a now absolutely pristine field. The Donegal game marked the official reopening of the pitch and Eamonn Fitzmaurice asked Vince to hand out the jerseys in the dressing-room.

This was his place, his house, his field. That was Eamonn's message.

And I'll always remember the team-talk beforehand, how

Eamonn put Vince at the centre of his message. 'Lads,' he said, 'this, of all days, is one not to lose in our own field with what that man has done for everyone here across the years.'

Vince was emotional handing out the jerseys, much as he tried to conceal it. And, after we'd won a bad-tempered game, I have this vivid memory of him slipping discreetly across to Eamonn to thank him for the honour. There was no great dialogue between them, but then there didn't need to be.

One year on, standing in a North Kerry graveyard, I felt so glad that he'd been honoured on those two occasions, given none of us had an inkling that he'd be leaving us so soon. Because Vince Linnane was a man I remain proud to have called a friend.

The day after I'd phoned Eamonn to confirm my inter-county retirement, I met Kieran Donaghy for lunch in The Killarney Park.

He said he'd just happened to be rolling through, but I reckoned he was looking to fish out information. So I stopped him before our conversation even started.

'Listen, I'm done,' I said. 'And Eamonn knows. I told him last night.'

Well, the eyes nearly jumped out of Star's head.

'You what? Are you serious? Listen man, it's probably just an appetite thing, cool the jets.'

He was gutted. I could see that instantly. Like most people in Kerry, he'd assumed I'd give it one last crack. Me stepping away had never really been factored into his own commitment to another year, and now I almost felt a need to reassure him that he'd made the right decision. We'd soldiered long and hard together, you see, and were probably considered the last of the old stock, along with maybe Donnchadh and, to a lesser degree, Darran.

I knew I could tell him my news in confidence then, but I also realized I'd disappointed him.

So I began talking about my waning energy levels against the palpable strength he seemed to take from basketball. I said it made perfect sense that he should go for it again.

And he kept repeating over and over, 'I know man, I know man . . .'

He didn't say it, but I knew he was really thinking 'I thought you'd be there with me!' We're the same age roughly, grew up together, competed against each other in county finals. By and large we had a shared history then, and I suppose it's human nature to want things to stay the same for ever, especially when you've known so many great times.

But, like most people, Kieran had no inkling of the struggles I'd been having to keep my body strong, the evening physio sessions at home with Ger Keane, the nursing of endless niggles, the slow, unmistakable sense of time (and mileage) simply catching up on me.

One of the things I'd said to Eamonn was that I was determined never to outstay my welcome as a Kerry footballer. I had no interest in being a bit-player. Maybe that makes me sound a little conceited, but if I couldn't be central to a team I was involved with, I just reckoned it was best I left the squad place open to someone who might be. If my county career just petered out, I knew it would torture me. And the more I thought about things, the more I came to feel that finishing up in Croke Park with one of the greatest, most cherished victories of my career might just have been pre-ordained.

Winning an All-Ireland with Dr Crokes had been the last real box I needed to tick.

And, while it wasn't a game I played particularly well in, while it wasn't one the team played particularly well in, the victory gave me a level of personal satisfaction that would have been pretty obvious to anyone looking at me at the final whistle. And I can't lie, scoring the goal was important to me.

Because the game was getting away from us until we got it, and I've always said that a sign of the best competitors in any sport is they still make a difference even when not at their best. I certainly wasn't at my best on St Patrick's Day 2017, but I've always had this inner voice when things aren't going well on a football field, reciting the same mantra.

All you need is one chance . . .

Killarney was a different town for me after that. I relaxed a lot more, settled into the natural beat of the place. For a start, I stopped worrying about walking from the bank to my car for fear of meeting somebody who might ask me the wrong question. And it's strange, once you step out of that inter-county bubble, just how unnatural it all looks in the rear-view mirror.

I don't regret a single day of my career in a Kerry jersey. But there's another life out there, and I've discovered it's got plenty to recommend it. Like in the work canteen on Monday mornings, I feel so much more free with the interaction now. It's a place where the GAA chat has always been intense with fellas like John O'Mahony, Kerry's biggest fan, Bobby Dwyer, branch manager in Killarney and devout Cork GAA man, Aidan Mangan, former inter-county referee, or the likes of former Kerry players Barry O'Shea, Stephen Stack and Pa Laide just rolling through, looking to cover all bases.

And, chairing it all, Sean Healy. Maybe the most passionate Listowel man I know.

The expression you'd hear most often there on Monday mornings is 'Did you hear?' Well, 2017 was the year I became a part of the 'Did you hear?' crowd.

Of course, I crossed the great divide too, signing up to a new life in punditry. Maybe, as some might see it, selling my soul to the devil. It's not how I see it, though a part of me did feel a little hypocritical about it at first.

Because in recent years I more or less closed my eyes and ears to TV and newspapers. God's honest truth, I'd never watch *The Sunday Game* any night that Kerry had played. We might have been in a Munster final the same day, but I'd stay away from it, preferring to watch whatever golf tournament was being shown on the same evening from America.

Why?

I suppose I'd signed up to that slightly neurotic attitude that modern inter-county involvement has come to nurture. One where you ask yourself 'Would watching the programme help me in any way?' If the answer was no, well then Des Cahill and the boys could get by fine without my attention.

I'd just stay in the bubble.

The odd time someone might say something that began trending on social media and, human nature being what it is, I'd end up tracking the segment down on RTÉ Player. Otherwise, zero interest. Trust me, I wasn't trying to build up any kind of siege mentality, any of this old 'us against the world' dynamic. I see why managers do that sometimes but it's never been my thing. I just don't buy into it.

When *The Sunday Game* made contact after my retirement in April, the first thing that struck me was that, finally, I could offer an unguarded opinion. I wouldn't have to be tiptoeing around stuff any more. I was no longer conflicted.

Yet straight away it was as if people became fixated on my likely onscreen relationship with Joe Brolly. On *The Ray D'Arcy Show* with Henry Shefflin in May, that was the question everybody kept asking: how I'd handle Brolly.

I could understand that, even if it interested me a lot less than people hoped.

Joe had taken a few pops at me over the years, and kept it going the week of my retirement. Basically, he seemed to see me as a bit of a choker. He'd backed up that view at different times by referencing the '02 All-Ireland final against Armagh; a Dr Crokes All-Ireland Club semi-final defeat to Crossmaglen; the trilogy of Kerry losses to Tyrone; the 2012 defeat to Donegal; and the 2013 loss to Dublin. Through all of these games, Joe seemingly located one common thread: I lacked a warrior mentality. To the best of my knowledge he's never seen me play in the Kerry county championship or in the Munster Club, yet he believes he knows me better than those who have.

'My point is he is not a leader,' he wrote once in the *Sunday Independent*. 'In adversity, he fails.'

Now Joe's words bothered me a lot less than they bothered Kerry people in general. They always took the bait. And I don't doubt that that's exactly what he wanted them to do. The more people are talking about Joe, the happier he clearly is. I get that. I sense he's comfortable personalizing something because he knows that's how to trigger a reaction.

So why say someone didn't play particularly well when you can just as easily label them a choker?

Personally, I've more interest in what Kerry people think of me after watching me for club and county over fifteen years than in anything Joe might choose to say just to get people's backs up. Sharing a TV studio with him won't ever change that.

The week of my retirement, a Trailfinders brochure came through the letterbox in Ardshanavooly. It seemed ironic timing.

Because, suddenly, the possibilities of summer had found a completely different emphasis in my head. The calendar was so much more open to me now. I mean, I've no idea what the South of France is like in July; I haven't an iota what Rome is like in

August. But I've every intention of finding out over the next few years now that football no longer has my schedule in a chokehold.

I'm not even entirely sure how much longer I'll stay relevant to Dr Crokes now.

Don't get me wrong, I still want to play the game as hard as my body allows me. That appetite hasn't gone. I suspect I'll always want to play with Crokes, but the day will come – potentially soon, too – when I'm just not at the level to play senior. When the young lads like Tony Brosnan and Gerard Kiely merit selection in Crokes' six best forwards ahead of me.

It would be easy for me to say that I hope to play on till I'm forty. But if I physically can't?

I wouldn't rule out playing for the Bs, given it was B and C football I was playing in my mid-teens, Tuesday-night games in the East Kerry League. Pride certainly won't be the reason for me stopping. My body will be.

You know Pat O'Shea went to America the Wednesday after our All-Ireland Club win, meaning he was missing for our first League match of the season against Rathmore, which we won by a goal. The following Tuesday I'd say he'd hardly touched back down in Shannon from Chicago when he sent out a group text. Just a single sentence: 'Training tonight 7pm!'

There was a poor turnout the same evening and that just made his blood boil. He called everybody together when it was over and expressed his disappointment. One of the things he said was 'If it's good enough for Colm Cooper to be here, why isn't it good enough for everybody else?'

The message Pat was sending out was it was time for us to park the past. Just eleven days after climbing our Everest, the wheels were turning for Crokes again. We purposefully changed the WhatsApp profile too, removing the image of Croke Park celebrations.

You know the poster of the winning team had the message 'Mission Accomplished' stamped across it. But I'm not sure that's ever entirely true in a GAA life. Because there's always another mountain to climb, always another target.

But I've other things I want to do with my life too. I'd love to get my golf handicap down to a single digit and, maybe above all, I want to enjoy family gatherings a little more. One of my big regrets is that I wasn't able to spend more time with my parents and enjoy stuff like christenings, First Communions and Confirmations in their company.

The number of times I said to Mike or Vince 'Look, don't plan for me to be there' is something I can never change now.

My family revolved around me far too much in the past. Everything was geared so that I was in a good place. It was treated as a bonus if I happened to get along to any family get-together. That's changed now. And the change is long overdue.

I have missed certain things more than others. I've missed the craic at the back of the bus, the face on Donaghy as all that BOOM BOOM stuff came pouring out of his headphones, the wind-ups, the butterflies in the stomach, the friendships.

Funny, I probably talk to Darran every second day, but I wouldn't dream of asking him about anything going on in the Kerry camp now. It's none of my business. Even close as I am to Donaghy, I had no idea if he was even travelling up to this year's League final because I simply wouldn't ask.

I know I've got to be careful about that and not end up erecting unnecessary barriers, but I'm outside the bubble now. Crokes is my only football family now. Because when Kerry stops, it stops.

The day after my retirement announcement, I went up to the grave in Aghadoe. It just seemed a natural thing to do, especially given my father's anniversary had fallen on the previous Sunday. I don't have any fixed times to go up there, but it's a place that gives me peace when I do. Sometimes just ten minutes up there can free a lot of the clutter inside my head.

I can't say that's because of a strong sense of religion, but I do believe in something. My mother always said, 'If you don't have your faith, you have nothing!' I used to envy her the conviction with which she'd say those words. I'm not a regular Sunday Mass-goer, and if you asked me to describe my faith I'd find it very difficult. But Aghadoe gives me a strong sense of my parents' spirit still alive, so clearly I'm not a non-believer.

You know maybe the hardest thing for me as a Kerry footballer was the standards I set myself. I had no interest in being a seven out of ten player. None. My attitude was that I didn't put in all that work to be chasing seven out of ten. It was unrealistic what I sought from myself, given how tight fellas might be marking me or how determined they would be to upset me. But I always reckoned it was better to come up short with a nine than with a six.

Often, of course, I failed to do that. The challenge was always to keep trying.

I played eighty-five Championship games for Kerry. I never tasted a Championship defeat in Killarney. I think I earned the respect of some of the best players I played either with or against. Those things I treasure.

The medals? They all ended up in the same USA biscuit tin. The All-Stars? On the front-room mantelpiece. It was always great to get them, but silverware was never the thing that made me proudest.

Maybe my longevity was.

To achieve what I did for so long, with all the attendant expect-ation and pressure, that was only possible because I became such a self-driven person. Did it make me cranky? Difficult to live with at times? One hundred per cent, it did that. If my family were honest, they'd tell you today, 'Fuck it was a nightmare at times trying to deal with that man!'

But they stuck with me through thick and thin. They never left me in any doubt that they were always in my corner. I can't ever forget that.

I won't.

Acknowledgements

I've had many blessings in my life, but none greater or more precious than my parents, Mike and Maureen. Thank you both for an amazing upbringing and for teaching me the right values.

We're a big clan and to my brothers and sisters – Danny, Mark, Mike, Vince, Geraldine and Karen – thanks for always being there for me through good and bad. I think we all know how lucky we were growing up in Ardshanavooly and I will always cherish the shared memories.

To my small army of nieces and nephews – Mark, Aaron, Jack, Liam, Mikey, Éanna, Christine, Ciara, Sarah, Grace, Aoife and Eve – I couldn't imagine life without you.

To the extended Cooper and O'Sullivan clans, a big thank you for all of the support and laughter along the way.

To Dr Crokes, my second family. Where do I begin? The journey we've shared has fulfilled me in ways that I know words will never adequately express. We've laughed, we've cried, we've laughed again. As the saying goes, 'It's been emotional!' And, hopefully, we've still some miles to go.

To my Kerry team-mates, it has been a pleasure. From the long nights training in Fitzgerald Stadium to fun-filled trips around the world, I know I've made friends over these last fifteen years that will last a lifetime.

To the four Kerry managers I played under – Páidí, Jack, Pat and Eamonn – I enjoyed every minute of your support, guidance and the unique intimacy of preparing for massive football showdowns. To all of the selectors, doctors and physios, thank you too. Your work was invaluable.

To three Kerry County Board chairmen – Seán Walsh, Jerome Conway and Patrick O'Sullivan – your passion for our county meant that nothing ever seemed a problem. Thank you for passing on that passion to those of us in the dressing-room.

To AIB, my employers since I left school. Thank you for the unflinching support you've always given me throughout my career, particularly through the difficult months of recovery from my knee injury in 2014. Specific thanks to the teams I have worked with in both Kerry and Dublin.

To Eamonn Keogh and Matt O'Neill for their help with supplying photos of family and Dr Crokes.

To Vincent Hogan and family, I am so grateful for your door always being open while I was in Dublin. Vincent, you have done a remarkable job on this book. Thank you.

To Céitílís, thank you for coming into my life and putting a smile on my face. Hopefully, there's a lot more to come.

And, finally, to the Kerry supporters. Thank you for the care and respect you've always shown towards me over the last decade and a half. It's been my privilege to wear the green and gold.

Picture Acknowledgements

Every effort has been made to contact copyright holders where known. Those who have not been acknowledged are invited to get in touch with the publishers. Photos not credited have been kindly supplied by Colm Cooper.

Section one

Page 1: The five Cooper brothers: © Eamonn Keogh (macmonagle.com).

Pages 2–3: First game: © Brendan Moran / SPORTSFILE; Battling with Armagh's Enda McNulty: © INPHO / Lorraine O'Sullivan; My favourite Kerry goal: © Morgan Treacy / INPHO; Colm with parents: © Eamonn Keogh (macmonagle.com).

Pages 4–5: With Tyrone's Ryan McMenamin: © Brendan Moran / SPORTSFILE; With Kieran Cahillane: © Eamonn Keogh (macmonagle. com); Aussie rules, with Dale Morris: © Ray McManus / SPORTSFILE.

Page 6: Scoring in the '06 All-Ireland against Mayo: © Oliver McVeigh / SPORTSFILE; Same goal, different angle: © Cathal Noonan / INPHO; Holding Sam Maguire cup with Declan O'Sullivan: © Brendan Moran / SPORTSFILE.

Page 8: Munster Championship '07: © Cathal Noonan / INPHO; Tackled by Graham Canty: © Matt Browne / SPORTSFILE; Celebrating with Pat O'Shea: © Paul Mohan / SPORTSFILE.

Section two

Page 1: On the bench: © Morgan Treacy / INPHO; Winning the ball against Anthony Lynch: © Donall Farmer / INPHO; With Sam Maguire in '09: © Stephen McCarthy / SPORTSFILE.

Pages 2–3: 'That's my boy!': © Eamonn Keogh (macmonagle.com); 2010 Munster semi-final v. Cork: © Dan Sheridan / INPHO; With Graham Canty, 2011 Munster final: © James Crombie / INPHO; Celebrating Munster Final win in '11: © James Crombie / INPHO; 2011 All-Stars: © Stephen McCarthy / SPORTSFILE.

Pages 4–5: With Stephen Cluxton: © Ryan Byrne / INPHO; Getting past the Dublin defenders in 2011 All-Ireland final: © Donall Farmer / INPHO; Celebrating a goal against Dublin: © Morgan Treacy / INPHO; With Jack O'Connor in 2012: © Diarmuid Greene / SPORTSFILE; Cruciate injury: © Paul Mohan / SPORTSFILE.

Pages 6–7: With Kieran Donaghy and Ger Keane after 2014 All-Ireland win: © James Crombie / INPHO; Getting my hands on Sam, 2014: © Cathal Noonan / INPHO; With Eamonn Fitzmaurice, 2015: © Ramsey Cardy / SPORTSFILE; With Philly McMahon in 2015 All-Ireland final: © Cathal Noonan / INPHO; Battling with Dublin's defenders, 2015 All-Ireland final: © Ryan Byrne / INPHO; After 2015 defeat against Dublin: © Donall Farmer / INPHO.

Page 8: Celebrating 2017 Dr Crokes' Club Championship with Pat O'Shea: © Brendan Moran / SPORTSFILE; Champions: © Piaras Ó Mídheach / SPORTSFILE; Lifting the Andy Merrigan Cup: © Brendan Moran / SPORTSFILE.

Index